APPEAL TO
EXPERT
OPINION

DOUGLAS WALTON

APPEAL TO EXPERT OPINION

Arguments from Authority

The Pennsylvania State University Press
University Park, Pennsylvania

Library of Congress Cataloging-in-Publication Data

Walton, Douglas N.
  Appeal to expert opinion : arguments from authority / Douglas Walton

    p.   cm.
    Includes bibliographical references and index.
    ISBN 0-271-01694-9 (cloth : alk. paper)
    ISBN 0-271-01695-7 (pbk. : alk. paper)
    1. Reasoning. 2. Authority. 3. Fallacies (Logic). I. Title.
    BC177.W315   1997
    160—dc21   96-39773
                                                                     CIP

It is the policy of The Pennsylvania State University Press to use acid-free
paper for the first printing of all clothbound books. Publications on uncoated
stock satisfy the minimum requirements of American National Standard for
Information Sciences—Permanence of Paper for Printed Library Materials,
ANSI Z39.48-1992.

For Karen, with Love

CONTENTS

Acknowledgments   xi

Preface   xiii

CHAPTER ONE:
THE PROBLEM OF AUTHORITY   1

  1. Peirce's Four Methods of Fixing Belief   3
  2. Science As the Modern Authoritarianism   5
  3. The Culture of Technical Control   9
  4. Different Conceptions of Scientific Knowledge   13
  5. Expert Testimony in Court   17
  6. A Complex Type of Argument   19
  7. Being Intimidated by Experts   22
  8. Questioning an Expert Opinion   23
  9. The Problem of Fallacies   28
 10. Finding a Middle Way   29

CHAPTER TWO:
HISTORICAL BACKGROUND   32

  1. Overview of Developments   33
  2. Plato on Socratic Questioning of Experts   35
  3. Aristotle on Dialectical Arguments   38
  4. The Medieval View of Argument from Authority   43
  5. Galileo's Challenge to Proof by Authority   46
  6. The *Port-Royal Logic*   48
  7. Locke's Account of *Argumentum ad Verecundiam*   52
  8. Bentham on Appeal to Authority   55
  9. The Meaning of *Verecundia*   57
 10. Where to Begin   60

CHAPTER THREE:
IDENTIFICATION OF THE TYPE OF ARGUMENT   63

  1. Appeal to Reverence   64
  2. Knowledge Versus Appeal to Authority   67
  3. Testimony of Authoritative Sources   69
  4. Varying Definitions of *Ad Verecundiam*   72
  5. The Ambiguity of 'Authority'   76
  6. Advertising Testimonials   79
  7. Position to Know   82
  8. Authority and Expertise   84
  9. Terminological Choice   86
10. Provisional Conclusions   88

CHAPTER FOUR:
FORM OF THE ARGUMENT   91

  1. Deductive Forms   92
  2. Probable Inferences from a Knowledge Base 96
  3. Inductive Forms   98
  4. Presumptive Forms   100
  5. Expert Systems   104
  6. Informal Logic and Expert Systems   107
  7. The Concept of an Expert   110
  8. Reliability and Bias—Subjective Factors   114
  9. Human and Machine Expertise   117
10. Evaluating the Form in a Context of Dialogue   120

CHAPTER FIVE:
DIALECTICAL ASPECTS   126

  1. The Case of the Deadly Radar Gun   127
  2. The Case of Lorenzo's Oil   134
  3. Reported Controversies   137
  4. Appeal to Expert Opinion in Political Debate 140
  5. The Context of Dialogue   144
  6. Style of Presentation   149
  7. The Secondary Level of Dialogue   153
  8. Critical Questions and Logical Form   157
  9. Drawing Inferences from Expert Opinion   159
10. Dialectical Structure of Appeal to Expert Opinion   164

CHAPTER SIX:
EXPERT TESTIMONY AS LEGAL EVIDENCE   167

  1. The Adversarial Setting of a Trial   168
  2. The Battle of the Experts   171
  3. Junk Science in the Courts   176
  4. The Go-It-Alone Expert   179
  5. Legal Criteria for Scientific Testimony   181
  6. Hearsay Evidence in Expert Testimony   185
  7. Science As a Body of Knowledge   188
  8. Solutions to the Junk Science Problem   192
  9. The Framework of Dialogue in a Trial   194
10. The Consistency Critical Question   197

CHAPTER SEVEN:
CRITICAL QUESTIONS   199

  1. Premises and Critical Questions   200
  2. Early Accounts   202
  3. Accounts in the 1970s   205
  4. Recent Accounts   208
  5. Personal Reliability and Bias   213
  6. The Trustworthiness Question   215
  7. Position to Know   217
  8. General Acceptance in a Field   218
  9. General Recommendations   222
10. Using Critical Questions for Evaluation   225

CHAPTER EIGHT:
EXPLAINING THE FALLACY   230

  1. Suspect and Fallacious Appeals   231
  2. Specific Defaults Cited   234
  3. Dogmatic Appeals to Authority   239
  4. The Halo Effect and Milgram's Experiments   243
  5. Institutional Setting of Authority   245
  6. Fallible Arguments Absolutized   247
  7. Confusing Two Types of Authority   250
  8. Profiles of Dialogue   253
  9. Subfallacies   255
10. Summary   257

Bibliography   263

Index   275

ACKNOWLEDGMENTS

During my lectures in courses over the years, whenever the topic of appeal to expert opinion as a type of argument came up, I have always sensed an enthusiasm and interest in this particular subject, both on my own part and that of the class. And although I began the project of collecting research material for a book on it many years ago, it has never been possible to complete the project until just this year. The main reason for the delay was the existence of such a huge mass of relevant literature on the subject in two main areas outside my own field: law and computer science. However, in the academic year 1993–94, the means were finally at my disposal—thanks to a Social Sciences and Humanities Research Grant—to finish my collection of this material and work through it. I would like to thank the Social Sciences and Humanities Research Council for funding this research and, in particular, for enabling me to employ Victor Wilkes to help with the collection of materials. It was this work that finally made the completion of the project possible.

Although I had previously written several papers and book chapters on various aspects of the argument from expert opinion, especially in connection with its status as a traditional informal fallacy in logic, it was made clear by this earlier work that a general systematic account of the normative structure of this type of argument would have to go into the kind of depth that could only be accomplished in a monograph. As early as 1974, John Woods and I (Woods and Walton 1974) sketched out the basis for such an analysis—clearly only a first step—that laid out a framework for research on this type of argumentation and identified the problems that needed to be addressed. In chapter 7 of Walton 1989a, a better developed and more useful account was given, that moved some way toward solving some of the problems. But it was far from evident that this was still anywhere near to the last word on the subject. In fact, it is clear from that account that many of these problems were very much unresolved at that point.

In two articles (Walton 1989b; 1989d), more refinements were given to the underlying structural basis of reasoned use of expertise as a type of argumentation. Here the results of expert systems technology, as developed by the recent advances in artificial intelligence, were shown to be helpful, and even essential, to understanding how appeal to expertise works as a distinctive kind of knowledge-based reasoning. Parts of these two articles, in revised form, have been reprinted in Chapter 4, and thanks for permission to use this material are given to the editors of *Argumentation,* and to Professor Fernand Vandamme, the editor of *Communication & Cognition.*

Many of the notes for this book were first written while I was a member of the research group "Fallacies as Violations of Rules for Argumentative Discourse" as a Fellow-in-Residence of the Netherlands Institute for Advanced Study in the Humanities and Social Sciences (NIAS) in 1989–90. I thank the staff and fellows of NIAS for their support that year—and in particular, the members of our research group on the fallacies—Frans van Eemeren, Rob Grootendorst, Scott Jacobs, Sally Jackson, Agnes Verbiest, Agnes Haft-van Rees, Charles Willard and John Woods. As well, for their comments and conversations, I thank Alan Brinton, Mark Weinstein, and Erik Krabbe.

On June 11, 1996, I was invited to give a talk, "Appeal to Expert Opinion," to the department of philosophy of the University of Groningen, Netherlands. During the discussions after this talk, some useful comments and suggestions were made that have improved various parts of this book. I would especially like to thank Theo Kuipers and John North for their questions and suggestions. During the Conference on Formal and Applied Practical Reasoning in Bonn, Germany, in June 1996, some conversations on artificial intelligence with Subrata Das, John Fox, Dov Gabbay, Rod Girle, Hans-Jürgen Olbach, John Pollock, Ray Reiter, and Lofti Zadeh turned out to be helpful for making revisions to Chapter 4.

Two reference librarians were extremely helpful to me in tracking down information: Linda Dixon of the University of Winnipeg Library and Graeme Rymill of the University of Western Australia Library. I would also like to thank Rita Campbell, for doing the index, and Harry Simpson, for helping me with the proofreading. Finally, I would like to thank the Department of Philosophy of the University of Western Australia for inviting me as a Research Associate in 1996 and providing facilities needed for the completion of the book, and the Oregon Humanities Center for facilities and support provided in 1997, when I was there in the capacity of Distinguished Visiting Research Fellow.

Special thanks are given to Amy Merrett for the word-processing of the text and figures of the manuscript.

PREFACE

Remarkably, the problem of evaluating appeals to expert opinion was posed as a logical puzzle as early as the fifth century B.C.—a puzzle that not only has never been solved, even as we approach the millennium year of 2,000 A.D., but that, until very recently, has not been given much attention in the mainstream of logic. Sextus Empiricus (c. second or third century A.D.) attributed the following argument to Anacharsis of Scythia (who supposedly left Scythia at the end of the fifth century B.C. to go in search of wisdom):[1]

> Who is to be the judge of skill?
> Presumably, either the expert or the nonexpert.
> But it cannot be the nonexpert, for he does not know what constitutes skill (otherwise he would be an expert).
> Nor can it be the expert, because that would make him a party to the dispute, and hence untrustworthy to be a judge in his own case.
> Therefore, nobody can be the judge of skills.[2]

As this clever argument suggests, there is an inherent difficulty in judging matters of technical expertise, even though we commonly do judge such matters and, in many cases, doing so is a practical necessity. The argument of Anacharsis indicates that when we do judge the worth of such matters, it is dubious whether we are using any rational criterion.

1. According to R. J. Hankinson, *The Sceptics* (London: Routledge, 1995), 321.
2. Sextus Empiricus, *Against the Logicians,* vol. 2 of *Sextus Empiricus* (works), Loeb Library edition, trans. R. G. Bury (Cambridge, Mass.: Harvard University Press, 1933), 29–31. This reconstruction of the argument of Anacharsis is based loosely on the translations of Bury and Hankinson (owing somewhat more to Hankinson's), and represents not the exact wording of the complete argument but what is taken (by the author) to represent a précis of the essential problem posed.

The argument of Anacharsis is a typical logical puzzle of a kind well known to sophists and philosophers of the ancient world. It has the form of a dilemma. No matter which option is chosen—and it seems that one option or the other must be taken—the same unpleasant (and unacceptable) conclusion follows. However, the premises of the argument do seem to be acceptable, and the argument has a structurally correct form (that of a dilemma). So how do we deal with this contradiction? If the premises are acceptable, and the argument has a structurally correct form (the dilemma is a valid form of argument), then the conclusion must (rationally) be acceptable, too. But clearly it is not.

A very similar and closely related problem may be expressed in the form of the puzzle of Anacharsis by asking the question: How can one rationally evaluate an appeal to expert opinion used to support an argument that has been put forward to support one side on a disputed issue? The problem, as the argument of Anacharsis indicates, is that the worth of such an opinion must either be evaluated by an expert in the field of the appeal or by a nonexpert (layperson). But the nonexpert is really in no position to evaluate the worth or acceptability of the opinion. He lacks the expertise. On the other hand, the expert, although she has the technical expertise to judge the opinion, becomes a party to the dispute, as soon as she chooses to support the contention of the one side or the other. Such a choice of sides on a controversial issue involves a compromise of objectivity by the technical expert. After all, even putting an opinion in lay terms involves a loss of strict technical accuracy. A biased expert cannot give an adequate or rationally compelling evaluation of an argument. So here again, there is a dilemma. The problem is: What is wrong with the argument?

The solution offered by this book is quite a long and detailed argument that provides an analysis of the structure of arguments based on appeals to expert opinion. One has to read the book to see what the solution is. Although it is simple enough to state the problem, it is not such a simple matter to solve it. The solution requires identifying three prior subproblems: (1) the logical form of appeal to expert opinion arguments; (2) the various rational ways of responding to the use of such an argument in a dispute; and (3) different contexts in which such arguments are used, in particular, how they can be used fallaciously to deceive people and to unfairly get the best of a partner in argumentation.

As difficult as it is for a nonexpert (or even another expert) to try to evaluate an argument based on an appeal to expert opinion, it is a task that is done all the time in everyday reasoning (often very badly, as this book demonstrates). The purpose of this book is to give methods that will help us to do it better.

1

THE PROBLEM
OF AUTHORITY

Many of the things we accept are, inevitably, accepted on the basis of authority. If I get a diagnosis of my illness from a physician, I may get a second opinion, but even that opinion has been put forward by a certified expert. I may look up accounts of my illness in a medical library, but these too are written by experts. Of course, we presume that these pronouncements are based on scientifically verified facts, but once again this assumption is only guaranteed by the experimenters being experts in the scientific field in question. If you think of it, in fact, nearly everything we believe is believable because it is based on the opinions of experts. In this age of specialization and professionalization, it is not possible to escape accepting things on the basis of authority.

We like to think, however, that we can make up our own minds individually and autonomously on what to believe, reserving the right to be skeptical and using our own best judgment on what to think with respect to those opinions that really matter. But how real is this cognitive autonomy, given the dominance of fields of expertise and scientific authority in modern civilization? Can the individual thinker really question the established views that constitute the wall of expert scientific opinion that surrounds him or her and have a rational opinion that differs from the accepted view? These questions represent the problem of authority, but the way the problem is felt and expressed in daily life has shifted in recent times.

The problem of authority has stereotypically been portrayed in modern times by the analogy of Big Brother—a centrally established politicoreligious elite that runs our lives and tells us what to think and how to act. The case cited as the paradigm is that of Galileo, forced by the Church to go on record as retracting his stated opinions because they contradicted Church teachings, even though they were genuine findings of scientific research. According to the modern viewpoint, religious dogma is the authority that is closing off rational thinking based on scientifically verified facts.

The postmodern view has shifted this modern stereotype of the problem of authority. The evil of modernity, which postmodernists take as their point of opposition, is the effort of the established elite to reduce and homogenize "difference" by making everyone look and think the same way (Cherwitz and Darwin 1995). From the postmodern perspective, the problem of authority is that the individual must struggle against a monolithic, centrally and rigidly imposed viewpoint. Modernity is just another one of these monolithic and centrally fixed systems of thought and opinion. According to the postmodernist viewpoint, science has no more claim to represent the truth or ultimate reality than any other collective viewpoint. The Enlightenment—based on Descartes' and Pascal's idea that the axiomatic method of reasoning (typified by Euclidean geometry) is the scientific method of thinking that is the only way to refute skeptical doubt—was the starting point of modern thinking that lasted up to the mid-twentieth century. Currently that view has been challenged by various forms of postmodernism. Yet if we no longer accept scientific method as the kind of thinking needed for cognitive autonomy, could science itself now be the source of the postmodern problem with authority?

The American philosopher and scientist Charles Saunders Peirce expressed the modern problem of authority as one of the "fixation" of belief (Peirce 1958a). The use of the term 'fixation' is particularly appropriate because, as skeptical philosophers have often observed, many of the most important decisions we make in our everyday lives—about what to do and what sort of personal goals to adopt—are made in a situation where there is little time to personally collect sufficient data so that one's conclusion is based on firmly established knowledge. Instead we have to assume and guess and, very often, trust or rely on the opinions of those who have presumably taken the effort to study the matter— the experts. So we have to "fix on" or accept certain opinions or beliefs as the best information or advice we have to act on for the moment. But there is also a widespread tendency to "fix" onto these beliefs too firmly— to treat them as "gospel," as beliefs that cannot be questioned.

1. Peirce's Four Methods of Fixing Belief

In his 1877 essay, "The Fixation of Belief," Charles S. Peirce outlined four ways that people arrive at "ideas that settle down in the minds of people as habits, customs, traditions," or commonly accepted opinions (Peirce 1958a, 91). The first is the *method of tenacity*: a steady and immovable clinging to beliefs an individual already has, by suppressing any doubts or wavering. The second, the *method of authority,* involves the community or state, which creates institutions to "keep correct doctrines before the attention of the people," to teach these doctrines to the young, and to prevent contrary doctrines from being expressed. Anyone who rejects such an established belief, according to Peirce is "terrified into silence." This method, Peirce tells us "has, from the earliest times, been one of the chief means of upholding correct theological and political doctrines" (102–4). Peirce thinks that the method of authority is both mentally and morally superior to the method of tenacity, as a method of fixing belief. The third method, the *a priori method,* rests not on "observed facts," but on propositions that seem "agreeable to reason" (105–6), based on the intellectual fashions at a particular time. *A priori* has the advantage that it is more intellectual than the first two methods, but it has the disadvantage that it is based on "taste" or "fashion." The fourth method, the *method of science,* is that of scientific investigation based on "real things, whose characters are entirely independent of our opinions about them" (107). Only this method, according to Peirce, allows for "bad reasoning" as well as "good reasoning," by testing whether the reasoning fits with "rough facts" external to the feelings and purposes of the method. The method of authority, for example, will always continue to suppress what is seen as "dangerous reasoning" in order to insure peace and security. Certain nonconformities are tolerated, Peirce tells us, but if you "let it be known that you seriously hold a tabooed belief," you "may be perfectly sure" of being treated with a brutal cruelty (109–10). Peirce thought that each of these four methods of fixing belief had its advantages. But he thought that the method of science is the only one to use if you wish your opinion to "coincide with the fact" (111). So, although Peirce made a conscious effort not to come right out and say that the method of science is the best method, it is clear that, in his opinion, it is the only one that (1) is based on reality, (2) is self-correcting because it is open to refutation on the basis of factual evidence, and (3) moves toward the real truth of a matter.

Peirce's four methods is a typically modern viewpoint that presents the heart of the matter as a Galileo-like conflict between the rational and falsifiable method of scientific investigation and the central authority of politicoreligious dogma or ideology. The problem, according to Peirce, is that the method of authority, unlike the method of science, is not open to correction. Instead, it is held into place rigidly by those in authority, who stand to gain by keeping the established doctrine as a monolithic bloc to be taught to the young as 'the truth.' Anyone who dares to question these doctrines, or suggest anything different, is terrified into submission.

This difference between the method of science and the method of authority that Peirce cites may not be as absolute as he portrays it, however—in relation to the modern situation, at any rate. Barry Marshal, the Australian physician who discovered that ulcers and gastritis are caused by the virus *helicobacter pylori* (that can be treated successfully with antibiotics in most cases), was strongly opposed by the scientific establishment when he tried to communicate the results of his research.[1] At first, Marshal's fellow scientists described him as a crackpot, and his efforts to gain acceptance for his theory were especially strongly opposed by the drug companies, who had billions invested in conventional ulcer medications. The conventional acid-lowering medications were the best-selling drugs of all time, whereas the use of antibiotics is a generic cure, so nobody can make a big profit from it. When this lone scientist first dared to question the established method of treating ulcers, he was penalized by the scientific community for daring to suggest anything so radical. It was only through considerable persistence against all kinds of opposition over a long period that he was eventually able to gain acceptance for his theory. Many doctors only investigated experimentally in order to demolish his theory. As results came in, however, Marshal's theory gained support. Still, after ten years, according to Marshal, only 10 percent of physicians were actually following his treatment.

Established doctrine in science can be a monolithic bloc that is hard to crack. It did change in the Marshal case, but it changed very slowly. On the other side, the authority of the political or religious type of dogmatic belief is not nearly so monolithic as it was in Peirce's time and in previous times. Such dogmas, particularly in democratic North America,

---

1. See David Suzuki, *The Nature of Things,* CBC Television, September 7, 1995.

now change very rapidly and are highly pluralistic in nature. What remains the same, however, as Peirce says, is that once one of these doctrines gets a firm enough hold politically, its proponents can be successful in using tribunals and reeducation penalties designed to knock back into line and terrify into submission anyone who might publicly question the doctrine or act in such a way as to appear to contravene it.

2. Science As the Modern Authoritarianism

From Peirce's view of the contrast between the method of authority and the method of science, it seems that the worst danger he postulated is the kind of conflict where religious or political authority is used to suppress scientific investigation or override scientific reasoning. This kind of situation remains both a danger and a reality in some countries. But in the western world at the moment, deployment of any kind of strong, central, and unified authority in either religion or politics has declined to a remarkably low profile. The prestige of science is enormous, and it is felt on all matters of practical reasoning and deliberation in one's daily life. For example, in advertising, deciding what products to buy, or in health, deciding what food to eat or medications to take, expert scientific opinion is uppermost in public opinion. In matters of personal conduct and lifestyle, opinions from social scientists seem to be the most widely used and powerful sources of advice in the setting of public opinion and conduct. Anyone who tries to dispute what is taken to be an established scientific opinion, finding, or method can be easily dismissed as a "crackpot" or "nut." It seems the mere opposition to a scientific viewpoint is enough to suggest that the dissenter is not someone who is thinking rationally. Or if anyone presents evidence, even of a kind that is compelling from a practical point of view, if this evidence is not based on a controlled study or some other form of finding that can be described as "scientific," it can be dismissed as "anecdotal." Thus, if there is a conflict between scientific evidence and an "anecdotal" finding, the assumption is that the scientific evidence is the only kind worth paying attention to.

It is ironic that Peirce contrasted the method of science with the method of authority, for now science has become the ultimate authority. The latest scientific findings on health, diet, and stress, or any matter pertaining to personal lifestyle are of intense interest to the public. Polls and other statistical findings are routinely used in making political and business decisions. A staggering quantity of legal evidence used in the courts consists of the testimony of scientific experts, DNA evidence being the latest example. The opinions of social scientists seem to be particularly influential in matters of personal conduct. For example, social scientists as expert scientific witnesses in trials commonly testify that criminals should not be held responsible because they were victims of their environment or of circumstances that they could not control. This type of statement is very much an ethical, political, and ideological one, with important social and even religious implications. But it is soberly treated as the scientific opinion of an expert.

Many people take these scientific findings and opinions quite seriously and act on them, even though the opinions often change rapidly and may be directly contradicted by other scientific experts. An excellent case study described by Cynthia Crossen is the oat bran mania of the mid-1980s (1994, 43–53). At a time when people were beginning to become concerned about the effects of cholesterol on heart disease, the results of some research partly funded by the Quaker Oats Company were published by a team at Northwestern University in the *Journal of the American Dietetic Association*. The study showed that, for 208 subjects, adding oat bran to their diet resulted in a significant drop in their cholesterol count. Quaker subsequently began advertising its cereals containing oat bran as cholesterol-lowering products that could reduce the risk of heart attack, and the media took up oat bran as a miraculous, life-saving ingredient in food. Oat bran was added to more than three hundred products, including potato chips, licorice, and beer. Then, in January 1990, a new study was published by two researchers from Harvard that concluded that oat bran does almost nothing to forestall heart disease (43–45).

In a case like this, the problem seems to lie not in any central authority telling people what to do, but in the partnership between science and corporate interests. One area where there is considerable confusion about who are the real scientific experts is food. A large commercial industry is devoted to advertising and promoting various foods and the basis of their argument is often that the particular food product they promote is healthy or nutritious. Advocates cited in food commercials are more often celebrities than experts. But many commercials feature appeals to expert opinions, for example, by physicians. Physicians often give expert advice on diet and nutrition, but in many cases their training has not qualified them to be specialized experts on these matters. Other persons do specialize in nutrition. According to Helen MacDonald, the term "Registered Dietitian" is legally protected, where "nutritionist" has no such protection, so almost anyone can claim to be a nutritionist or an expert on nutrition (1985, 188). Generally, however, a person with a serious claim to expertise would have a university degree in human ecology or home economics. However, there are many spurious claims made to expert opinion advice in the area of food, diet, and nutrition. Ads commonly claim that some food or vitamin will "help" cure a condition like acne or herpes. MacDonald cites her experience of interviewing an author who made a number of claims about how vitamins could help various common ailments: "In his book there are sections that describe what each of the vitamins, nearly-vitamins, and minerals can do for you. Quite a number of them are cited as aids to memory. The interesting thing was that many of my questions couldn't be answered because it had been a while since the book was written and he couldn't remember."

MacDonald cites this particular book as an example of the many dubious claims about diet and health made by so-called experts in nutrition who do not really have any academic or professional qualifications at all.

> The aforementioned book is but one example of the nutrition misinformation being foisted on an unsuspecting public by unscrupulous instant "experts," people who wouldn't recognize 1,25 dihydroxycholecalciferol if they had a snoutful of it. In fact, it looks very much as if we are becoming a nation of nutritionites. A nutritionite—not my word, by the way, but that of one of the foremost nutritionists, Jean Mayer—is no nutritionist. According to Dr. Mayer, "The nutritionist is aware that some parts of that package of knowledge encompassing nutrition are firm and factual—but there are still some pieces missing. The nutritionite, unencumbered by questions or the nuisance of governmental or professional regulations can feel free to give no end of advice. Out of a sound base of ignorance coupled with considerable conceit and misunderstandings of nutritional axioms plus delusions, the nutritionite expounds and bamboozles." (176)

People seem willing to accept such advice and arguments, even if the supposed expert really has no serious or legitimate (or very little, at best) claim to expertise. Perhaps the reason is that the proposed remedies are easy and painless, and, presumably, not likely to cause harm even if they don't work.

On October 17, 1990, a lecture on nutrition was given by a woman whose credentials included a Ph.D. from the International University of Nutritional Education in Huntington Beach, California. The speaker,

Nancy Appleton, was introduced by the provincial minister of education as "a researcher, author and professional whose theories were based on sound scientific research." In the lecture, Appleton claimed that people should not eat sugar, because it causes food allergies, diabetes, tooth decay, arthritis, heart disease, and cancer. A critic claimed, however, that the International University of Nutritional Education is one of many names used by a California diploma mill that had granted diplomas to his dog and cat. Contacted at her Santa Monica home, Appleton did not respond to this charge, only saying that she did have a bachelor of science degree from UCLA, and that "helping a lot of people get well" is "what it's all about" (Krueger 1990, 1). The University of Winnipeg subsequently reported that they had nothing to do with the lecture, and that Appleton was invited by the Canadian Natural Hygiene Society, who had rented the lecture hall.

The problem posed by this kind of case is that the area of food and nutrition tends to be interdisciplinary in nature, and it may be hard to say, in a given case, which fields are most relevant. The controversy about the claim of Linus Pauling (a Nobel Prize winner in biochemistry) that large doses of Vitamin C are the best remedy for the common cold was complicated by the fact that Pauling was neither a physician nor an expert on nutrition. Where there are several different scientific fields that bear on a problem, it becomes harder to sort out appeals to expert opinion.

According to physicist and science policy observer John Ziman, giving the Royal Society's Medawar Lecture, a new framework for the production of knowledge called "postacademic science" is emerging, where research is done by interdisciplinary teams instead of individual scientists, and the problems are chosen by the funding bodies. Kam Patel reports that

> Professor Ziman argued that in postacademic science, research is directed toward specific ends and relates to problems that will not have been set by individuals themselves or even by the teams. The choice of problems to be worked on operates at the level of the bodies funding science. "All policy talk about foresight, priorities, accountability, etcetera is really focused on 'problem choice.'"

In postacademic science, most research work arises out of problems "arising in the context of application that is determined by corporate and government bodies," and that, according to Ziman, "could mean a decline in scientific objectivity" (Patel 1995, 7).

According to Crossen (1994), this decline is now a reality as more and more research is funded and carried out by industries that have a financial stake in the outcome of the research. The modern situation is that popular respect for scientific research as a backing for an opinion is quite high. This viewpoint is reasonable for, as Peirce pointed out, scientific research uses hypotheses that are open to correction, or even refutation by empirical findings and tests that can be duplicated by other investigators (Peirce 1958b, 132–33). But on the other hand, this respect for science, like anything else, can be exploited by those who want to make a profit, or to advocate a particular point of view as a public policy.

More and more, advocacy groups use reported scientific findings to support their arguments and find this type of argumentation successful in the manipulation of public opinion. But at the same time, the public becomes more aware that these practices are being used as public relations techniques. These developments have led to a postmodern decline in respect for scientific objectivity.

3. The Culture of Technical Control

Scientific terms and concepts are defined in an empirical way, based on the collection of data from experiments or widely reported findings collected by statistical methods and verified by the use of blind studies and control groups. Once a concept is accepted as scientifically valid, it is hard to challenge its objective existence. But the recently expanding list of scientific "syndromes" makes one wonder if the terms used in science really are defined in a value-free objective way.

Dr. Harald Schrader, a neurologist at the University Hospital in Trondheim, Norway, questioned drivers in Lithuania, a country that does not have personal injury insurance for drivers, and where medical bills relating to automobile injuries are paid by the government, to see whether they suffered from whiplash (chronic whiplash syndrome, indicated by headaches and neck pains after a rear-end collision). According to Dr. Schrader's findings, when drivers in Lithuania were asked about their symptoms, no difference in reported headaches and neck pain was found between those who had been in a rear-end collision and those (in a control group) who had not. No genuine cases of chronic whiplash turned up (Grady 1996, D8). By contrast, in Norway, there is a patients' organization of 70,000 people who claim to have the chronic disability of whiplash syndrome. The leader of this organization even threatened to sue Dr. Schrader when his study was published. If Dr. Schrader's findings are right, chronic whiplash syndrome, despite its impressive medical definition as an objective event of compressing of vertebrae in the spine, would seem to be a socially constructed concept built on the reported complaints of individuals in a particular legal system of insurance claims. Many examples of such syndromes suggest the same conclusion. Scientific terms and concepts, supposedly based on empirical reports, can really be based on human values and interests, disguised within the "objective" shell of the scientific display of statistics and empirical data.

Those holding the postmodernist viewpoint sketched out above have recently begun to question the modern assumption that science is free of cultural bias. The following case described by Anthony Flint indicates the kind of questions that are being debated (1995, D8):

Case 1.1:   Biology students once learned that a sperm swims toward the passive egg of the female, pounds on the walls and breaks down the damsel's defenses. Conception was not so much a union as a vanquishing.

Today's researchers see it differently. The egg, they say, sends out messages to guide the sperm, participating actively in the process, until sperm and egg find each other and merge.

Yet because scientists came to the lab with preconceived labels for the microscopic players—sperm as aggressive male, egg as passive female—it has taken a long time for them to see what was really going on.

The postmodernist critics have taken this questioning to a deeper level of critique, some even drawing the extreme conclusion that the standards of rationality in scientific and reasoning (including logic) are socially constructed assertions put forward by a social group (the scientists) who have an interest in defending them. But even those who stop short of this extreme conclusion have been impressed by the "deconstruction" of cases like Case 1.1, which indicate a cultural bias in how scientific results are presented. There has been a shift from the modern assumption that science represents an objective picture of reality to a postmodern view that science is just another perspective that represents reality in an instrumental way that is useful for scientific investigation. Perhaps the cultural bias is not in the methods of the underlying scientific research itself but in how the outcome of the research is "presented." Such bias is easy to find, particularly in looking through social science textbooks, which now carefully present the "politically correct" point of view, whereas not so long ago the bias in the presentation of their theories and findings seemed to have quite a different spin on it.

In the general postmodernistic view of things, each group has its own bias and its own special interests, and this situation of subjective points of view is normal and acceptable. In fact, it is portrayed as an ideal, called "difference." The modern idea was that authority was a problem because government, religion, the establishment, or the "military-industrial complex" had a monolithic grip on enforcing the beliefs that the public adhered to, on matters of personal conduct and lifestyle. Thus to be a "conformist" was a bad thing, and to be against the central authority came to be regarded as a fashionable counterculture stance. The postmodern view has retained the opposition to any monolithic central agency enforcing life style choices, but the reality of the situation has shifted somewhat. Now we have different advocacy groups, with arguments that are not universally credible, trying to use the media and other resources to get their views lodged into public opinion and into the bureaucracies of the legal system, government regulations, the universities, or other institutions that have rules and regulations that affect everyone.

Advocacy groups try to use science in particular to get their views fixed in place in governments, courts, universities, and other bureaucratic systems to set penalties in place for disagreeing with their views and rules of how things ought to be done. Science is just another institution to be "cleansed" of opposing views and "corrected" to suit the interests of the advocacy group. The view of any particular group is that science had been used to oppress and victimize them in the past, so now science can legitimately be used to support their interests.

The postmodernist view still looks back to, as a focal point of opposition, the modern situation of a religion or strong central government imposing a monolithic centralized viewpoint on everyone, using some firmly fixed ideology to dictate to everyone on how they should live, and what values they should hold and act upon. But the postmodernist view, unlike the modern view, does not exempt science from this critique. Richard Cherwitz and Thomas Darwin express this postmodern attitude very clearly.

> The postmodern attitude takes as its primary task theorizing, preserving, and celebrating difference. The great evil of modernity, to which postmodernity reacts, is the systematic effort by those in control to impose order on 'society' by forcibly reducing and homogenizing the myriad differences that characterize life.

On this reading, modernity is best exemplified by totalitarian
regimes that attempt to make all citizens look and think alike.
Argument is but one of the many weapons of homogenization in
the arsenal of totalitarian oppressors. (1995, 199)

According to the postmodernist viewpoint, any argument, even one
based on scientific expertise, represents an attempt to suppress difference by exerting a monolithic control. Expert opinion based on scientific rationality is just another attempt to homogenize individual thinking
to suppress difference. According to extreme versions of the postmodernist view, rational argument of any sort is just another bias or point
of view used by its exponents to advance the interests of their own
established groups. Scientific argument is no exception. Science is seen
as a central, monolithic fixed body of doctrine established by and for an
elite (the scientists). It is rigid and fixed, in the sense that it is beyond
refutation by nonexperts. On this extreme view, science is seen as just
another advocacy-based point of view that lays claim to objective rationality but is really biased and subjective, advocating the interests of its
members. After all, science is based on models that are useful and
reflect an instrumental point of view that does not necessarily correspond to reality.

It is not just the more extreme proponents of postmodernism
who have difficulties with science as representing rational thinking.
Daniel Yankelovich argues that what he calls the "culture of technical
control" is undermining the ability of the public and the experts in
democratic countries to make rational decisions on how to deal with
the serious problems they currently confront. The culture of technical
control assumes rightly that policy depends on highly specialized knowledge and skills possessed only by scientific and technical experts. By
using this premise as its base the culture of technical control draws the
conclusion that the only solution to the serious problems faced in
democracies is through "public education" through the media (1991, 9).
The idea is that the expert scientists are the ones who have the knowledge, so they are the only ones that can solve these problems. The public can then be "educated" through the media on how to implement the
correct solutions.

One problem with the culture of technical control is that it assumes
that the public is incapable of the level of reasoning and deliberation
needed to deal with these problems. The assumption is that if you are
not a scientific expert, then you have no say in deciding what to do on
matters of public deliberation, even in a democracy (except to implement the conclusions arrived at by the experts). A second problem is

with the culture of technical control is that we now have social scientists (and all kinds of scientists) who are all too ready and willing to tell us how to make decisions and conduct deliberations in our personal and political lives; a subproblem is that they frequently disagree with each other. Even worse, they seem to change their advice rapidly as each new scientific research finding is published, indicating a different opinion. Understandably, the public is beginning to treat the announcement of new scientific findings on such matters with considerable skepticism. However, it is difficult to question any proposition that has been announced as a research finding of scientific experts in a technical domain of knowledge.

4. Different Conceptions of Scientific Knowledge

According to one normative model of the kind of argument characteristic of scientific investigation, science is a cumulative buildup of knowledge, based on premises that are solidly established and verified by objective evidence and conclusions drawn from these premises only by rigorous logical proofs. To say that an argument is *cumulative* in this model means that the line of argument or demonstration always moves forward, and that (ideally, at least) there is never any need to retract a proposition, once it has been established (Walton 1995). The inquiry is a normative model of ideal of correct argument that has frequently been taken to represent scientific argumentation.

The model of argument as inquiry is also frequently identified with the philosophical viewpoint called foundationalism. It was most clearly expressed in modern times by Descartes' method modeled on geometric reasoning, of starting with indubitable premises, and drawing inferences only by steps that allow no possibility of going from truth to falsehood. In fact, it was Descartes' generalization of the inquiry as a geometrical method to a general method that could characterize all reasoning that is reliable and valuable, both in science and philosophy, that is the characteristic of modernity. This modern style of thinking, which took scientific research to be the only kind of thinking that really represents reality, and is not susceptible to skeptical doubt, was even more sharply represented by Pascal. In his satirical work *Lettres Provinciales,* Pascal ridiculed the idea that casuistic reasoning based on "probability" (so-called), an old idea going back to the Greek notion of *eikos* (or plausibly seeming to be true), could be a reliable way of reasoning in everyday ethical deliberation or in philosophical discussion.

Instead, Pascal, in his book *De L'Esprit Geometrique* (translated as
"Reflections on Geometry and the Art of Persuading"), pronounced that
what is called "the art of persuading . . . is nothing more, strictly speaking, than the methodical carrying through to their conclusion of a
complete set of satisfactory proofs" (Gleason 1966, 319). By "satisfactory proofs" Pascal meant the geometrical method used by Euclid in
geometry—starting from self-evident axioms, deducing theorems by
deductive steps of argument, and using only previously proved propositions as premises.

This idea of using the inquiry as the model of reasoning in science
was known to Aristotle, who called the inquiry the demonstration
(*apodeixis*). But Aristotle (unlike Pascal) did not ridicule the idea of
persuasive or dialectical reasoning as a serious and worthwhile kind of
thinking that could be used to raise questions and conduct enlightening
philosophical and practical discussions. In fact, in *Topics* (101a30–35),
Aristotle wrote that the kind of reasoning he called dialectical was not
only useful for conversations but also for raising questions about the
fundamental axioms used in demonstrations in scientific proofs.

But with Descartes and Pascal, founders of the Enlightenment that
ushered in the characteristic modern way of thinking, the old idea of
the dialectical use of reasoning in Aristotle was lost entirely. Nobody
thought of logic or methodical reasoning in dialectical terms anymore,
and logic came to be identified with Aristotle's syllogistic, and subsequently with the mathematical version (propositional logic) of the old
Stoic logic. As dialectic faded away, the inquiry model of scientific reasoning became identified with objective logical reasoning generally.
Anything else came to be categorized as "subjective," and therefore of
no real worth as "proof" or correct reasoning.

But with the advent of postmodern thinking some questions need to
be asked. Does the model of the inquiry represent scientific research
generally, or is it better seen as representing a normative model that
only advanced research on a thoroughly studied subject in a highly
developed field can hope to approximate? Could there not also be a
prior *discovery stage* in this line of development, where hypotheses are
guessed at and questioned, preliminary to "weeding out" at later stages
of refinement, prior to mathematically precise formulation, and verifi-
cation or falsification? Peirce thought that there was an earlier "guess-
ing" stage where promising hypotheses were selected out for testing on
a basis of which one seemed to better explain the data. Peirce also
thought of scientific knowledge as being in a state of perpetual criticism—never entirely beyond questioning or falsification by new developments or findings. Such a nonstatic conception of scientific knowledge

as being in a continually changing process of development is at odds with the modern Pascalian view of science as a set of solidly established self-evident propositions and subsequent propositions inferred by the highest standards of deductive proof.

One might think that Peirce, like Aristotle, would leave some room for questioning conclusions derived from the findings of technical experts in a domain of scientific knowledge. But during and after Peirce's time, respect for science as the basis for all authority on what and how to think was in the ascendancy. It is clear that Peirce took a dim view of not only the method of tenacity and the method of authority, but also what he called the "*a priori* method." Unlike science (in Peirce's view), this method is based on the "intellectual fashions" of a particular time. Aristotle also thought that dialectic was based on *endoxa,* or popularly accepted opinions, but he did not find this a reason to reject dialectic and indeed thought that this feature was part of its value.

In the postmodern era, however, we are beginning to question the Pascalian view that science, modeled by the inquiry types of argumentation, is the only kind of reasoning that is of any worth, and that is based on reality and gives a way to truth. The various critiques and revelations of cultural bias cited above have cast doubt on the modern view, to some extent. But the problem is that the prestige of science is still so enormous that it is difficult for many people to even question opinions or findings supposedly based on scientific research or thinking at all. And if they do, what they are doing in even asking such questions, seems (along Peircean lines) to be thinking of an inferior and merely popularistic sort.

Readers may think these differing views of the place of science in determining how we should reason is a purely philosophical controversy, but in fact the issue very much affects practical matters relating to appeal to expert opinion as a working type of argument. Huber, in his controversial book *Galileo's Revenge: Junk Science in the Courtroom* (1991), claimed that relaxed standards for expert testimony in civil cases were causing bad verdicts in product liability suits. Giannelli has also shown how pervasive the use of expert opinion evidence has become in criminal cases (1993, 112). DNA profiling is the best known example, but other sophisticated instrumental techniques include neutron activation analysis, atomic absorption, mass spectrometry, voice prints, bite mark comparisons, hypnotically refreshed testimony, and voice stress analysis. Social science research has introduced "syndrome" evidence, like rape trauma syndrome, battered wife syndrome, and child abuse accommodation syndrome.

In one case, a woman shot her husband in the back six times and, as he was lying on the garage floor, asked him how long it would take him to die and spoke of inheriting his money (see Case 6.5). Three psychiatrists testified in court that the woman was in "a robotic or disassociative state" during the time of the shooting, but later seemed to become her own self again. A jury of eleven women and one man found, on the basis of "the psychiatric testimony by three eminent doctors who have nearly 75 years of practice among them" and who agreed that the defendant was "in a state of automatism at the time of the shooting" (Mitchell 1996, A7), that the defendant was not guilty of murder. This case illustrates how scientific syndromes have been stretched to cover cases that, in the past would clearly have been seen as instances of wrongdoing for which the perpetrator was responsible.

The *Frye* test for expert testimony, the traditional legal criterion, required that scientific testimony must include proof that the principle on which the testimony is based must be "sufficiently established to have gained general acceptance in the field to which it belongs." But the new ruling, Federal Rule of Evidence 703, now often supersedes *Frye* and requires only that the bases for an expert's opinion be "of a type reasonably relied upon by experts in the particular field" (Imwinkelried 1993, 60). The new ruling allows in many kinds of new scientific techniques that are not yet well established by all the practitioners in a given field of science (see Chapter 6, section 5).

In a famous trial, *Daubert v. Merrell Dow Pharmaceuticals* (1992), ruling whether Benedictin causes birth defects in human beings, the Supreme Court "repudiated the notion that scientific knowledge is a static body of propositions that are immutably true." According to the Court, the criterion of "good science" is not what the conclusions are, but how they are reached (Imwinkelried 1993, 62). This view of science was cited as a reason for favoring the newer and more open criterion of expert scientific testimony over the more conservative *Frye* ruling (see Chapter 6, section 5).

Clearly the law is having difficulty dealing with expert testimony used as evidence in the courts. The fact that expert evidence is so ubiquitous in current court cases, and the evident fact that scientific experts can easily be found to testify for both sides of a trial—the findings of the one group of experts contradicting those testifying for the other side—suggests that some way of rational thinking or judging arguments other than purely scientific reasoning in a field of technical expertise is needed to evaluate claims made on the basis of expert testimony. In evaluating expert testimony, then, the question is whether we are appealing to some kind of rational argumentation other than scientific reasoning in a field of technical expertise.

5. Expert Testimony in Court

The main problem with the authority of science relates not so much to internal matters of how scientific reasoning is used in scientific research within a discipline to arrive at conclusions (though this is part of it) as to the more subtle but more crucial problem: how the results of this research are communicated to a wider community of users who are not experts in that discipline. This problem is more subtle because it involves two frameworks of communicative discourse in which the same sequence of reasoning is used. First, there is the internal scientific reasoning itself that led to a particular conclusion within the scientific discipline or research investigation. Second, there is the bringing forward and using of that conclusion and explaining the line of reasoning that led to it in a communication exchange between the scientific expert and the user. This second framework of discourse seems to require a kind of reasoning or rational thinking that is not itself scientific.

Particularly in the use of expert scientific opinion as evidence in a court of law, one can see the duality of two very different frameworks of argument. As part of the normative model of the inquiry in a scientific investigation, an impersonal testing and cumulation of evidence is supposedly what matters in an argument. Partisanship, advocacy, personal attack, and self-interest are supposed to be irrelevant as evidence. Any evidence that such matters are playing a role in acceptance or rejection of a hypothesis, or in drawing conclusions from it, would (or should) be regarded as bias—a serious breach of professional standards of research.

The legal framework of evidence is quite different. Attacking the character of a witness—a highly personal matter—is a legitimate and important kind of evidence. In fact, our legal system is based on an adversarial framework, where the clash of arguments between self-interested advocates is seen as the basis of the argumentation that enables conclusions to be drawn and findings to be made. The purpose of each side is to assemble the evidence that supports its contention and attack the evidence put forward by the other. By its nature, this approach is quite different from scientific research, where it is important to look at all the relevant evidence, to test a hypothesis, and to go whichever way the outcome of the test indicates.

The oddity of juxtaposing these two frameworks of argument appears when we confront the situation of a scientific expert testifying in court. The expert witness is paid by one side to support the argument of that side. It does not always work out completely that way in practice, but generally it does. And in many cases, it looks like the scientific evidence is tailored to fit the needs and requirements of the lawyer's case. Among the more notable types of cases that have been prominent in recent publicized trials are those where the scientific testimony of the expert witness for the one side flatly contradicts the scientific testimony of the expert witness for the other side. Other notable cases (such as that of the Menendez brothers) are those where a social scientist or psychiatrist presents evidence that the accused in a criminal trial was suffering from some kind of syndrome, in an ever-growing list of such syndromes, so that he or she cannot be held accountable for the harm caused (Giannelli 1993, 112). In some celebrated cases, the view was even put forward that nobody is ever responsible for their actions, according to the social-scientific view of behavior that stresses changing the behavior rather than laying the blame. This point of view is directly at odds with the purpose of a criminal trial, which is to decide whether the accused is "guilty" or not.

The postmodernist perception that a scientific opinion can contain an interest, a bias, or a point of view is then justified strongly by the experience of dealing with appeal to expert scientific opinion in the courts. To begin with, science is not a static body of knowledge. And when scientific knowledge is applied (or someone attempts to apply it) to the particulars of a given case, there may need to be presumptions made about circumstances that are not known or cannot be quantified precisely.

Are we then to agree with the extreme postmodern conclusion so often drawn nowadays that a scientific opinion is just another subjective bias? We should go on a bit further in our examination before quickly leaping to this thesis of extreme relativism. What has become apparent is that the appeal to expert opinion involves two different kinds or uses of reasoning: (1) the reasoning used by the expert in a technical domain of knowledge to arrive at a particular conclusion and (2) the kind of reasoning that needs to be used by the nonexpert who is engaged in a deliberation or persuasive argument that needs to be partly based on, and informed by, the advice of the expert. Unless there is room for this second type of rational argument to ask intelligent questions in cross-examining an expert, then there is no hope of proceeding in a rational manner when confronted by problems like cases where what the experts say is implausible or when one expert flatly contradicts another. What of the problem of getting a second opinion that flatly contradicts the advice given by our family physician? How does one proceed to act rationally in the face of such a contradiction on the part of the scientific experts? If there is a way to proceed—and there must be—it represents a kind of rational thinking or judging arguments that is external to Peirce's way of fixing belief by the method of science.

6. A Complex Type of Argument

Appeal to expert opinion is a complex type of argument because the roles of the two chief parties involved are somewhat at cross-purposes. The user is trying to get some information from the expert. But he, the user, is not himself an expert in the field of the inquiry (at least, typically). Nevertheless, the user has to try to understand what the expert is saying or means to say. The expert is trying her best to impart information or give advice to the user of a kind he will be able to understand, despite his lack of technical knowledge. So the expert is engaging in a kind of scientific or technical reasoning in her field of expertise, and then trying to convey the conclusion of this reasoning (and perhaps explaining how she got it) to the user.

A potentially confusing aspect of arguments based on authority is the tendency to identify them with more basic kinds of argumentation. Initially, it is easy to identify expert opinion-based arguments with knowledge-based scientific reasoning. But this identification is a mistake. The internal knowledge-based reasoning used by a scientific expert or by an expert practitioner of a skill has recently been modeled or duplicated by expert systems (see Chapter 4, section 5). Scientific argumentation (according to Aristotle and especially Pascal) also has its own structure as a form of inquiry in a scientific discipline where hypotheses are verified or falsified empirically, and theories are expressed in a mathematical form. Neither of these kinds of reasoning, however, represents the dynamic of appeal to expert opinion as a type of argument. The latter is typified by the use of scientific or knowledge-based reasoning by a partner in dialogue who is generally not herself a scientist or an expert in the field of the argument. Thus, seeing appeal to expert opinion as being a kind of scientific inquiry or knowledge-based reasoning is simplistic.

The problem I confront in this book is not whether scientific research is open to challenge because of its internal methods of reasoning or its findings but rather one of what use is made of these findings when they are reported to or used by a wider public of individuals who are not themselves scientists (or at any rate, are not concerned with research in a particular scientific discipline relating to the matter at hand). The problem is that once a scientific finding is announced by the working scientists, a "spin" can be put on it when it comes to applying it to wider use, teaching it in a school or university, or relating it to decisions of personal or public affairs (as noted in Case 1.1, above).

It is easy initially to identify appeal to expert opinion as a type of persuasion. However, this approach is also too simplistic. As Bruce Lincoln (1994) points out, authority, despite its superficial commonality with persuasion, is something quite different.

> Even when authority does work with and through words, it does so in a very different fashion than persuasion. Thus, one persuades by arguing a case, advancing reasoned propositions, impassioned appeals and rhetorical flourishes that lead the hearer to a desired conclusion. In contrast, the exercise of authority need not involve argumentation and may rest on the naked assertion that the identity of the speaker warrants acceptance of the speech, as witness the classic pronouncements of paternal authority *in extremis:* "Because *I* said, so," and "Because I'm your father, *that's* why!"

Although the potential for persuasion is always implicit within authority, the two things are generally different. Authority, according to Lincoln functions as "a time-saving device or a shorthand version of persuasion" (1994, 5). The person consulting the expert does not have direct access to the scientific evidence or the skilled experience that the expert has. The expert must communicate her opinions and advice in a way that the user will find comprehensible. This communicative exchange may involve persuasion, to some extent, but the core of it should be a transfer of information or advice from one party to another. The user party typically also must play a role in the dialogue by asking intelligent questions directed to the statements made by the expert.

Thus the type of argument involved is neither simply the internal reasoning of the expert as a scientific inquiry nor simply a type of persuasion. It is a dialogue (dialectical) exchange between two parties where one asks a question and the other presents some previously established line of scientific or expert reasoning as the basis of the assertions made to the other. Presumably, the questioner is seeking information in the form of expert advice in order to best deliberate on how to proceed in some situation where expert advice would be useful in helping to determine a prudent course of action. Or, in other cases, an expert opinion could be used for other purposes in other types of dialogue. For example, in a trial, an expert could testify to present evidence that would be useful to a jury in trying to decide which attorney, the prosecution or the defense, has fulfilled the requirements of the burden of proof legally deemed appropriate for this kind of case.

All in all, then, various types of dialogue could be involved in a given case where appeal to expert opinion is the form of argument being used in a case. A systematic survey of six basic types of dialogue that are common frameworks of argumentation has been given in Walton and Krabbe (1995, 80; see also Fig. 4.3).

Initial Situation / Main Goal	Conflict	Open Problem	Unsatisfactory Spread of Information
Stable Agreement/ Resolution	Persuasion	Inquiry	Information Seeking
Practical Settlement/ Decision (Not) to Act	Negotiation	Deliberation	
Reaching a (Provisional) Accommodation	Eristic		

Fig. 1.1. Systematic Survey of Dialogue Types

The goal of the eristic type of dialogue is to get the best of the other party by any (verbal) means, even if it includes fallacious personal attack arguments and similar tactics. The goal of persuasion dialogue is for each party to rationally persuade the other party that her (the first party's) thesis is true based on premises that are commitments of the second party. The expert consultation type of dialogue is a sub-species of information-seeking dialogue where the purpose is for the questioner (who is not an expert in the field in question) to get information requiring technical expertise from a genuine expert in a domain of scientific or technical knowledge.

The complexity is that a sequence of argumentation in a given case can involve a shift from one type of dialogue to another. For example, an appeal to expert opinion could be an argument exchange in an information-seeking dialogue based on a prior inquiry in a scientific field that is then used in a persuasion dialogue as evidence to back up a disputed contention. Evaluating the argument in such a multiple framework of uses means going beyond Peirce's method of science as the only really reliable or rational way of fixing assent, and countenancing other conversational frameworks of argument as being normative standards for judging reasoning as well. This viewpoint of multiple perspectives, or multiple types of dialogue, is a kind of relativism. But it does not sanction the extreme postmodernist view that all viewpoints are equally valid or rationally acceptable.

7. Being Intimidated by Experts

The primary problem of appeal to expert opinion is to evaluate particular cases of the use of appeal to expert opinion in argument by some normative standards that will generally enable us to evaluate the argument as strong or weak and, in particular, to spot its weak points. The problem faced by all of us, on a daily basis, is how to evaluate and generally deal with expert opinion when we have to make practical decisions about things like going to the dentist, buying a car, consulting a financial adviser, and so forth.[2] We tend to be intimidated by experts, not only because they so often use technical jargon but because we ourselves (if we are not experts in the field in question, which is generally the case) are not in a good position to really understand the expert's reasons for advocating a particular conclusion or recommending a particular course of action. Thus we quite rightly feel powerless, and feel we lack the resources necessary to deal with this kind of problem.

Caplan describes the feeling of helplessness all of us have experienced at some time or another, when confronted with this problem.

> Virtually every adult has felt inadequate and helpless when dealing with authorities and experts who seem to have the information we need or the power to help us. We've all had some maddening experience such as listening hard but not understanding when a doctor or lawyer tells us about our medical or legal situation, when a psychologist or teacher interprets our child's test results, or when a person we've hired to repair our home or car doesn't quite fully explain why we supposedly need expensive work done. Even if we don't feel foolish asking them to explain better, we may feel helpless, because we don't know where or how to begin asking questions.

Caplan's book, *You're Smarter Than They Make You Feel,* is designed to help anyone who has been treated badly by experts like physicians,

2. Also included here should be instances where we have to deal with expert opinions in our jobs; for example, lawyers who have to examine scientific experts in court.

lawyers, or teachers, and who feels frustrated and powerless. Her own advice is based on the psychology of empowerment rather than on an approach of informal logic or critical thinking. But she expresses the nature of the problem as one of critical thinking when she writes that we "don't know where or how to begin asking questions" (1994, 4). The crux of the problem is to formulate a general account of the right questions to ask when confronted with an appeal to expert opinion.

The problem of dealing intelligently with arguments based on expert opinion is not just a psychological one. Psychology can help by teaching us to be more assertive, to take control of the situation, and be less intimidated by experts. But the problem is one of judgment and reasoning— of evaluating arguments based on expert opinion by identifying the strong and weak points in such an argument, so that we can judge its rational acceptability—as opposed to other alternative hypotheses or proposed courses of action. But as section 6 showed, this problem is a subtle one. We cannot just concentrate on the internal reasoning of the scientific expert or the persuasion aspect of how the expert puts her point across in an attempt at communicating informatively to a layperson who has consulted her. We have to realize that such a dialogue exchange is a composite of these two contexts of argument.

In order to give a useful normative evaluation of appeals to expert opinion as arguments, then, we cannot just look at the form of the argument and judge the argument as valid if it has the right form, as we might in traditional logic. We need to take the form of the argument into account, but we also need to see the argument as a communicative exchange involving a sequence of questions and replies between two parties, one of whom is an expert in some field of knowledge or some skill and the other of whom is (typically) not. In other words, the kind of structure needed to normatively evaluate particular instances of appeal to expert opinion arguments is dialectical, meaning that it involves a dialogue or communicative exchange between two parties. Moreover, it is not a simple type of dialogue, and the goals of the two parties in the exchange are generally not the same.

8. Questioning an Expert Opinion

In the conduct of everyday life, the actions we take, the decisions we make, and the beliefs we accept are commonly based on the authority of experts. Even though ours is an era where there is less deference to any single central religious or political authority, we do very often go along with the authority of expert opinion. Not only are most of our important and central beliefs based on scientific authority but, as Haskell notes, we routinely defer to the authority of experts in all sorts of common decisions.

> Living as we do in a society of specialized occupations and advanced technologies, we find that deference to experts is woven into even the homeliest routines of everyday life. We make jokes about the inaccuracy of the weatherman's forecast, yet we allow it to shape our plans and our choice of wearing apparel, even when our own glance out the window reveals no hint of the weather he predicts. When my car won't start and the mechanic says it is because of a faulty voltage regulator, I do not ask him to recite all the evidence and reasoning that led him to that conclusion, but trust his judgment and get on with my life—either that or go to a different mechanic. My dentist aggravates me by his habit of explaining little and presuming much, but even after I have stopped him and made him explain the options available to me, I usually find that I am drawn, in spite of its great expense, to the treatment he knew was best all along. Having never compared an alloy crown with one made of gold, how can I alone judge which is best for my aching tooth? (1984, 9)

A typical situation of having to deal with expert opinion is a consultation with our physician or dentist. Even understanding what he or she is telling you is likely to be quite difficult. You do not want to appear ignorant, but he or she may be explaining the problem in a way that makes no sense to you and using terms that are not familiar, or even comprehensible. He or she may be talking fast, and you probably find it hard to even remember exactly what he or she just said. If you try to take notes, you may even be diagnosed as an "obsessive-compulsive" (irrational) person. You know that you can ask questions, but after all, he or she is the expert, and you don't want to suggest that you lack confidence in his or her medical and scientific knowledge.

However, the problem is not entirely a psychological one—that you are intimidated by the expert and need more self-confidence or self-esteem. The normative problem is more specific to the case: you need to know what questions to ask, how and when to ask them, and what conclusions to draw from the answers you get (or do not get). These are normative and dialectical questions, not psychological ones. But they are not only logical in the traditional (narrower) sense. They have to do with how an argument was used as part of the question-reply sequence of interactions in a communicative exchange. In this case, the exchange is an advice-giving expert consultation dialogue. A layperson is trying to get advice from an expert and the expert is trying to give that advice —to communicate it. Thus, the dialogue exchange is (ideally) a collaborative effort where both parties can expect to benefit, if things go well. Too often, however, this kind of exchange does not go very well, and misinformation or, even worse, confusion and misunderstanding are the results.

The problem is a difficult one because you—as a layperson—are not an expert in the field in question, and therefore it is inherently difficult for you to grasp the information the other party is trying to convey and the arguments he or she is using. But it is vitally necessary to make the effort, because if you do not even try you will likely come off the worse for it. Indeed, many people even have to confront this type of situation in their jobs or professions. For example, a lawyer who has the job of cross-examining an expert medical witness in court may not herself be a physician. Even so, she has to make the effort to learn a little bit about the subject-matter of the cross-examination. She has to appear confident before the judge or jury and take a leading role in the questioning of the witness. This is not an easy thing to do successfully, but it is a skill that can be learned and improved upon. The first step is realizing that normative evaluation of arguments from expert opinion is a distinctive and legitimate task of skilled communication and reasoning, and that it is a common and necessary part of everyday life; it makes the job easier. It is something we are already doing on a daily basis. But it is something we need to learn to do better.

What needs to be recognized, contra Peirce and the modern way of thinking about rationality, is that rational thinking outside science is both possible and necessary, and that this kind of rational thinking can meet normative standards of adequacy as good and reliable reasoning. More and more, the ridiculous excesses of abuses of appeals to expert opinion in the courts—indeed, in all walks of life—make it clear that many so-called results of scientific research need to be critically questioned and put in some kind of context where their real import for deciding how to proceed (for example, on legal and political questions) can be assessed rationally. This task of dealing with expert opinion arguments has become more urgent, more commonplace, and yet more difficult in recent times. More pressure is being put on the legal system by claims to expertise that are highly controversial and need to be critically questioned.

In the late 1980s a wave of therapists calling themselves "traumatists" began using a technique of putting patients under hypnosis to get them to recall repressed memories of childhood sexual abuse. A typical scenario is outlined by Gardner (1993, 371).

Case 1.2:   A woman in her thirties seeks therapy for symptoms ranging from mild depression, anxiety, headaches, or the inability to lose weight, to more severe symptoms like anorexia. Her therapist, having succumbed to the latest mental-health fad, decides almost at once that the symptoms are caused by repressed memories of childhood abuse. Profoundly shocked by this suggestion, the woman vigorously denies that such a thing could be possible. The stronger her denial, the more the therapist believes she is repressing painful memories.

The patient may be hypnotized, or given sodium amytal, or placed into a relaxed, trancelike state. Convinced that a childhood trauma is at the root of the patient's ills, the therapist repeatedly urges the woman to try to remember the trauma. If she is highly suggestible and eager to please the therapist, she begins to respond to leading questions and to less obvious signs of the therapist's expectations.

After months, or even years, images begin to form in the patient's mind. Shadowy figures threaten her sexually. Under continual urging, these memories grow more vivid. She begins to recognize the molester as her father, or grandfather, or uncle. The more detailed the visions, the more convinced both she and the therapist become that the terrible truth is finally being brought to consciousness. To better-trained psychiatrists, these details indicate just the opposite. Childhood memories are notoriously vague. Recalling minute details is a strong sign of fantasizing.

As the false memories become more convincing, the patient's anger toward a once-loved relative grows. The therapist urges her to vent this rage, to confront the perpetrator, even to sue for psychic damage. Stunned by their daughter's accusations, the parents vigorously deny everything. Of course they will deny it, says the therapist, perhaps even suppress their own memories of what happened. The family is devastated. A loving daughter has inexplicably been transformed into a bitter enemy. She may join an "incest survivor" group, where her beliefs are reinforced by hearing similar tales. She may wear a sweatshirt saying, "I survived."

The problem posed by this kind of case is that the therapist is a scientific expert of some sort—a psychiatrist, a psychologist, or at least someone with credentials as a certified therapist. So even though there may be no corroborating evidence in the form of photographs, testimony by others, physical evidence, or a history of sexual misconduct, the therapist's testimony is expert scientific evidence in a court of law. But is it "evidence" that is reproducible or falsifiable by some test that can be carried out by other investigators? There have been grave doubts on this score, expressed forcefully by the False Memory Syndrome Foundation, a group of distinguished psychologists and psychiatrists who do not agree that recovered memory should be counted as reproducible scientific evidence.

Although therapy is typically more an art than a science, and therapists are more motivated to make their clients feel good than to differentiate between truth and fiction in their client's narrative, the outcome of therapy is regarded as expert scientific evidence. If the presumption is that something is "science," or has been found by a scientific investigation, it is extremely hard for anyone who is a nonscientist to question it. Anyone who overtly questions or disagrees with scientific evidence can be presumed to be "kooky" or a crackpot—the questioning being a sign of being psychologically unstable.

Surely there is a basis for comparison between the expert scientific testimony in these cases and the European witch craze of the sixteenth and seventeenth centuries, where the trials of people alleged to be witches or individuals who had made a pact with the devil were aided by experts who supplied the esoteric details (Trevor-Roper 1967, 97). The Dominicans had demonological manuals used by theological experts who determined guilt based on evidence of a kind that was difficult or impossible to question. Confessions could be extracted by torture and then used as evidence. Signs of fear, or a person's being old or ugly, were taken as evidence of guilt.

The difference is that in the sixteenth and seventeenth centuries, the official religion was the authoritarian viewpoint that could not be questioned. Anyone who questioned the officially accepted religious view was labeled a "heretic. " Heresy, or being against the Church, was sufficient for a person to be arrested on the grounds that he or she might have made a secret pact with the devil. Such a person had to be "re-educated," and was prosecuted for this purpose in an inquisitorial procedure in which he was presumed to be guilty, once accused. In the modern period, science became the new authoritarianism, and to question official scientific views or findings would be enough to throw one's rationality into question.

9. The Problem of Fallacies

Appeal to authority has traditionally been treated as a fallacy by logic textbooks. Other kinds of authority have been covered under this heading: the authority of powerful institutions, like religious authority, government authority, or legal authority, for example. But primarily the textbooks have been concerned with the kind of appeal to authority used in the appeal to expert opinion as an argument. Often not distinguishing clearly between these different kinds of authority, and perhaps influenced by the Big Brother view that central dogmatic authority is the big problem, these textbooks have tended to see the appeal to authority type of argument as generally fallacious. By 'fallacious' is meant not only an incorrect argument but also a type of argument that is inherently deceptive in that it tends to fool people into accepting a bad argument as a good one. This view of appeal to authority as being a fallacy was especially dominant in the modern, postwar textbooks, persisting into the late 1960s and early 1970s (as we will see in subsequent chapters).

The era of the late 1960s and early 1970s was a time of positivism in the universities. Scientific reasoning was the criterion of truth, and the idea that appeal to authority was a fallacious type of argumentation was readily acceptable to students; this assumption needed no argument. Pascal's triumphant modern viewpoint was the conventional wisdom of the time. However, that attitude has been shifting gradually. One event that signaled the swing over to the opposed postmodern point of view was the development of expert systems technology. It then seemed evident that there was a scientific way of processing expert opinion reasoning. No longer was appeal to expert opinion rejected, in the popular view, as a method of reasoning to a conclusion that had no status at all as rational thinking. It could now be accepted as having some sort of status or credibility as a form of rational thinking.

Reflecting that change in thinking, the more recent textbooks have rated appeal to expert opinion as a type of argument that can be reasonable in some cases but fallacious in other cases. This newer approach is more balanced, but it poses a problem. What criteria should we use to evaluate an appeal to expert opinion in a given case so that we can determine whether it is fallacious or not? This question states the central normative problem of appeal to authority in a nutshell. Although these newer textbooks have now taken the step of attempting to provide some guidelines to their readers, the problem is that they exhibit little agreement. Their accounts, although some of them have merit, are not based on any systematic research into the structure of the appeal to expert opinion as a distinctive type of dialectical argument.

What is needed is a recognition that appeal to authority is an extremely powerful and commonly used type of argumentation that affects the most intimate decisions we make in our everyday deliberations, not only in the law courts and in politics but in virtually all our reasoning on anything that matters. Accordingly, much more care and attention needs to be paid to understanding how this type of argument is a genuine and legitimate method of gaining a rational person's assent. Even more important, we need guidance on how to rationally question and criticize arguments based on the authority of expertise.

10. Finding a Middle Way

The problem with the treatment of appeal to expert opinion in the logic textbooks of the past has been that logic, as a subject, has tended to raise expectations of great precision and definiteness. A proposition is said to be "true" or "false." An argument is either "valid" or, if not, then it is "invalid." Such evaluations are supposed to be based on definite and clear evidence, resulting in a decisive outcome. Normally, a mathematical decision procedure, like a truth table, is used. Hence logic has ignored or pushed to the sidelines, evaluation of "subjective" arguments like appeals to expert opinion that need to be judged as presumptively strong or weak in a given case, depending on how the argument was used in that case.

Along came the extreme postmodernist reaction, which rightly perceived the contextual and dialectical nature of everyday arguments like appeal to expert opinion, but used this premise to leap to the conclusion that no single objective "deconstruction" of the argumentation used in a given case is possible. Suspicious about claims to any kind of "authority," the extreme postmodernist is wary of the claims of any kind of objective standard of "correct" thinking. This postmodernist declares that any attempt to study, analyze, or evaluate arguments based on appeal to expert opinion would only reflect the bias of the investigator, perhaps creating a bias for either traditional standards of rational discourse favored by a logical elite or standards of scientific rationality, making an advocacy for the interests of the scientific elite. These relativistic conclusions are a defeatist message, declaring (in advance) that any attempt to investigate this subject is doomed to failure.

The problem with appeal to expert opinion as a type of argument is

that people in the past have tended to swing to extremes. The modern
viewpoint has tended to assume that the method of science is the only
kind of thinking that has validity and represents the truth. This view
tends to defer to authority too much, thinking of the expert in absolute
terms, as someone who knows everything about his or her subject and
who, consequently, cannot be questioned with any credibility by a nonexpert. The postmodernist viewpoint, going to the other extreme, rejects
authority as an elitist conception and refuses to defer to it at all. The
problem with this pendulum reaction is that appeal to expert opinion
as a type of argument cannot be evaluated reasonably. We need to seek
out a middle way between these extremes if it is to be analyzed as a
rational and useful kind of argument. Expert opinion needs to be
treated as an argument that has some weight of presumption in its
favor, but is not absolute, and is inherently open to critical questioning.

A dialectical viewpoint that allows for several different frameworks
of rational discourse, as indicated in the types of dialogue in Figure 1.1,
concedes that scientific findings based on the model of the inquiry do
have standing as evidence or as conclusions of an important kind of
reasoned argument. But that does not make them sacrosanct or beyond
questioning. In many cases, a scientific opinion may need to be challenged by the dialectical kind of argumentation used in a persuasion
dialogue—say, in a case where the scientific experts disagree, or in a
case where the problem cannot be resolved exclusively by means of
applying scientific evidence. Thus, the same argument could be acceptable as used in one context of dialogue, but should be regarded as questionable if used for a different purpose.

It is difficult for us to accept this middle way when evaluating arguments. People want to see the argument as either unconditionally valid
and trustworthy or as inherently fallacious. The idea seems to be that
logic must be on firm ground, and an argument, if it is to be acceptable,
must be clearly and decisively valid beyond all doubts. But the problem
with this approach is that, by default, arguments based on authority
are tossed into the "fallacious" or worthless category because of the possibility that they can be deceptive and misleading—they are sometimes
powerfully persuasive even when they turn out to be groundless and
flawed.

The ironic thing about the advent of the postmodernist way of thinking is that it fixates on a modern view of things that is now in the past,
warning of the dangers of authoritarianism and elitism of entrenched
interests and biases marked as objective knowledge. But there is just
as much danger in the new situation in which the postmodernists advocate a thoroughgoing relativism in which all standards of objective

rationality are declared to be culturally biased. Moreover, the steps we need to take to advance beyond this situation of being trapped in multiple subjectivities, where all arguments are equal, are precisely the ones that the extreme postmodernists tell us are impossible to take. Instead of being trapped in these polar opposite extreme views of rationality, what we really need is a balanced attitude toward authority. We need to accept what we hear from the experts provisionally, on a presumptive but critical basis. We need to critically question what the experts tell us, but generally to presume that if our critical questions are answered properly, that what the experts say is acceptable—not unconditionally true or verified beyond question, but plausibly true and acceptable (tentatively)—as a basis for reasoned action and commitment (subject to correction if new, relevant information should come in).

To begin this seeking of a middle way of treating appeal to expert opinion, we need to understand how the current situation of extreme views came about. To do this, I turn, in Chapter 2, to the historical roots of the subject. In subsequent chapters, my goal is to provide an analysis of the structure of appeal to expert opinion as a type of argument that can be evaluated dialectically as stronger or weaker in particular cases. My goal is to define and justify criteria for normative evaluation of these arguments.

2

HISTORICAL
BACKGROUND

The *argumentum ad verecundiam,* the fallacy of appeal to authority, has long had a secure place in the curriculum of introductory courses in logic and critical thinking. But it is a difficult fallacy to teach to students, the way it is normally presented in the logic textbooks.

The initial problem is that the word *verecundia* is difficult to explain to introductory students because it does not mean 'authority,' as the student expects. As Hamblin notes (1970, 42), it means 'shame,' 'shyness,' or 'modesty,' and most often is translated by the textbooks as 'reverence' or 'respect' (see section 9; also Chapter 3, section 4). But what have all these terms got to do with fallacious appeals to authority? There is an explanation, as we will see shortly. It is hard to explain this connection to students, however, without leaving the impression that the Latin term is only an idiosyncratic, outdated terminology, characteristic of the antiquated and undeveloped state of this admittedly neglected branch of logic. A second, even more serious, problem is that, although the *argumentum ad verecundiam* is usually classified as a fallacy, arguments based on a premise that appeals to an expert opinion (the main type of appeal to authority arguments stressed in the examples given by the textbooks) seem like they could be reasonable, that is, nonfallacious arguments, in many cases. This possibility seems to open up a large and unsettled question: When are such arguments fallacious, and when are they not? A third problem, even prior to that of evaluating such arguments, is that of identifying them as a distinctive species of argument. 'Authority' could mean many things (see Chapter 3, section 5). Although usually taken by the textbooks to refer to the authority of expertise—obviously religious authority, legal authority, and so forth—'authority' represents kinds of authority different from expertise that could also be used to back up an argument.

As the first step toward working out solutions to these problems, this chapter outlines the main lines of historical development that lead up to the way the *argumentum ad verecundiam* has been treated in the twentieth-century logic textbooks.

1. Overview of Developments

It was only in the late nineteenth and early twentieth centuries that argument from authority commonly came to be treated as a fallacy in the logic textbooks. It was not included in Aristotle's list of fallacies in *On Sophistical Refutations,* his book on fallacies. It is only in the modern textbooks, such as Watts's *Logick* (1725, 466) that we begin to see it listed as a fallacy. There never has been much scholarly literature on appeal to authority as a form of argument, and what does exist tends to be treated very briefly in most of the textbook accounts. But in the past (generally before the eighteenth century) when it was mentioned, appeal to authority was treated as a reasonable type of argument, though not a conclusive one. Even in the ancient world, it was broadly accepted as a legitimate and reasonable credible type of argumentation. As Hamblin put it, "Historically speaking, argument from authority has been mentioned in lists of valid argument-forms as often as in lists of fallacies" (1970, 43). In fact, as I will point out, there is plenty of evidence that argument from authority was accepted in logic as a valid, or at least reasonable, form of argument in both the ancient and medieval periods.

What then happened to make it a fallacy? There are two things to be taken into account. The first factor is that Locke, in his *Essay Concerning Human Understanding* (1690), claimed to have invented the expression *argumentum ad verecundiam,* using the term to refer to a distinctive species of argumentation where one party in dispute tries to exploit the respect of the other party in order for an established authority to make him submit to the first party's argument (see section

7). There is no evidence that anyone prior to Locke used the expression *argumentum ad verecundiam* in this way, to refer to a distinctive type of argumentation of this kind, so we presume Locke did in fact invent this phrase (Hamblin 1970, 161). Locke did not describe this type of argument as (inherently) fallacious, but textbooks did subsequently interpret his account this way. Here then is the origin of the *ad verecundiam* expression, and it is after Locke that it took on the tendency to be classified as a fallacy.

The second factor is the rise of empirical science in western Europe and the resulting conflict with the accepted use of appeal to authority as a conclusive type of argument almost beyond challenge—particularly the authority of Aristotle and the authority of the Church—that had been prevalent in the Middle Ages. This clash between acceptance of dogmatic appeal to authority versus scientific experimentation as a criterion of evidence came sharply into focus in the trial of Galileo by the Catholic Church after he rejected the Ptolemaic conception of the universe in favor of the new Copernican hypothesis. Galileo based his argument partly on appeal to the authority of ancient sources, but also based it on his observations of the planetary motions (Martin 1991).

The rise of science brought with it a kind of positivist way of thinking, to the effect that knowledge should be based on scientific experiment and mathematical calculation and that all else is "subjective." This way of thinking brought along with it the corollary that the argument from authority is inherently questionable as a type of argument and has no real place as serious scientific evidence to justify a claim to knowledge. By the early twentieth century, the prevailing climate of opinion had made it become possible to dismiss argument from authority as a fallacy in the introductory textbooks without having to worry about students seriously questioning this claim.

It is hard to know exactly how to interpret these historical developments, however. As Hamblin notes, although "at various historical periods arguments from authority have been especially disliked," this has not so much been for the reason that this type of argument is being condemned (1970, 43). It may be because certain authorities have been distrusted and replaced by new authorities. Perelman and Olbrechts-Tyteca cite several cases in point.

> Often argument from authority seems to be under attack, but the challenge is really to the *person chosen as authority*. Thus, Pascal derides argument from authority when the authority is that of "men of influence," but has no hesitation in invoking the authority of St. Augustine. Similarly, Calvin rejects the

authority of the Church, but admits that of the prophets. (1969, 307)

It may be a more subtle interpretation to observe then that while the scientific culture often seems to be the basis of the attack on authority as a type of argument, what has really happened is that science has become the new authority. This may now be changing once again, however. In the late twentieth century, we have witnessed the beginning of an erosion of the bedrock of established facts that can be taken as the ultimate authority. Along with the idea that science is in a process of continual correction and improvement, there has come a greater acceptance of appeal to expert opinion as a fallible but legitimate type of argumentation, as indicated in Chapter 1.

2. Plato on Socratic Questioning of Experts

The ancient Greeks did not have professional experts in the same way that we are familiar with this concept today, such as scientists with university degrees and so forth. But they did have skilled craftsmen of various kinds that were acknowledged as specialists, like carpenters and stonemasons. Physicians were recognized as persons having a specialized skill. And at least one science, mathematics, was recognized as a discipline of exact knowledge.

In the Platonic dialogues, Socrates quite often alludes to the idea that if one person wants to get the most authoritative opinion on some matters relating to one of these crafts (*technai*), then the opinion best sought is that of another person who is skilled in that craft. Typically Socrates does not state that he is using a form of argument called appeal to expert opinion in these passages in the dialogues. He only uses the argumentation to prove various specific points. But in so doing, he appears to implicitly acknowledge that appealing to an expert's opinion does have a kind of status as a type of argument that is reasonable.

For example, in the *Laches*, Socrates asks Melesias: "If you were deliberating about the gymnastic training of your son would you follow the advice of the majority of us, or the opinion of the one who had been trained and exercised under a skillful master?" (184e; Plato 1961, 128). Melesias answers, "The latter Socrates, as would surely be reasonable." Socrates replies that his one vote "would be worth more than the votes of all us four." Socrates goes on to add that "a good decision is based on knowledge" and that the first question to ask when deliberating on an issue is "whether there is any one of us who is an expert in that about which we are deliberating," and if so, we should take his advice (185a; Plato 1961). This kind of passage, where Socrates bases his line of argument that those who have knowledge or mastery of special skills are the best sources of an opinion that falls into their special area of expertise, is fairly common in the Platonic dialogues.

For example, in the *Charmides,* Socrates uses a long and complex sequence of argumentation to conclude that wisdom is a kind of knowledge about knowledge. His thesis is that wisdom is a kind of second-order knowledge that does not necessarily imply a first-order knowledge of a given subject or discipline. Socrates' line of argument is very subtle, and it is not necessary to try to follow it through fully here. But if we examine part of it (171a–171d), the appeal to the opinion of a knowledgeable source can be perceived as an implied type of argument Socrates is relying on.

> The wise man will indeed know that the physician has some kind of science or knowledge; but when he wants to discover the nature of this he will ask, What is the subject-matter? For each science is distinguished, not as science, but by the nature of the subject. Is not that true?
> Yes; that is quite true.
> And medicine is distinguished from other sciences as having the subject-matter of health and disease?
> Yes.
> And he who would inquire into the nature of medicine must pursue the inquiry into health and disease, and not into what is extraneous?
> True.
> And he who judges rightly will judge of the physician as a physician in what relates to these?
> He will.
> He will consider whether what he says is true, and whether what he does is right in relation to these?
> He will.
> But can any one appreciate either without having a knowledge of medicine?
> He can not.
> Nor any one but the physician, not even the wise man, as appears; for that would require him to be a physician as well as a wise man?
> Very true.

> Then assuredly, wisdom or temperance, if only a science of science, and of the absence of science or knowledge, will not be able to distinguish the physician who knows from one who does not know but pretends or thinks that he knows, or any other professor of anything at all; like any other artist, he will only know his fellow in art or wisdom, and no one else.
>
> That is evident, he said. (Plato 1936, 34–35)

Actually, even the provisional conclusion that Socrates reaches at the end of this part of the argument is interesting with respect to appeal to expert opinion as a type of argument. Socrates is making the point that a nonexpert in a given field, such as medicine, will not be able to distinguish between a physician who really knows something and a physician who only thinks or pretends he knows but does not. He makes that point that the cross-examining an expert by a nonexpert (in the same field) is at best a process of guesswork that does not result in a conclusion based on knowledge (at least in the sense of first-order knowledge in the field in question).

But, apart from any other interpretations that might be made of this interesting passage in the *Charmides,* it does reveal that Plato presumed that an expert such as a physician does possess a kind of specialized knowledge that gives his opinion special status when he is consulted and asked for that opinion by someone who is not an expert in medicine. It implies that the lay questioner does have a reason for accepting the opinion in such a case, or at least takes it as having a preferred status as an opinion solicited from a source that possesses knowledge.

Of course, this point of view does not imply that the layperson then has knowledge of this opinion, at least first-order knowledge, in the sense that the physician has. And in fact, Socrates emphasizes that this is not the case. The conclusion of his argument, at this point, in fact emphasizes the logical gap between the nonexpert questioner and the expert source. The former is not in a position to distinguish between the real knowledge-based opinion and the phony one, with any basis of first-order knowledge. This argument emphasizes the tenuousness of appeal to expert opinion. On the other hand, the Socratic method of rational argument, which Plato called 'dialectic,' consisted in Socrates questioning the experts on various matters of philosophical importance and finding out (by deriving contradictions and absurdities from arguments based on premises accepted by the experts) that the opinions of the experts were highly questionable. Hence Socrates' famous Socratic wisdom: He claimed not to possess knowledge himself, but only to be

wise in the sense that he knew that he did not know anything (in contrast to the experts, who claimed to know things, but whose claims
could be shown to be questionable).

The method of questioning used by Socrates, especially in the earlier
dialogues, is sometimes called *elenchus,* often referred to as *exetasis* or
"scrutiny" (R. Robinson 1953). According to Robinson, *elenchus,* in the
wider sense, is the Socratic method of "examining a person with regard
to a statement he has made, by putting to him questions calling for further statements," in order to "determine the meaning and the truth-
value of his first statement" (sometimes by leading to contradictions
and difficulties). Robinson claims that the use of this method is so common in the early dialogues that "we may almost say that Socrates
never talks to anyone without refuting him" (7). Thus Plato certainly
believed that a layperson can critically examine the opinion of an
expert in a field of knowledge who has put forward this opinion as
something that is known to be true, or is accepted in a field of expert
knowledge.

3. Aristotle on Dialectical Arguments

Aristotle recognized the worth of the argument from appeal to expert
opinion in several places in his writings. In the *Topics* (III. I. 116a12–23),
Aristotle discusses which is the better or more desirable of two things.
One of his criteria is that the more desirable thing is more likely to
be chosen by the expert in any particular line, such as medicine or
carpentry.

> First, then, that which is more lasting or secure is more desir-
> able than that which is less so: and so is that which is more
> likely to be chosen by the prudent or by the good man or by the
> right law, or by men who are good in any particular line, when
> they make their choice as such, or by the experts in regard to
> any particular class of things; i.e., either whatever most of
> them or what all of them would choose; e.g., in medicine or in
> carpentry those things are more desirable which most, or all,
> doctors would choose or, in general, whatever most men or all
> men or all things would choose, e.g., the good: for everything
> aims at the good. You should direct the argument you intend to
> employ to whatever purpose you require. Of what is 'better' or
> 'more desirable' the absolute standard is the verdict of the

better science, though relatively to a given individual the standard may be his own particular science. (Aristotle 1928, 383–85,
quoted in Ross)

For example, if you want to know whether a particular course of treatment is better than another one, you should ask what most, or all doctors, would choose. If your purpose is the recovery of your health, then
you need to decide what is better or more desirable for that purpose.
The way to answer this question, according to Aristotle, is to seek the
opinion of an expert, which is, in this case, a doctor.

Aristotle also recognized appeal to authority of various kinds as a
"topic," or commonly used kind of inference warrant, in *The Art of
Rhetoric* (II. 1398b12–1399a5):

Another topic is that from a previous judgment in regard to the
same or a similar or contrary matter, if possible when the
judgment was unanimous or the same at all times; if not, when
it was at least that of the majority, or of the wise, either all or
most, or of the good; or of the judges themselves or of those
whose judgment they accept, or of those whose judgment it is
not possible to contradict, for instance, those in authority, or of
those whose judgment it is unseemly to contradict, for
instance, the gods, a father, or instructors; as Autocles said in
his attack on Mixidemides, "If the awful goddesses were content to stand their trial before the Areopagus, should not
Mixidemides?" Or Sappho, "Death is an evil; the gods have so
decided, for otherwise they would die." Or as Aristippus, when
in his opinion Plato had expressed himself too presumptuously,
said, "Our friend at any rate never spoke like that," referring
to Socrates. Hegisippus, after having first consulted the oracle
at Olympia, asked the god at Delphi whether his opinion was
the same as his father's, meaning that it would be disgraceful
to contradict him. Helen was a virtuous woman, wrote Isocrates,
because Theseus so judged; the same applies to Alexander
(Paris), whom the goddesses chose before others. (Aristotle
1937, 309)

Here Aristotle recognizes several types of argumentation that carry
some weight as reasonable inferences. One is the inference, 'If the
majority accept *A*, then *A* is (plausibly) true.' Another is the inference
'If the wise accept *A*, then *A* is (plausibly) true.' Both these inferences
can have three different forms, depending on whether it is all the wise

(or the majority), or most, or the good that are referred to. These two types of argumentation correspond to what later became known as *ad populum* (appeal to popular opinion) arguments and appeal to authority arguments.

Moreover, Aristotle distinguishes several different types of appeal to authority arguments. One is the judgments of "those in authority," such as "gods, fathers, or instructors." This appears to be more of a kind of administrative or institutional authority of a superior who gives orders or commands. Another authority referred to is Socrates himself, or to how Socrates spoke. Then the oracle at Delphi is mentioned, and then the gods and goddesses are mentioned.

When Aristotle writes of the judgment of "the wise" (*sophoi*), he would probably include the opinions of experts in the arts and crafts, including physicians or carpenters. But we have to be careful here, because Aristotle had a carefully worked out theory of wisdom, distinguishing between theoretical wisdom (*sophia*) and practical wisdom (*phronesis*).[1] Also, in his view, knowledge is not necessarily the same thing as wisdom (wisdom being a kind of second-order knowledge, or knowledge about knowledge, as elaborately defined in the *Nicomachean Ethics*). Such distinctions between knowledge and wisdom are probably somewhat alien to the modern reader. In the late twentieth century we certainly recognize the authority of expert opinion in legal rules of evidence as having a special status as a type of argumentation. But the notion of any designated group, such as philosophers, as being "wise" or sources of wisdom, over and above any expertise based on knowledge of a discipline, is not one that has general acceptance. People would generally be highly skeptical about any such assumption at the present time. Without going into these matters further, suffice it to say that Aristotle did recognize arguing from a premise of what is said by the wise or those who have specialized knowledge of a field as a distinctive type of argument that can carry a weight of plausibility (*eikos*).

In Aristotle's logic, a *demonstrative argument* is one where the premises are known to be true and the conclusion inferred is (therefore) also known to be true. This is to be contrasted with a *dialectical argument,* where the premise (proposition) is generally accepted as true but is not known to be true or false.[2] In the *Topics,* Aristotle writes, "A dialectical proposition consists in asking something that is

---

1. The best source here is probably the *Nicomachean Ethics* 1140b11.
2. This distinction is made very clear right at the beginning of the *Topics* (100a25–100b22), where Aristotle defines generally what he means by reasoning (*syllogysmos*). Note especially that his definition of dialectical reasoning is based on premises that are generally accepted opinions (*endoxa*), which includes reference to those of "the wise."

held by all men or by most men or by the philosophers, i.e., either by all, or by most, or by the most notable of these, provided it be not contrary to the general opinion; for a man would probably assent to the view of the philosophers, if it be not contrary to the views of most men" (I. 104a8–11). Thus dialectical propositions or *endoxa,* opinions that are generally accepted (Evans 1977, 77), which are the basis of dialectical arguments, are views or tenets that are "reputable" (Barnes 1980, 500), and have a general presumption in their favor. But they are not known to be true (or false), and are subject to questioning and discussion.

What is especially interesting here is that Aristotle explicitly classifies opinions based on expert opinion as dialectical propositions.[3] In the *Topics* (104a33–37), he classifies the views of "those who have made a study of these things" as having dialectical status: "Clearly also, all opinions that are in accordance with the arts are dialectical propositions; for people are likely to assent to the views held by those who have made a study of these things, e.g., on a question of medicine they will agree with the doctor, and on a question of geometry with the geometrician; and likewise also in other cases." So, for Aristotle, expert opinions have a special status as premises that are acceptable in dialectical argument. It would seem that, in Aristotle's logic, arguments based on expert opinion can be reasonable arguments, at least in the type of argument Aristotle called dialectical. But what exactly is the goal of dialectical argument for Aristotle? This question has been a hard one for Aristotle scholars to answer, and it has led to various con-

---

Reasoning is a discussion in which, certain things have been laid down, something other than these things necessarily results through them. Reasoning is *demonstration* when it proceeds from premises which are true and primary or of such a kind that we have derived our original knowledge of them through premises which are primary and true. Reasoning is *dialectical* which reasons from generally accepted opinions. Things are true and primary which command belief through themselves and not through anything else; for regarding the first principles of science it is unnecessary to ask any further question as to 'why,' but each principle should of itself command belief. Generally accepted opinions, on the other hand, are those which commend themselves to all or to the majority or to the wise—that is, to all of the wise or to the majority or to the most famous and distinguished of them. (Aristotle 1928, 273–74)

According to Evans (1977, 80), it is Aristotle's view that dialectical arguments are concerned with matters where there is *aporia* (perplexity; being at a loss), in cases where there are conflicting points of view, or where a satisfactory explanation of the matter is lacking.

3. On this point, there is a definite point of contrast between Plato and Aristotle. According to R. Robinson (1953, 79) Plato expressed a "strong belief in the value of experts" in the dialogues, but his method of dialectic did not recognize authority.

flicting views, surveyed in Bolton (1990), Devereux (1990), and Smith (1993). But Aristotle, in the *Topics* (101a26–101b4), gives us some indications when he tells us that dialectic is useful for three purposes: mental training in disputation, casual conversations when dealing with people in everyday arguments (many of which are based on popular opinions), and discussing the basic principles (axioms) of a science. Since a demonstrative argument must presuppose these first principles and cannot itself be used to prove them, dialectical argument has an important function in this third use.

According to Guthrie (1981, 155), not all dialectic is competitive because Aristotle, in addition to discussing dialectic as used by those skilled in competitive disputation, also mentions (*Topics* 172a30–172a34) that even unskilled arguers use dialectic, or what he calls *peirastic* (examination) arguments to test the pretentious. What Aristotle seems to suggest here is that dialectic has a use for critically questioning or examining the opinion of an expert who we think to be pretentious and whose opinion we may be somewhat doubtful about accepting at face value. Guthrie actually cites two uses or subcategories of dialectic, which he calls *peirastic*, or "testing and probing," and *exetastic*, or "examining critically" (155). These two types of arguments are very interesting from the point of view of analysis of arguments based on appeal to expert opinion because they suggest there is a special type of argumentation (or two special types) used within such an argument when the layperson critically questions the basis of the expert opinion by probing the expert's reasoning behind her stated opinion.

But is peirastic argument a species of dialectical argument, or is it a separate type of argument in its own right? In *On Sophistical Refutations*

The principle that the answerer must say what he really thinks is a part of the principle that dialectic recognizes no authority. Neither party may accept a proposition from anyone else, however near or great. The only authority is what seems true to us two here and now. 'The question is not who said it, but whether it is truly said or not' (*Chrm*. 161C). 'As long as we ourselves agree about it, we can say good-bye to other men's opinions' (*Plts*. 260B, cf. *Phdr*. 275BC). 'Let us not consider him, since he is not here' (*Men*. 71D). Another man's dictum can become an authority only by his being present and persuading us of its truth. If Protagoras could get his head above ground, he would very likely persuade us otherwise; 'but we must take ourselves as we find ourselves, I think, and always say what we believe' (*Tht*. 171D, cf. *Hp. Mi*. 365CD). Plato never raised the question whether this principle conflicts with his strong belief in the value of experts, and his demand that men shall obey the expert statesman.

Thus while Plato and Aristotle both recognize appeal to authority as a type of argumentation, their views of dialectical argument as a type of reasoning that is used in drawing conclusions from what an expert says appear to be different, in some respects.

(165a38–165b12), Aristotle defines dialectical and peirastic (examination) arguments as two distinct types of arguments. However, as Guthrie indicates, Aristotle seems to think of peirastic arguments as a subclass of dialectical arguments (155). Hamblin writes that Aristotle is not sure whether these are two types of arguments or one, and "in different places he makes each a subclass of the other" (1970, 59). Although Aristotle leaves us dangling on these questions, it is interesting to see that he recognized argument from appeal to expert opinion, as well as arguments critically questioning an appeal to expert opinion.

According to Aristotle, then, arguments from expert opinion are not conclusive or demonstrative, but neither are they inherently fallacious. He sees them as somewhere in between: an important species of dialectical argument (and subspecies or different kind of argument elusively called 'peirastic') that can be used constructively, but could also possibly be abused.

4. The Medieval View of Argument from Authority

Windelband contrasts Greek and medieval conceptions of appeal to authority as an argument: "The *appeal to authority* often makes its appearance in Greek and Hellenistic philosophy in the sense of a confirmation and strengthening of an author's own views, but not as a decisive and conclusive argument." However, in the medieval period, "even scientific thought . . . no longer gave itself credit for the power of truth [and] subjected itself to the authorities of antiquity and to religious institutions" (1901, 219, 221). The religious documents of the Old Testament in particular were regarded as a historically accredited authority. Of course, the truth still had to be extracted from these sources by interpretation and argument. But, generally, the appeal to authority was regarded as quite different as a type of argument from what it was taken to be by the Greeks. It now becomes a much more ultimate, finalistic type of argument that is not open to critical questioning in the way the Greeks would have thought appropriate.

Argument from authority was recognized in medieval logic as a reasonable form of argument. For example, in the *Introductiones in Logicam* of William of Sherwood (or Shyreswood), first printed in the thirteenth century, we find argument from authority listed as an *argument from extrinsic grounds,* where part of the argument lies "outside the dialectical problem."

> *From Authority.* Since authority considered as a dialectical
> ground consists in something that is said, it comes first from the
> logician's point of view (Est autem locus ab auctoritate primus
> quoad logicum, cum consistat in dicere); for authority, properly
> so called, is the confirmed opinion of some wise man or, alter-
> natively, a saying worthy of imitation (sententia ymitatione
> digna). 'Authority' is being used broadly here, however, in the
> sense of a judgment, or something said by several wise men
> (Sumitur tamen hic communiter ut et iudicium, ut dicatur dic-
> tum plurium sapientium). (William of Sherwood 1966, 93)

William gives the following example:

Case 2.1:   Everything said by the astronomers to be revolving is
            revolving.
            The heavens are said by the astronomers to be
            revolving.
            Therefore, the heavens are revolving. (93)

Another example given by William is also worth noting:

Case 2.2:   Aristotle does not mention more than four causes.
            Therefore, there are no more than four causes. (92–93)

Interestingly, Case 2.2 is an argument from negative evidence, evidence
of a kind that could be classified as an *argumentum ad ignorantiam* as
well as an *argumentum ad verecundiam*. Today we would be inclined
to think of this as an inconclusive, weak kind of argument from lack of
evidence. However, William seems to treat it as a conclusive type of
argument.

William had put the argument in Case 2.1 in the form of a syllogism-
like argument that could be classified by present standards as a deductively valid type of argument. He even goes so far as to propose an
elaborate syllogistic form of the argument in Case 2.2:

Case 2.2a: No things said by Aristotle not to be are.
           More causes than four are said by Aristotle not to be.
           Therefore, there are no more causes than four. (94)

This treatment is ironic. Aristotle, who had treated appeal to authority as an inconclusive dialectical type of argument that is inherently
open to questioning and discussion, was now being treated as a kind

of ultimate authority. His name was being appealed to a source of opinion in a type of argument that was presented as being deductively valid, and in a way that made it seem very much like a conclusive sort of proof.

A few years after the time of William of Sherwood, Peter of Spain, who became Pope John XXI and died in 1277, wrote a logic book, *Summulae Logicales,* that had more influence on later thought than William's writings (Kneale and Kneale 1962, 234). In a selection from Peter of Spain's writings on topics,[4] Kretzmann and Stump (1988, 243) find a topic Peter called "The Topic *From Authority*":

> Authority, as the term is used here, is the judgment of a wise man in his own field of knowledge. Hence, 'from the judgment of a thing' is the usual designation for this Topic.
>
> The Topic *from authority* is the relationship of an authority to that which is proved by the authority. For example, 'An astronomer says that the heaven is revolvable; therefore, the heaven is revolvable.' Where does the Topic come from? From authority. The maxim: Any expert should be believed in his own field of knowledge.

In the translation of the *Summulae Logicales* of Dineen (Peter of Spain 1990, 66), the maxim in the last sentence quoted above is translated, "All experts are trustworthy in their own field." Although the *Summulae Logicales* has a good deal on the subject of fallacies (treated in Aristotelian fashion), there is no mention of an *ad verecundiam* fallacy or fallacious appeals to authority. According to Kneale and Kneale (1962, 234), Peter of Spain's logic textbook, the *Summulae Logicales,* was widely used in the Middle Ages, and remained in use as late as the seventeenth century. Thus appeal to authority as a reasonable type of argument does appear to be known in the medieval period as a distinctive type of argument in logic in the tradition of the Aristotelian topics.

Perhaps what is most interesting here is that appeal to authority is not treated under the heading of fallacies in the logic textbooks (and 'fallacies' was a widely used heading in the textbooks of this period), but under the heading of reasonable, but plausible types of arguments (topics).

---

4. *Topoi* (or "topics"; see section 3 above) are argument structures used by Aristotle and subsequent commentators to find arguments for use in a speech and test the plausibility of the inference in an argument.

5. Galileo's Challenge to Proof by Authority

In the medieval period, the argument from authority reached its high point: it seemed to be taken as a kind of conclusive proof or disproof of a proposition. However, in keeping with the observations of Hamblin (1970), and Perelman and Olbrechts-Tyteca (1969), it could be that certain sources, namely Aristotle and the Scriptures, were chosen as being the authorities and any other sources or arguments disagreeing with them were discounted. When the works of Greek science and philosophy were rediscovered in western Europe, they had an understandable impact on academic life. Citing the opinion of the respected ancient authors on a scientific question came to be a form of appeal to authority that strongly influenced the scientific beliefs of the time. The belief that the earth was the center of the cosmos was the popular view of the time, apparently supported by Greek science. In particular the theory of Claudius Ptolemy, a second-century-A.D. Alexandrian Greek astronomer, stated that the planets moved in an eccentric path around the earth.

One step in the evolution of this period of determining scientific belief by appeal to authority was the appearance of a book in 1543 by Nicolaus Copernicus, who studied the ancient writings and found that Greek scientists had suggested that the sun, not the earth, was the center of the cosmos. He invented a model, using perfect circular motions, to develop this hypothesis. Subsequently, Johannes Kepler (1571–1630), reinterpreted the data and, using more accurate data from Tycho, concluded that the orbits of the planets around the sun were elliptical. In 1609, Galileo built a telescope, inspired by reports of one having been made in the Netherlands, as well as published observations that, he believed, supported the Copernican theory. However, Galileo soon found out that his view was strongly opposed by the scholars and churchmen of the time on the grounds that it was contrary to the authority of the Bible. History had reached a point of clear conflict between the institutional authority that prevailed at the time and the claims of empirical science. Drake expresses the nature of this conflict concisely:

> The age into which Galileo was born was one in which the power of authority was uppermost in every sphere of activity— political, religious, and philosophical. It was therefore virtually impossible to attack that power in one sphere without disturbing it in others. To Galileo it was clear that in matters of scientific investigation, authority as such could not be allowed any

weight; observation, experiment, and reason alone could establish physical truth. (1967, 64)

When Galileo published his *Dialogue on the Two Chief Systems of the
World* in 1632, rejecting the Aristotelian-Ptolemaic system, he was
ordered by the pope to Rome, then tried by the Inquisition and, after
making a formal renunciation of the Copernican theory, was sentenced
to life imprisonment (commuted to house arrest) for the last eight years
of his life.[5]

Galileo's own view on appeal to authority as a type of argument, as
expressed in the *Dialogue* was that appeal to authority is "no substi-
tute for reasoning." Galileo recognized appeal to authority as a reasonable type of argument but emphasized that it had to be carried out in
a reasonable way. "If one is appealing to an authority, it is more adequate to look not only at the authority's conclusions but also at his
reasons and arguments" (Finocchiaro 1980, 174). In the *Dialogue* (ll.
346–349), Galileo wrote:

> Aristotle's authority is misused by the Peripatetics when they
> follow him in a specific conclusion he reached rather than in the
> manner whereby he arrived at it. The advantage of following
> his procedure is that one can apply it to a novel situation to
> reach novel conclusions when conditions have changed. For
> example, since Aristotle argues that the earth is at the center of
> the world because it is the center of celestial revolutions, it is
> reasonable to conclude that, if it could be shown that the sun
> and not the earth is at the center of celestial revolutions, then
> he would conclude that the sun and not the earth is at the cen-
> ter of the world; the novel situation here would be one where
> the available evidence made it more likely that the sun rather
> than the earth was at the center of celestial revolutions. In
> other words, the follower of the spirit of Aristotle, as opposed to
> the blind follower of his letter, should be able to see that the
> proposition that the center of the world is the center of celestial
> revolutions is more basic than the proposition that the earth is
> the center of the world, and from this to prefer the former in
> cases of conflict. (Galileo 1967, 128)

Curiously, then, Galileo's view of the argument from authority was
very much like Aristotle's. Both saw it as a useful but inherently

5. Finocchiaro (1989) gives a full and revealing account of the whole sequence of
events, including the most important primary sources of information.

questionable and nonconclusive argument. Both saw it as a kind of argumentation that could be reasoned with, questioned, and checked against other evidence and countervailing argumentation. Both were supportive of the idea of viewing an argument as a dialogue exchange of views. It is ironic, then, that Aristotle should have been held up as an authoritative source used to try to shut down Galileo's questioning of the accepted scientific view.

Once scientific thinking became established as the accepted framework of knowledge, however, the say-so of any authority could come into conflict with scientific findings, based on observation and experiment. According to this new way of thinking, which we have now come to accept, the opinion of the authority must give way in such a conflict. The "subjective" opinion of the authority must give way to the hard evidence of scientifically verified, "objective," knowledge. This new conventional wisdom, where scientific knowledge has priority over an authority's opinion, suggested that appeal to authority may not be very reliable as a type of argument.[6] This, in turn, made it possible that such an argument could be misleading, sophistical, or fallacious.

6. The *Port-Royal Logic*

Arnauld's *The Art of Thinking*, usually called the *Port-Royal Logic*, originally published in 1662, defined the *sophism of authority* as committed when "we accept something as true on authority insufficient to assure us of this truth." Arnauld's account of how this fallacy works appears to be psychological. Man's mind is "weak and befuddled," and often goes by superficial external appearances.

> To understand how common these sophisms are we need only reflect that when the majority of men hold one opinion rather than another, they hold this opinion not for any weighty or essential reasons but because the position has certain extraneous aspects which are deemed more likely to accompany truth than falsity. This habit of man is easily explained. Man's mind for the most part is weak and befuddled, full of clouds and false lights. The inmost truth of things is often deeply

---

6. Of course, it was not "new" at all, because it corresponded exactly with Aristotle's own view of the matter, as outlined in section 3 above. But it was "new" as a generally accepted view, especially in contrast to the previous generally accepted view of argument from authority.

hidden, but external appearances are readily perceived. And since man inclines to what is easiest, he nearly always finds himself of an opinion which possesses these external appearances of truth.

The main external signs of truth are taken to be: (a) the authority of a proponent and (b) the manner of propounding. These external signs are potent persuaders and overwhelm nearly every mind (1964, 286).

Although Arnauld goes on to indicate how the weakness of the human mind leads people to reason fallaciously from authority, as a religious thinker he also claims that appeals to the authority of the universal Church on matters of religion are not fallacious and are even "completely decisive":

God, willing that a knowledge of the mysteries of faith be accessible to the simplest of the faithful, had the goodness to accommodate himself to this weakness of the human mind. He did not make this knowledge depend upon the individual examination of each point proposed for belief, but instead he gave as a certain sign of the truth the authority of the universal Church, a sign so clear and evident that it relieves the mind of the perplexities which necessarily arise from a close consideration of these mysteries. Thus, in matters of faith the authority of the universal Church is completely decisive. The universal Church cannot err. We fall into error only when we wander from the Church's authority and refuse to submit ourselves to it. (286–87)

Even this type of conclusive authority can be "presented in a wrong manner" according to Arnauld. Some people try to "spread their doctrines by sword and bloodshed," but "any reasonable person will reject whatever is urged in so offensive a manner and not even the most stupid will listen" (289).

The type of authority cited by Arnauld above is religious authority, or perhaps even more specifically, the institutional authority of the "universal Church," as he calls it. However, Arnauld does appear to acknowledge the distinction between this type of authority and the type based on expert knowledge (in secular matters). He even argues that in a conflict between the two, religious authority should be given higher value as a weight of argument. Here he is inclining more back toward a medieval view on the conflict between religious authority and the evidence arising from scientific observation and reasoning.

> That the authority of the devout be preferred to the authority
> of the sage even in secular matters stems in part from piety's
> being more discernible than sagacity and in part from men's
> dislike of making distinctions. Qualifications perplex men; they
> would everything be black or else white. If a man can be trusted
> in one thing, he is to be trusted in all; if questioned in one, then
> questioned in all. Men love shortcuts and absolute statements.
> But this love is unreasonable. No one person is an authority in
> all matters. To conclude that because a man is grave, he is there-
> fore in all things intelligent and clever is to reason poorly. (288)

Arnauld's analysis of the fallacy of appeal to authority seems to be psy-
chologistic in nature. The fallacy is portrayed as one of giving in to
superficial appearances, concluding that an opinion is true just because
the person who asserts it has a "grave" appearance.

Above, Arnauld also makes the suggestion that there is a kind of
"halo effect" about authority: if an authority "can be trusted in one
thing, he is to be trusted in all." This principle suggests that we tend to
over generalize with appeals to authority. If a person is an expert in
some narrow, well-defined area of expertise, that position gives her a
certain air of authoritativeness or credibility. Hence we may be inclined
to give her opinion on some unrelated subject (in which she is not an
expert) much more weight than it really deserves. We will see in
Chapter 8 the importance of these observations in giving an analysis of
the *ad verecundiam* fallacy.

In chapter 13 of part 4 of *The Art of Thinking,* Arnauld formulates
an important rule for determining when to accept an appeal to authority. He begins by distinguishing between necessary truths, that is,
theorems in geometry, and truths that "relate to existing things, especially to human and contingent events" (340). Then he asks, with
respect to the latter type of statements, how should one decide which is
true, if two authorities give conflicting accounts. Let us say that on one
account a certain historical event was said to occur, but that according
to another account it did not occur. Arnauld gives the following rule for
deciding:

> How then shall I decide to believe in the occurrence of the one
> rather than of the other if I judge them both possible? I shall
> decide according to the following maxim: *In order to judge of
> the truth of some event and to decide whether or not to believe in
> its occurrence, the event need not be considered in isolation—
> such as a proposition of geometry would be; but rather all the*

circumstances of the event, both internal and external, should be considered. I call internal circumstances those which belong to the event itself; external circumstances, those which pertain to the persons by whose testimony we are led to believe in the event's occurrence. If the circumstances of the event are such that like circumstances are rarely accompanied by falsity, we are naturally led to believe that the event is true. And it is proper that we be so led, especially in the conduct of life where no greater certainty than moral certainty is demanded and where in many cases we must be satisfied with choosing the most probable.

But if on the contrary the circumstances of the event are such as are not infrequently accompanied by falsity, reason requires either that we remain in suspense or that we consider as false what has been told us if there is no further indication that the event has occurred—even though we do not consider the event an utter impossibility. (341–42)

This rule will turn out to be very significant in our evaluation of appeal to authority as a type of argument because it takes into account something that frequently happens in cases where this type of argument is used. Often there is objective evidence available, giving us circumstances that can either conflict with or support the account of the matter given by the authority. In evaluating the argument from authority, we can use this evidence to support or undermine it, whichever way the evidence goes.

Another important factor in many cases is that the authority may have made other pronouncements on the same subject, statements that may either support or be inconsistent with the opinion currently in question. This too is a type of evidence that can be used to evaluate the evidential worth of an appeal to authority in a given case. Arnauld was the first to state these criteria for judging the worth of an appeal to authority as an argument. Thus his account is very significant, but it was, by and large, overlooked by the logic textbooks and dictionaries of philosophy, who tended to quote Locke's description of the *argumentum ad verecundiam* in their description of the fallacy of appeal to expert opinion.

But, in another way, the *Port-Royal Logic* was influential. In its account of the kind of reasoning described as being used for "coming to understanding," the *Port-Royal Logic* offered two methods: (1) *demonstration,* where thoughts are ordered in a sequence based on first judgments or axioms, that are known immediately to be true, and conclusions, judgments that follow deductively from the axioms and (2) *discovery* and search for axioms by skillful selection. However, as Dickoff and James pointed out, little is said in the *Port-Royal Logic* about discovery, "simply because very little can be said" (Arnauld 1964, xliii). Both in its central use of the model of geometrical demonstration and its having little to say about the method of discovery, the *Port-Royal Logic*, supported Pascal's elevation of the scientific demonstration as the only kind of thinking that represents reality.

7. Locke's Account of *Argumentum ad Verecundiam*

Locke's account of the *argumentum ad verecundiam* in his *Essay Concerning Human Understanding* was published twenty-eight years after the *Port-Royal Logic,* and according to Hendel, Locke was "certainly cognizant of the *Logic*" (1964, xix).

Locke's *Essay,* published in 1690, but probably written about 1671 (Hamblin 1971, 159), is generally thought to be the first occurrence of the term *argumentum ad verecundiam,* used to denote a type of argumentation of the kind subsequently treated in logic textbooks. Locke claims to have invented the term and, as we shall see in Chapter 3, many of the logic textbooks follow Locke's terminology in their accounts of the *argumentum ad verecundiam* as a fallacy. The passage in question in Locke's *Essay* occurs in the chapter 17, 'Of Reason', in book 4, and is omitted in many editions because it seems to be parenthetical to the main discussion (Hamblin 1970, 159). Hamblin (159) quotes the passage in full, from the Yolton edition (1961, 278–79). In this famous passage, Locke claims to have invented the *argumentum ad ignorantiam* as well as the *argumentum ad verecundiam.* He also defines the *argumentum ad hominem*—a type of argument he acknowledges as being already known under that name—and contrasts these three types of argument with another type he calls *argumentum ad judicium.* Section 19 of the *Essay,* where Locke defines *ad verecundiam,* and section 22, where he defines *ad judicium,* are quoted below.

> 19. Before we quit this subject, it may be worth our while a little to reflect on *four sorts of arguments* that men, in their reasonings with others, do ordinarily make use of to prevail on their assent, or at least so to awe them as to silence their opposition.

First, The first is to allege the opinions of men whose parts, learning, eminency, power, or some other cause has gained a name and settled their reputation in the common esteem with some kind of authority. When men are established in any kind of dignity, it is thought a breach of modesty for others to derogate any way from it, and question the authority of men who are in possession of it. This is apt to be censured as carrying with it too much of pride, when a man does not readily yield to the determination of approved authors which is wont to be received with respect and submission by others; and it is looked upon as insolence for a man to set up and adhere to this own opinion against the current stream of antiquity, or to put it in the balance against that of some learned doctor or otherwise approved writer. Whoever backs his tenets with such authorities thinks he ought thereby to carry the cause, and is ready to style it impudence in anyone who shall stand out against them. This I think may be called *argumentum ad verecundiam.* (Hamblin 1971, 160)

Note that Locke does not describe the *argumentum ad verecundiam* as a fallacy. As Hamblin puts it, Locke describes it and the other arguments as "assent-producing devices, sophistical or otherwise" (160), and Locke does not condemn them but "stands poised between acceptance and disapproval" (161). Locke does indicate clearly, however, how the *argumentum ad verecundiam* can be used fallaciously as a sophistical tactic in some cases, by taking advantage of the "respect" and "submission" of the other party.

Locke also indicates that the *ad verecundiam* is to be contrasted with another type of argument called the *ad judicium.*

22. *Fourthly,* The fourth is the using of proofs drawn from any of the foundations of knowledge or probability. This I call *argumentum ad judicium.* This alone of all the four brings true instruction with it and advances us in our way to knowledge. For: (1) It argues not another man's opinion to be right because I, out of respect or any other consideration but that of conviction, will not contradict him. (2) It proves not another man to be in the right way, nor that I ought to take the same with him, because I know not a better. (3) Nor does it follow that another man is in the right way because he has shown me that I am in the wrong. I may be modest and therefore not oppose another man's persuasion; I may be ignorant and not be able to produce

> a better; I may be in an error and another may show me that I
> am so. This may dispose me, perhaps, for the reception of truth
> but helps me not to it; that must come from proofs and argu-
> ments and light arising from the nature of things themselves,
> and not from my shamefacedness, ignorance, or error. (160)

Only the *ad judicium* is based on "knowledge and probability" directly,
whereas the *ad verecundiam* is merely based on an inference from the
"shamefacedness" of the other party in a discussion. Thus the *ad verecundiam* is portrayed as a type of argument that is inferior to the *ad
judicium* type. The *ad verecundiam* can "dispose me . . . for the recep-
tion of truth," but it does not "help me" to truth. Locke seems to suggest
that the *ad judicium* is the more direct or reliable type of argumentation
so that, in any conflict between the two, the *ad verecundiam* should
give way to the evidence that is the "light arising from the nature of
things themselves." Locke seems to suggest that the *ad verecundiam* is
a subjective type of argumentation, as contrasted to the more objective
ad judicium.

Of course, Locke was an empiricist, and his general viewpoint
reflects the empiricist orientation of modern experimental science. In
any conflict between a conclusion drawn from the opinion of an authority and a finding drawn from the "light arising from the nature of
things themselves," the latter type of *ad judicium* argument wins. It
was Locke's account of the *ad verecundiam* that became so influential
in the treatments of the appeal to authority fallacy in the modern logic
textbooks. The early textbooks, beginning notably with Watts's *Logick*
(1725), adopted a broadly Lockean style of description of the *argumentum ad verecundiam* in their sections on fallacies. However, they
most often changed Locke's account significantly, suiting it to their own
uses. For example, the entry for *argumentum ad verecundiam* given in
Watts's *Logick* translates *argumentum ad verecundiam* as "address to
our modesty."

> When the Argument is fetch'd from the Sentiments of some
> wise, great, or good Men, whose Authority we reverence, and
> hardly dare oppose, 'tis called *Argumentum ad Verecundiam,* an
> Address to our *Modesty.* (466)

As Hamblin notes, this description is "subtly altered in perversion of
Locke's original intentions" (1970, 164). For one thing, the *argumentum
ad verecundiam* is now described as a fallacy, without mentioning or
recognizing that it could be a reasonable kind of argument in some

cases. For another thing, *verecundia,* which seemed to mean something like "respect" for an established authority in Locke's account, has now come to be translated as "modesty." The variability and lack of clarity in these multiple variations on the Lockean account came to pose a big problem in the modern logic textbook treatments of the *ad verecundiam.*

Before returning to some clarification of the meaning of the term *verecundia,* however, let us examine one other account of the fallacy of appeal to authority.

8. Bentham on Appeal to Authority

The first part of Bentham's *Handbook of Political Fallacies,* first published in 1816, is entitled "Fallacies of Authority." Bentham begins with an analysis of authority giving four factors for determining the weight of an argument from authority.

> What on any given occasion is the legitimate weight or influence to be attached to authority, regard being had to the circumstances surrounding the person who is claimed to be the authority? The answer depends upon: (1) the degree of relative and adequate intelligence of the person in question; (2) the degree of relative probity of the same person; (3) the nearness or remoteness between the subject of his opinion and the question in hand; and (4) the fidelity of the medium through which such supposed opinion has been transmitted, including both correctness and completeness. (Bentham 1971, 17–18)

This analysis, although it was generally not noticed or acknowledged by subsequent logic textbooks that treated the appeal to authority as a fallacy, was a significant step forward. It suggested that the appeal to expert opinion could be treated as a type of argument that has a certain "weight" or "influence" depending on certain factors regarding the "circumstances" of "the person who is claimed to be the authority." These factors, here clearly stated for the first time as such and organized as criteria for evaluating appeals to authority are: (1) the knowledge, skill, or "adequate intelligence" of the authority, (2) the sincerity or "degree of relative probity" of the authority, (3) the field, or subject of the authority's opinion, and its relationship of "nearness or remoteness" to the "question in hand," and (4) the "medium through which the supposed opinion has been transmitted," that is, the text of discourse quoted or interpreted by the arguer who has used the authority's alleged opinion to support his side of the dispute. All four of these factors are key requirements in the framework for evaluation of the appeal to authority as a type of argumentation given in Chapter 7. As we will see, given the scattered and uneven treatment of appeal to authority as an argument by so many of the logic textbooks, it is remarkable that Bentham's early analysis of it was accomplished in such a systematic way, bringing together several of the most important factors.

Bentham, like Arnauld and Locke, took a balanced, middle-of-the-road approach to arguments resting on appeal to authority; not condemning them as universally fallacious but seeing them as arguments that can have a "weight" or "persuasive force" when used properly.[7] Bentham writes that the legitimacy of this persuasive force, or its "deficiency," depends on the four criteria above (18). Bentham also distinguishes four types of "probable degrees of legitimately persuasive force" of arguments from authority: (1) professional status (scientific or professional opinion), (2) power, (3) opulence, and (4) reputation (19). This classification will turn out to be less significant in our analysis, but it does indicate that Bentham distinguished between the authority of professional or scientific expertise and the institutional type of authority associated with power to command obedience.

Bentham, like both Arnauld and Locke, recognized that argument from appeal to authority is inherently different as a type of evidence from appealing directly to the factual information or direct evidence available in a case. He recognized that the one type of evidence can be weighed against the other, and like Locke, saw that as the factual (*ad judicium*) type of evidence becomes available in a case, it becomes less necessary or useful to rely on the evidence gotten by appealing to the opinion of an authority.

> The need for the legitimately persuasive force of authority, that is—the probability of comparatively superior information on the one hand, is in inverse ratio to the information of the person on whom it is designed to operate, on the other. The less the degree in which each man is qualified to form a judgment on any subject on the ground of specific and relevant information, or direct evidence, the more cogent the necessity he is under of trusting, with a degree of confidence more or less implicit, to indirect or

7. In this, remarkably, Arnauld, Locke, and Bentham all seem to be in basic agreement (very broadly) with the point of view expressed by Aristotle, although none of them indicates any awareness of Aristotle's views specifically, in connection with their treatments of appeal to authority as a type of argument.

circumstantial evidence. (23)

In fact, Bentham even claims that the appeal to authority should be judged "fallacious evidence" if direct evidence is available, but the arguer continues to rely on the "inconclusive" evidence furnished by the appeal to authority. On the other hand, "no fallacy can be alleged" (23–24), where the opinion of a "professional person" or scientific authority is cited on an issue beyond the competence of the audience to judge correctly on the basis of the direct evidence available.

Up to this point, Bentham's analysis of appeal to authority is very useful, and the logic textbooks would have done well to make more use of it. But the rest of his treatment of the subject is less successful (25–82). As Hamblin notes (1970, 165), the work was ghost-written by two other authors under Bentham's name (first Dumont, in French, and then revised and translated into English by Bingham). Perhaps because it was cobbled together by three people, the system of classifying and organizing the various types of fallacies seems to wander, and gives an impression of eccentricity.

Bentham tried to bring the interests of the general public into his analysis, actually defining the fallacy in these terms:

> The most fallacious use of authority is in instances where the debaters are capable of forming a correct judgment on the basis of relevant arguments, but in which the *opinion,* real or supposed, of some person whose profession or other particular situation involves an interest opposite to that of the general public, is brought forth in the character of an argument in the place of such relevant arguments as ought to be furnished. (1971, 25)

Bentham's aim of formulating a practical analysis of appeal to authority that would be useful to parliamentarians and legislators was a noble idea. But, unfortunately, his treatment of the subject is so sketchy and wandering that it is not surprising that subsequent generations made little use of it, sticking instead to Locke's account as their point of departure.

9. The Meaning of *Verecundia*

A peculiarity of the modern treatment of the *ad verecundiam* fallacy is that it draws all kinds of un-Lockean conclusions from descriptions of the *argumentum ad verecundiam* loosely based on the language and spirit of Locke's account. Modern students are not, in general, familiar with the term *verecundia,* and it is no doubt quite a leap for most people to try to connect this term, especially given the various ways it is translated, to the argument from appeal to authority.

The *Oxford Latin Dictionary* lists five meanings for *verecundia:*

> *uerecundia* ~ae, *f.* [VERECVNDVS + -IA]
> 1. An attitude of restraint (arising from respect for others or a proper humility on one's own part), modesty. (b) defence, respect (for a particular person, etc.) (c) (w gen. of gd.) reluctance (to do something) arising from such a feeling.
> 2. Lack of forwardness due to oversensitivity, uncertainty, etc., diffidence.
> 3. A sense of shame (consequent on, or inhibiting, dishonourable or disgraceful conduct).
> 4. A sense of shame (in the face of what is coarse or indecent), modesty.
> 5. (in general) Moderation, restraint. (Glare 1982, 2035)

We can quite clearly see how meaning 1, and to some extent also meaning 2, expresses the kind of attitude that fits nicely into Locke's account of the *argumentum ad verecundiam* as a distinctive species of argumentation. However, if one does not know this, it would be difficult to get any clear, coherent, and useful explanations of the *argumentum ad verecundiam* from the modern sources.

The dictionaries of philosophy—like many of the logic textbooks—as we will see in Chapter 3, tend to translate *argumentum ad verecundiam* as the argument appealing to "respect" or "reverence." The entry in Flew specifically cites Locke's account.

> *argumentum ad verecundiam.* (Latin for: argument appealing to respect.) The label, introduced by Locke (*Essay IV* [xvii] 19), for an appeal to respect for and for submission to someone's authority, where the authority is understood as not being authority relevant to the particular area in question. (1979, 21)

This entry seems to presume that (1) it is the fallacy of *ad verecundiam* being defined and (2) it occurs where the authority is not relevant to the area in question. Neither of these presumptions is consistent with Locke's account of the *argumentum ad verecundiam.*

The dictionary entry in Reese also defines the *argumentum ad verecundiam* as appeal to respect, but singles out respect for the famous as the defining characteristic.

> The Argument from Authority (*Argumentum ad Verecundiam*) [is] the fallacy committed in appealing to the feeling of respect people have for the famous in order to win their assent to a conclusion. Not every appeal to authority commits this fallacy, but every appeal to an authority with respect to matters outside his special province commits the fallacy.
>
> "These pills must be safe and effective for reducing. They have been endorsed by Miss X, star of stage, screen and television." (1980, 168)

This account is somewhat different from Flew's, because (presumably), Miss X is not an authority on these pills at all, so the argument is more of an appeal to celebrity status. Reese defines the argument in terms of "respect people have for the famous," which is of course different from, and narrower than Locke's account. Also, both the Flew and Reese entries characterize the fallacy as an appeal to an authority that is outside, or not relevant to her field or "special province." This too goes beyond, or is different from Locke's account. Reese, however, explicitly states that not every appeal to authority is a fallacy.

Angeles, like Flew, defines *argumentum ad verecundiam* as a fallacy, but as a dualistic kind of argument that can either be an appeal to authority, or as an appeal to reverence or respect for those in authority. Here it now means two fallacies, instead of the unified type of argument described by Locke.

> *Fallacy of argumentum ad verecundiam (argument to authority or to veneration).* (a) Appealing to authority (including customs, tradition, institutions, etc.) in order to gain acceptance of a point at issue and/or (b) appealing to the feelings of reverence or respect we have of those in authority, or who are famous. Example: "I believe that the statement 'You cannot legislate morality' is true, because President Eisenhower said it." (1981, 96)

The entry in Runes defines *verecundia* as respect, once again, and specifically, respect for authority of various kinds.

> *Argumentum ad verecundiam*: An argument availing itself of human respect for great men, ancient customs, recognized institutions, and authority in general, in order to strengthen one's point or to produce an illusion of proof. (1984, 34)

Here the word 'fallacy' is not used, but it is clear from the use of the phrase "illusion of proof" that the fallacious use of the argument is being referred to. However, the disjunction at the end allows also for the possibility that one could use such an argument nonfallaciously, to "strengthen one's point." Of all the dictionary definitions, this last one probably changes or distorts Locke's account the least.

10. Where to Begin

We have seen in this chapter that although the leading accounts of the argument from authority are fairly consistent in treating it as a fallible but useful kind of argument—and some of them have particularly insightful things to say about it—on the whole, no well worked-out analysis of it as a type of argument has been established. The most compelling account of it is that of Locke (who gave it a Latin name at least) and it is this account that was adopted by the logic textbooks, even if it was most often changed and subtly distorted in the process.

Locke's account, as brief as it is, seems to give the best overall picture of how this type of argument, in principle a reasonable one, can so often be used as a sophistical tactic to take advantage of the "diffidence" or "modesty" (*verecundia*) of someone who is not very sure of himself when confronted by the opinion of an expert authority, a "learned doctor" in an established position of eminence. We can all sympathize with this kind of situation and are familiar enough with it in our personal lives. The person who is appealing to the expert opinion can back up his argument by using the classic put-down to the other party: "Well, you're not an expert, are you?" This seems to leave the other party no room to reply effectively. If he tries to pit his own opinion against that of the expert, he looks bad (immodest, presumptuous). Note also, once again, that Locke does not claim this type of argument is a fallacy and treats it in a balanced, middle-of-the-road way. Nevertheless, the way he sketches out his brief description of this type of conversational exchange, he makes it clear that there is a very real scope for potential abuse in this kind of argument, and how the abuse works as a persuasive or effective sophistical tactic.

Locke is not describing the kind of case where the alleged authority is not a genuine expert in a field of knowledge or where she is an expert in the wrong field for the opinion cited. Both these failures could be factors. But in the kind of case he cites, the authority cited could be a genuine expert and in the right field, but even so the argument from expert opinion could be used fallaciously to browbeat the other party into surrendering prematurely. What Locke's account suggests is that when the *ad verecundiam* argument is used fallaciously, it is not just a weak or inadequately documented appeal to expert opinion. It is more like a decisive blocking or shutting-down type of move in argumentation that blocks off the respondent's ability to raise any further questions or meaningfully or effectively take part in attempting to support his side of the issue any further in the dialogue. But while Locke paints a convincing picture of a common type of situation in argumentative discourse, he offers no analysis of the specific form of the *ad verecundiam* as a well-defined type of argument. According to his account, it is a characteristic type of exchange of argument: moves between two participants (or three, if you include the authority) in a dialogue framework.

The idea of evaluating an argument as a contribution by two parties to a dialogue receded into the background of logic once Aristotle's syllogistic logic (and modern propositional and quantificational logic) became the dominant models of logical argument. As outlined in Chapter 1, the Euclidean model of demonstration, using deductive logic to infer theorems from axioms in an ordered sequence of inquiry became, in the modern period, the model of scientific reasoning of a kind that represented the only kind of argument really worth anything as a way of getting to the truth. Can the ancient Greek dialectical concept of an argument as a dialogue exchange be reborn in a modern form that would make it useful for evaluating arguments like appeal to expert opinion? In Chapter 4, section 10, the foundations for a new dialectical theory of argument for use in evaluating the form of appeal to expert opinion in a context of dialogue are set out. Prior to getting to this stage, however, appeal to expert opinion must be identified as a distinctive type of argument with identifiable premises and conclusion.

Our first problem is to identify the type of argument associated with the *ad verecundiam* more exactly, as it is conceived by the current logic textbooks. And then beyond that, we must analyze this type of argument by first giving it some sort of standard form in order to determine what the constants and variables in its structure should be. Of course, we have noticed already that William of Sherwood cast the argument from authority in the form of a deductive (syllogistic) argument (1966, 94). Another proposal might be that it is a kind of inductive argument. Laplace (1795) attempted to construct an inductive calculus of testimony. He considers the case where a witness reports on the color of a ball she has drawn from an urn full of black and white balls. Laplace then has various probabilistic rules; for example, we could multiply the probability of drawing a certain ball by the probability that this witness is lying, from our experience of his past record of deceit (109–10). As Hamblin notes, "Laplace's calculus of testimony is probably useless," but still, it does suggest that the project of exploring the logical form of the *argumentum ad verecundiam* is a potentially useful project, "however imponderable the factors in practical cases" (1970, 218). Here then is the beginning point of our inquiry into the usefulness of the various possible accounts of the logical form of the argument from expert opinion, carried forward in Chapter 4.

Before we get to that point, however, Chapter 3 will survey the various contemporary accounts of the *ad verecundiam,* to further narrow down the target of analysis.

3

IDENTIFICATION OF THE TYPE OF ARGUMENT

In order to orient oneself in this subject, it is useful to get a feel for how the logic textbooks have standardly treated the *argumentum ad verecundiam* as a distinctive type of argument. A sampling of these textbooks, from the beginning of the twentieth century to the present, will convey the target concept of the kind of argument the texts are concerned about, and a sense of what they take to be important in teaching students how to handle this type of argument.

The standard treatment of fallacies has been sharply criticized by Charles Hamblin (1970). But Hamblin's survey has, in turn been criticized by Ralph Johnson as being somewhat too hard on the textbook authors (1990). Although Hamblin clearly had a good point that serious study of the fallacies has been a neglected area of logic, still, in the case of *ad verecundiam,* it will become apparent that the insights of the textbooks are, in some instances, well worth paying careful attention to, despite the conflicts and uncertainty in their treatment of the subject.

Although it is interesting to see how strongly so many of these textbooks dismiss the *argumentum ad verecundiam* as fallacious, the primary focus of this chapter is not on evaluation—that will come later—but on identification of the *ad verecundiam* as a distinctive type of argumentation. Of course these two things are closely connected, and some of the textbooks, as we will see, define this type of argument in such a way that it is inherently fallacious. There is much evidence of disagreement, however.

1. Appeal to Reverence

Many of the older textbooks, and even some of the more recent ones, define the *argumentum ad verecundiam* as appeal to reverence or veneration of "great names." This is seen as an emotional appeal, as contrasted with proof, logical argument, or evidence. These textbooks take their cue from Locke's notion of reverence, but they tend to be stronger than Locke in evaluating the *argumentum ad verecundiam* as a fallacious type of argument.

James Edwin Creighton characterizes the *argumentum ad verecundiam* as a form of argumentation that excludes consideration of the arguments for or against a position, thus in effect defining it as fallacious.

> The *argumentum ad verecundiam* is an appeal to the reverence which most people feel for a great name. This method of reasoning attempts to settle a question by referring to the opinion of some acknowledged authority, without any consideration of the arguments which are advanced for or against the position. It is, of course, right to attach much importance to the views of great men, but we must not suppose that their opinion amounts to proof, or forbids us to consider the matter for ourselves. (1904, 170)

Creighton concedes that sometimes it is right to attach importance to the opinions of "great men," but nevertheless as a type of "proof" he characterizes this kind of argumentation as inherently fallacious. You get the impression he wants to make some concession to the argument from the "views of great men," but generally waives the concession aside as exceptional or peripheral, portraying the appeal to expert opinion as not a method of reasoning that provides legitimate argumentation or proof, advanced for or against a position.

The brief account of the *argumentum ad verecundiam* given by John Grier Hibben is highly negative, describing it as "logically" not an argument at all.

Argumentum ad verecundiam.—This is an appeal to the sentiment of veneration for authority,[1] instead of an appeal directly
to the reason. The weight of great names is with some persons
the most convincing of all arguments. Logically it is not an
argument at all. It may serve to confirm the truth, but it does
not establish it. (1906, 163)

Some concession is made to this type of argumentation by saying it
"may serve to confirm the truth." But many negative aspects are
emphasized: (1) it is defined as appeal to a "sentiment" of veneration,
suggesting an emotional appeal, contrasted with an appeal "directly to
the reason," (2) it is classified as "not an argument at all," at least logically, and (3) it is said not to establish truth. This certainly makes the
argumentum ad verecundiam appear to be a fallacy. It describes it as a
type of argument that is seriously defective on three counts, from a logical point of view.

Daniel Sommer Robinson defines *argumentum ad verecundiam* in
terms of reverence for a person or institution, and even goes so far as
to identify this type of argumentation with propaganda.

The *argumentum ad verecundiam* is an argument which claims
a proposition or belief should be accepted because it has been
held by some highly revered person or institution. Thus all pro-
pagandists like to show that their views are *Christian*. Pacifist
arguments are a conspicuous example.

Robinson sees propagandistic *ad verecundiam* argumentation as a fallacy used by both sides in disputes on religion.

Case 3.1:   Thus it has recently been argued that the belief in im-
            mortality and the belief in a personal God are dying out
            because a large per cent of the answers from a group of sci-
            entists, who were asked whether they held these beliefs,
            were negative. There is practically no value in such argu-
            ments. In nearly every case they are pure propaganda.
            (1947, 198)

Robinson's attitude toward the *argumentum ad verecundiam* could be
described as dismissive. It is not absolutely or always a fallacy, but it is

---

1. The use of the word 'sentiment' may suggest a reference to the 'moral sentiment'
notion of Adam Smith and David Hume.

in "nearly every case," and so can generally be presumed to be fallacious as a type of argument, whenever it is encountered.

Albert M. Frye and Albert W. Levi do not even mention expertise in
their account of the *argumentum ad verecundiam,* and define this type
of argument exclusively as an appeal to reverence.

> *The appeal to reverence* (the *"argumentum ad verecundiam"*) . . .
> simply names the emotion or sentiment an argument may be
> intended to create in a listening or reading audience so that the
> proposition at issue will be believed (or disbelieved). The senti-
> ment is reverence—for a tradition, a doctrine, a nation, a creed,
> a great name, etc. In the United States of America, whenever
> there is a proposal that would bring this nation into closer
> relations with other nations, especially European, opposition
> speakers invariably invoke the name of George Washington and
> remind the people of his Farewell Address. (1969, 222)

Because they see the *ad verecundiam* as an emotional appeal—that
being the way they define it—Frye and Levi classify it along with other
fallacious appeals to emotion like "appeal to pity" and the like.

Such argumentation types have traditionally been classified as fallacious by the logic textbooks on the grounds that they are subjective
emotional appeals to popular enthusiasm, fear, pity, and so forth, and
therefore have only rhetorical value, and no real value as evidence, based
on knowledge or verifiable facts (Hamblin 1970, chap. 1). Some textbooks explicitly claim that the kind of information you get from an *ad
verecundiam* appeal to authority is not even evidence. Lionel Ruby
takes this position, and even adds that citing an authority is an evasion
of rationality. Under the heading of the appeal to authority under "eva-
sions of rationality," the following description is given.

> This evasion has the following structure: Jones says that P is
> true. When asked, Why? he answers, "Because X says so." Now,
> P (the *probandum,* or proposition to be proved) should be
> proved by adequate evidence, but the fact that X says it is true
> is not *evidence* for its truth. The citing of authority is an evasion
> of the law of rationality. (1950, 128)

Ruby admits that "sensible people must rely on authority for many of
their important decisions," but insists that such beliefs are not knowledge, and are not based on *evidence*—only someone's say-so (128).

2. Knowledge Versus Appeal to Authority

Other textbooks define *argumentum ad verecundiam* as appeal to authority, and admit it as a legitimate kind of argument or evidence, in some instances, but contrast it, in Lockean fashion, with the kind of evidence gained by inquiry into knowledge. These texts stress, however, that basing arguments on appeal to authority can be a serious obstacle to knowledge, in many cases.

In Thomas Fowler's *The Elements of Inductive Logic*, we find the use of argument from authority as a natural kind of reasoning arising from long-standing common practices, but one that is almost always fallacious in an educated society, where people think for themselves. According to Fowler, it is natural to infer by a process of induction by simple enumeration that if the opinions or predictions of a person or group of persons are found verified by subsequent facts, that this person or group should come to be accepted as an authority, because their prediction was based on knowledge. However, he warns that generally such a principle is "rash" and "unwarrantable" as an inference.

> It is on this principle that a savage, or even an uneducated man in a civilized community, will trust implicitly any person for whom he has conceived a general respect. In nine cases out of ten he probably acts more wisely in trusting to such a person than in trusting to himself. But the same habit of mind, which is a virtue among uneducated men and in primitive states of society, becomes one of the most serious obstacles to progress and knowledge when men, either individually or collectively, have attained that stage at which they are able to inquire for themselves. (1870, 269)

The suggestion here is that the argument from authority is characteristic of primitive or uneducated reasoning, whereas in modern society, people must learn to think for themselves, instead of relying on authority. Now we have knowledge, it is no longer sufficient to simply trust the authority of some other person whom you respect. Now we must think for ourselves.

According to this suggestion, the appeal to authority as a type of argument is essentially irrational or unenlightened—a "serious obstacle to progress and knowledge." It is suggested that appeal to authority may be contrasted with knowledge, or inquiry into the facts of a matter, and that arguments based just on authority are inferior to arguments based on inquiry into knowledge.

Fowler does not totally reject arguments from authority, but definitely sees them as inferior, and even dangerous. The problem, according to Fowler is that, even within his or her proper area of expertise, a person's authority is apt to become "tyrannical and irrational," unless constantly confronted with facts and external criticism (270). He cites Jeremy Bentham as backing his claim that too often in the history of thought, an "undiscriminating submission to the authority of past generations," based on "respect for a great name," like Aristotle or Galen, has blocked the progress of knowledge based on observation (271).

These early textbooks convey an attitude of suspicion or mistrust toward the *argumentum ad verecundiam,* and admit it as a legitimate type of argumentation only grudgingly, and with very careful limitations. In general, it is quite clear that these textbook authors see evidence based on scientific knowledge as very important to emphasize, and they worry about arguments based on authority as being in conflict with arguments based on scientific knowledge.

John Veitch defined the *argumentum ad verecundiam* as "an appeal to one's reverence for authority—one's modesty in face of a great author or his opinion." This kind of argument, Veitch acknowledges, can sometimes be appropriate, as for example, when we accept the opinion of a doctor of medicine, or the analysis of a "recognized chemical expert" (1885, 546). However, the more basic question, according to Veitch, is "not whether the conclusion was accepted, but whether it was the conclusion to be accepted." The fallacy comes in when people "shut themselves out from the fullness of human knowledge" by falling into "exclusive acceptance and worship" of authorities (547). Veitch is suggesting that appeal to authority has only a relative or provisional status as a kind of argument, against the higher standard of human knowledge at a given historical time. Implicit here is the Lockean contrast between *ad verecundiam* and other subject-based kinds of arguments with the objective type of evidence or argument Locke called *ad judicium.* Some texts explicitly refer to Locke's account, but many go their own way, taking a broadly Lockean line.

James Hyslop characterized the *argumentum ad verecundiam* as a species of person-directed argument that is valid when the party to whom the appeal is addressed accepts the cited source as authoritative, and otherwise not. Hyslop defines an *argumentum ad rem* (argument to the thing or matter) as "an argument directed correctly to the issue." An argument which ignores the issue, "but which nevertheless may be useful in influencing an opponent" is called *an argumentum ad personam* (1899, 174). Then the *argumentum ad verecundiam* is defined as a species of *argumentum ad personam* that appeals to an authority accepted by the opponent.

> The *argumentum ad verecundiam* is an appeal to authority, or body of accepted doctrines. It is valid for producing conviction when the authority is accepted by the persons to whom the appeal is addressed, but it is not *ad rem* proof, and when not accepted by anyone is still more glaring as an *ignoratio elenchi* [evasion of the issue]. (175–76)

Hyslop's analysis, although reminiscent of Locke's in outline, is original and significant in its own right. The several forms of subjective argumentation he distinguished, including *ad populum, ad hominem* and *ad ignorantiam,* as well as *argumentum ad verecundiam,* are said to "have the legitimate use of driving a man to define his position" even though "they do not accomplish real proof, and to that extent evade the issue" (176).

3. Testimony of Authoritative Sources

Those textbooks that define the *argumentum ad verecundiam* in terms of the attitude of reverence are emphasizing the point of view of the party or audience to whom the argument is addressed. What is emphasized here is the emotional reaction of awe, or respect for authority, that makes an arguer vulnerable to this sort of appeal. Other textbooks have tended to define *argumentum ad verecundiam* more in terms of another participant involved, the authority or learned person who is cited as the source of the opinion. This individual has properties that evoke certain attitudes, or has certain characteristics that define the *ad verecundiam* as a distinctive type of argumentation.

   In dealing with tricks and tactics of persuasion of the kind where appeals to the dignity of an authority is exploited, Robert Thouless concentrated not so much on the attitude of reverence or awe of the listener or person to whom the argument is directed. Instead, he concentrated on a property of the speaker or of the source cited. Thouless defined *prestige* as "the acknowledged dignity of authority possessed by Cabinet ministers, bishops, prize-fighters, successful authors, and other famous men" (1936, 88). He acknowledged that the prestige suggestion of authorities was "beginning to lose its force," and was beginning to meet with "a more critical intelligence" even in his day. But he was inclined to advocate an attitude of mistrust of appeals to prestige because it is so easy to exploit it deceitfully by the power of suggestion or innuendo.

> We should be inclined to distrust all suggestion by prestige and not merely that based on false credentials. The prestige of professors and learned men has been used to crush many movements of scientific discovery at their beginning. The authoritative voice of the learning world put off the acceptance of Harvey's discovery of the circulation of the blood for a whole generation, as it had previously delayed the acceptance of Copernicus's discovery of the earth's motion. Lister's discovery of the use of antiseptics in surgery was similarly opposed by established medical authority within the memory of men now living. In our own days we have heard the thunders of established authority against the revolutionary psychological discoveries of the great Viennese psychotherapist, Professor Freud.

Thouless thought that because of the general subservience to prestige suggestion that is natural, we have to make an effort to cultivate an attitude of critical alertness to counterbalance it.

> While reasonably grounded learned authority can be a force of great value and is indeed our principal protection against the cruelties of commercial exploitation by humbug and quackery, yet it has been too often in the past a force opposing the advance of knowledge. Its power to do this (as also the power of the quackery which it should suppress) can only be rendered harmless when men lose their subservience to prestige suggestion. (108)

The basis of the appeal to authority as a type of argument here is prestige suggestion. Presumably this is such a powerful force in persuasion because of the *halo effect*: we tend to trust experts, and in general to presume that what an authority says is likely to be reliable.

Max Black took the approach that appeal to authority is a form of appeal to testimony, a form of argumentation that is generally an acceptable, and widely accepted, ground for many of our most common beliefs (1946, 232–56). According to Black, such appeals are based on trust.

> When a person is alleged to be qualified to speak on a certain topic, he is commonly called an authority on that topic. To be

"qualified" to give testimony in a certain field is to have quali-
ties which *generally* ensure the truth of the statements made.
Testimony by an authority consists of statements made by a
person whom there are general reasons to trust.

Black adds, however, that not all testimony is to be trusted, and he
gives criteria for distinguishing between reliable and unreliable appeals
to authority.

Among the most useful tests of qualification applied to alleged
authorities are *recognition by other authorities* (especially as
evidenced by such official signs of respectability as titles, diplomas, and degrees) *agreement with other authorities,* and *special
competence* ("being in a position to know"). (233)

Among other factors mentioned by Black are (1) the established credibility of the testifier, based on past judgments, (2) the dogmatic or
undogmatic aspect of how the appeal to authority is used, and (3) the
prestige of the authority, a factor that is hard to resist, and which we
should be on guard against abuses (234–35). The idea of testimony is
very interesting as a basis for the *ad verecundiam* type of argument,
indicating that the authority is acting as a "source," who passes along
information or knowledge that was (presumably) once original data.
    William Kilgore distinguished between two types of appeals as evi-
dence to support a conclusion: appeal to authoritative sources and
appeal to original data, both of which can be reasonable in context.

Fallacies Misusing Appeals to Authoritative Sources. The use of
statements from authoritative sources as evidence to support a
conclusion does not in itself constitute a fallacy of argument.
The views and opinions of qualified authorities can have significance when evidence is weighed. Problems do emerge if the
point at issue is in dispute among different competent authorities; in such cases we must appeal to original data. In basic
research the appeal to an authority relative to a point at issue
would not be accepted as adequate or satisfactory evidence.
(1968, 59)

Kilgore does not use the expression *argumentum ad verecundiam* at
all, and he generally presumes that arguments using authoritative
sources as evidence are nonfallacious. An interesting and nontradi-
tional aspect of Kilgore's treatment is that whether an appeal to an

authoritative source has significance as evidence is said to depend on the context in which the argument was used (see Case 3.9). In basic research in a scientific inquiry, appeal to an authority would not be accepted as a satisfactory kind of evidence, whereas in another context, the same appeal could legitimately carry some weight as an argument.

Peter Facione and Donald Scherer make an important point in saying that when an authority *vouches* for a particular proposition, we accept this as an argument in favor of the proposition on the presumption that the authority would be able to provide an acceptable proof for it on demand. Thus the appeal's reasonableness depends on its use as a voucher to stand in for evidence that, presumably, could be given if requested.

> It is not necessarily a fallacy to cite authorities. If the authorities are used, it is, logically, only to facilitate things. It is supposed to save having to reproduce the entire proof for something. Instead of the whole proof the reliable authorities give their word. They *vouch* for the conclusion's being true, but they could have given the proof. They should be able to supply an acceptable proof upon demand. An authority is really only as good (reliable) as what he or she can prove upon demand. What Einstein might say about physics was, accordingly, highly plausible because presumably he could have substantiated his assertions about physics. (1978, 315)

This is an important point, because it provides a rebuttal to the objection that appeal to the opinion of an expert authority is not evidence, and is therefore inherently evasive, untrustworthy or fallacious. It can be conceded that it is not direct, scientific or "hard" evidence, of the kind that is based on observations, etc. directly. Nevertheless, it can be maintained that, to be reliable or trustworthy, it needs to be based indirectly on objective evidence, that can presumably be produced if requested.

4. Varying Definitions of *Ad Verecundiam*

At the outset of the discussion, a terminological question of some importance needs to be kept in mind. Does the phrase *argumentum ad verecundiam* refer to the fallacy of illicit (incorrect, erroneous) appeal to authority? Or does *argumentum ad verecundiam* refer simply to the use of the opinion of an authority in argument? The latter could, in principle, by a reasonable (nonfallacious) type of argument, or use of opinion in argument. If so, then by the second usage, an *argumentum ad verecundiam* could be, at least in some instances, a reasonable argument as opposed to a logical fallacy.

The accounts of Kilgore, Black, and Facione and Scherer begin to suggest that the type of argument underlying the *ad verecundiam* may not be fallacious *per se,* or generally. The tendency for this point of view to become more common in the more recent textbooks posed a terminological dilemma. Many of the textbooks were defining the *argumentum ad verecundiam* as the emotional appeal to reverence, prestige, awe, etc., or in a way that presumed that it is a fallacy. Other textbooks understand the phrase *argumentum ad verecundiam* less literally and more generally, as referring to appeal to authority, or to an authoritative source, in argumentation (typically, an appeal to expert opinion). What we seem to have is a type of argument that is seriously fallacious, but is also legitimate (reasonable or nonfallacious), when not being exploited as a fallacy.

We are brought virtually to contradiction in the account of *ad verecundiam* given by Robert Kreyche.

> APPEAL TO REVERENCE (*argumentum ad verecundiam*). The irrelevancy of this type of appeal is manifest when someone, instead of weighing a question on its intrinsic merits, attempts to awe his listeners by invoking the authority of tradition or of those upholding it. This is, of course, a perfectly legitimate type of appeal, but one easily subject to abuse. (1961, 280)

When you define this type of argument as an "appeal to reverence" that attempts to "awe" listeners instead of "weighing a question on its intrinsic merits," and then categorize it as an irrelevant appeal, it certainly sounds like it is fallacious. It then appears incongruous to add, without further explanation, that this type of appeal is "of course . . . perfectly legitimate," even if "easily subject to abuse." This seems like too much of an abrupt about-face. An attempt to awe listeners by invoking the authority of tradition sounds like it is a good way off from being "perfectly reasonable." Quite a few of the textbooks seem to operate on the presumption that their readers will generally accept the *argumentum ad verecundiam* as a fallacy, without having to justify this classification too strenuously.

One tactic used by textbooks to get readers to accept an account of *ad verecundiam* as a fallacy while only dealing with it very briefly is to cite its use in support of an opinion that would be strongly condemned. Latta and MacBeath (1956, 379–80) use this technique to dismiss *argumentum ad verecundiam* in a few lines.

Case 3.2:   The *argumentum ad verecundiam* consists in appealing to authority instead of establishing our contention on its merits. If one were to argue against the abolition of slavery on the ground that Aristotle regarded it as justifiable, or that it was sanctioned by the Christian church, one would be guilty of this fallacy.

Using this type of example is a way of heading off any inclinations students might have to question whether appeal to authority is always fallacious as an argument.[2] In light of the possibility of nonfallacious appeals to authority in argumentation however, this way of building the fallaciousness into the definition of the phrase *argumentum ad verecundiam,* while characterizing it as "appealing to authority," is highly questionable.

Other textbooks also find ways to effect a quick dismissal of *ad verecundiam* as fallacious appeal to authority. James Carney and Richard Scheer treat the appeal to authority fallacy as being the same as the *ad verecundiam* fallacy. According to their account, the fallacy is a simple one (1964, 25–26).

Case 3.3:   The *ad verecundiam* fallacy (appeal to authority fallacy) occurs when one supports a view by appealing to the endorsement of the view by someone who is not in fact an authority on the subject matter being considered. Thus if someone argues that Soviet Russia will take over the United States before 1970 and supports this claim by citing the fact that Mr. X says they will, and Mr. X is not an authority on the Cold War and the world situation, this would be an instance of the *ad verecundiam* fallacy. If, on the other hand, Mr. X is an expert in the field, the argument would be correct.

This suggests, incorrectly, that all instances of support of a view by appealing to the endorsement of someone who is, in fact, an authority on the subject matter would be correct arguments.

Incidentally, another terminological problem is that many textbooks,

2. This tendency tends to prevail more in the textbooks that deal with the *ad verecundiam* in a brief space of half a page or so.

like Kreyche (above), include appeals to tradition as instances of the *argumentum ad verecundiam,* while others like T. Edward Damer treat appeal to tradition as a separate style of fallacy from appeal to authority (1980, 92). W. Ward Fearnside and William Holther treat appeal to tradition as a subspecies of appeal to authority (1959, 89). This is another question of how to define or identify the *ad verecundiam* as a distinctive type of argumentation.

What seemed to emerge in more and more of the modern textbooks as a practice was to define the *ad verecundiam* as appeal to authority (or to equate the two), and to stress expert opinion as the kind of authority that is (primarily) meant. While stressing the fallacious appeals to expert opinion, the textbook would go on to concede that going on the say-so of an expert can be a reasonable (nonfallacious) type of argument in some cases, provided that certain abuses are not committed, e.g., appealing to the opinion of someone who is not really an expert, or who is only an expert in a different field from that in which the expressed opinion lies. In the more recent textbooks, one tends to find more of a balanced approach, where the fallacious and nonfallacious kinds of arguments that appeal to expert opinion to support a claim are both illustrated.

William Werkmeister represents a turning point for the *ad verecundiam.* He defined it not as appeal to reverence, but as the "attempt to justify or validate an idea by quoting some 'authority' in its support" (1948, 60). Although Werkmeister characterized this type of argumentation as a fallacy on grounds that it is irrelevant as evidence, he nevertheless emphasized that "not all appeals to authority are irrelevant" when backed up by expert knowledge and reasoning (59–60). Werkmeister made a very important point, for the first time in the textbook treatments of the *ad verecundiam,* by distinguishing, in a balanced way, between critical and uncritical uses of appeals to authority to support an argument. He took the view that a critical appeal to authority can be of value as an argument, if based on an appeal to genuine knowledge that can be independently verified (61).

Case 3.4:   Not all appeals to authority are irrelevant. When an expert is quoted in his own special field, his "authority" is worth a great deal. But the value of such a quotation even in this case depends not so much on his "say-so," but on the fact that in this particular field his knowledge is to be trusted more than our own. His knowledge and reasoning, however, are trustworthy only to the extent to which they can be checked and verified through established methods of analysis or experimentation. Einstein may well be quoted as an authority on matters pertaining to theoretical physics, and Eisenhower is an authority on military strategy. But when Einstein is quoted as authority in the field of economics, or Eisenhower in the field of literature, they are out of their special fields and have no longer any authoritative standing. To accept anything they say in these fields merely because *they* have said it, is to commit the fallacy of *argumentum ad verecundiam.*

Werkmeister explained the *ad verecundiam* fallacy as committed when an authority is appealed to merely as an "authority" in an uncritical way. But he made the point that if the authority is competent in a field of knowledge, and if the arguer appealing to this expert opinion can back the appeal critically, showing why it should be accepted, then the *ad verecundiam* can, in principle be a correct (nonfallacious, justified) type of argument.

5. The Ambiguity of 'Authority'

Another puzzle is the inherent ambiguity of the concept of authority, which could mean many different things in different contexts. According to Richard De George, "Being an authority in a field of knowledge is different from being an authority in public life, though in both instances we refer to people as authorities" (1985, 12). In still different senses, we cite the authority of the Bible, or we may say that someone speaks "with authority" or that his statement is "authoritative." In some instances legal authority and the authority of expertise can be combined, as in a coroner's report, for example. These complications suggest that analyzing the *argumentum ad verecundiam* may not be as simple as it may initially appear.

When the textbooks define *argumentum ad verecundiam* as "appeal to authority," there are several major kinds of appeals that might be included under this heading. One important meaning of 'authority' is what we might call *administrative authority,* the right to exercise command over others or to make rulings binding on others through an invested office or recognized position of power. A second significant meaning of 'authority' is expertise in domain of knowledge or skill. Patrick Wilson calls this second meaning *cognitive authority,* which he defines as a relationship between two individuals where what the one says carries weight or plausibility, within a certain domain or field of expertise, for the other individual (1983, 13). De George states that a person may be an authority in two principal, essentially distinct ways: "he may be an authority in a certain field of knowledge, or he may occupy a certain position which carries with it certain rights or powers" (1985, 13). These two meanings of the term 'authority' are distinct, in the sense that an appeal to authority in argument could be of the one kind without necessarily being an appeal to the other meaning of 'authority.'

Although the two kinds of authority are essentially different in nature, they can be combined in the same individual in some cases. For example, a physician may have the authority to certify a person as fit to possess a driver's license according to the legally required medical standards, determined by the physician's examination. The doctor's conclusion is based on his medical knowledge and skill, and his authority, in this respect, is the cognitive authority of expertise. However, the physician's ruling is also a case of the exercise of administrative authority, because it is his standing as a licensed physician that makes his ruling authoritative, and gives him the right to make this officially binding pronouncement.

J. M. Bochenski distinguishes between two types of authority. An *epistemic authority* is an expert in a field of knowledge, i.e., "one who knows better." A *deontic authority* is a superior or commander who sets rules concerning what should be done. While Bochenski thinks of these two kinds of authority as distinct from each other in principle, nevertheless he thinks that they sometimes coincide: "For example, the professor, who is primarily an epistemic authority for the student, is, at the same time, a deontic authority in the field of rules concerning the operations in the lab" (1974, 71). Here the one individual represents both kinds of authority.

John Woods and Douglas Walton distinguish between *de facto authority,* which is the authority of expertise based on a claim to special knowledge in a field of skill, competence, or factual knowledge, and *de jure* authority, which is the authority to perform actions or make rulings based on a titular or administrative position or role (1974, 146).

It seems appropriate then to distinguish between two broad types of authority that are basically different in function, import, and logical structure in argumentation. The *cognitive (epistemic, de facto)* type of authority is a relationship between two individuals where one is an expert in a field of knowledge in such a manner that his pronouncements in this field carry a special weight of presumption for the other individual that is greater than the say-so of a layperson in that field.

The cognitive type of authority, when used or appealed to in argument, is essentially an appeal to expertise, or to expert opinion. By contrast, the *administrative (deontic, de jure)* type of authority is a right to exercise command or influence, especially concerning rulings on what should be done in certain types of situations, based on an invested office, or an official or recognized position of power.

In evaluating the reasonableness of appeals to authority in argumentation, it can be easy to confuse these two meanings of 'authority.' This confusion may suggest that any appeal to expert opinion of the cognitive type is somehow so binding and forceful—"authoritarian" in the "bad" or "overbearing" sense—that it can only be challenged with the greatest difficulty. Accordingly, the use of an appeal to cognitive authority in argument may be greeted with suspicion, hostility, or resentment. Another suspicion raised by confusing the two is that all appeals to sources of authority are inherently subjective, and therefore irrelevant to any serious investigation into the real facts in an inquiry. Perhaps it is these suspicions that have been behind the modern tendency to generally treat the *argumentum ad verecundiam* as a fallacy. Another worry articulated by Woods and Walton is that confusion between the two types of authority can be encouraged by political or religious leaders to invest themselves with infallibility and power to suppress opinions that they wish to portray as heretical, disloyal, or radical (1974, 147). Despite these genuine and reasonable worries about the misuses of authority, both types of authority have legitimate and reasonable functions in decision-making and argumentation.

The present inquiry will treat as secondary the concept of administrative authority and concentrate primarily on the analysis of the reasoned use of expertise (cognitive authority) in argumentation. This way of proceeding is suggested by two factors. One is the clearly evident emphasis the informal logic textbooks have put on the appeal to cognitive authority in their treatments of the *argumentum ad verecundiam*. The other is the inherent interest of the appeal to expert opinion as a type of reasoned argumentation in its own right. As will become clear later however, the study of the *argumentum ad verecundiam* is tied to the concept of administrative authority in essential ways, and in the end we will see this concept come up again in an important way.

An important general difference between appeals to epistemic and deontic authority is worth noting. As several of the textbook accounts cited so far indicate, epistemic appeals to authority are best treated as a form of argument that only *generally* ensures the truth of a proposition asserted, subject to qualifications, such as how controversial the proposition is or what other experts say (Black 1946, 233). Deontic appeals to authority, in contrast, often tend to be highly conclusive arguments. For example, if a minister says "I now pronounce you man and wife" in the appropriate circumstances, then it follows absolutely that it is true that you are now man and wife, i.e., married.[3] For this reason alone, the ambiguity between the two meanings of 'authority' can be a source of difficulty.

6. Advertising Testimonials

Many textbooks classify the use of testimonial appeals in advertising under the category of the *argumentum ad verecundiam* or fallacious appeal to authority. *Introduction to Logic* by Irving Copi is a case in point.

> Advertising "testimonials" are frequent instances of this fallacy [*argumentum ad verecundiam*]. We are urged to smoke this or that brand of cigarettes because a champion swimmer or midget auto racer affirms their superiority. And we are assured that such-and-such a cosmetic is better because it is preferred by opera singers or movie stars. Of course, such an advertisement may equally well be construed as snob appeal and listed as an example of an *argumentum ad populum*. But where a proposition is claimed to be literally *true* on the basis of its assertion by an "authority" whose competence lies in a different field, we have a fallacy of *argumentum ad verecundiam*. (1953, 61)

This classification is questionable, however, as a general rule. Some commercials do use expert authorities; for example, physicians to endorse medications advertised on television. But many of these commercials use movie stars or other celebrities to promote products that these famous or glamorous people cannot truly be said to be expert authorities on. It is not their authority, at least in the sense of expertise that is being appealed to, but more their glamour, personal appeal, or perhaps fame, or even their likability as a well-known and loved entertainer. In some cases, an appeal to authority or expertise may be partly involved, but that does not seem to be the whole story of what is being appealed to.

3. Such a pronouncement is sometimes called a *performative utterance,* which has the property that saying makes it so.

Gerald Runkle defines the *argumentum ad verecundiam* as the appeal to the feeling of reverence toward a "great respected person."[4] The kind of argument he has in mind seems to be more appeal to celebrities than to experts, as indicated by the example of Joe DiMaggio praising a particular coffeemaker. Runkle rejects this argument as fallacious on the grounds that DiMaggio, while an expert ballplayer, has no special competence in the field of coffeemakers.

> This appeal, so obviously fallacious, must be very effective, for great sums of money are spent to foster it. Athletes and movie stars, all highly regarded by the people, are paid well to endorse all kinds of products. Karl Malden's opinion on travelers' checks is irrelevant to the question whether they should be purchased. Bill Russell is no authority on telephone calls. And what is Joe Namath's special competence in popcorn poppers or pantyhose? Jim Lovell, ex-astronaut, is paid to endorse a life insurance company! The strangest instance of this fallacy occurred in an advertisement extolling the merits of a recording tape. The "authority" appealed to is dead and was dead before tapes were even invented, yet: "If Beethoven were alive today, he'd be recording on 'Scotch' brand recording tape." The ad goes on to say that Beethoven was a genius, "but he was even more than that. He was a pro." Like Russell and Namath, presumably. (1991, 32)

The problem with this approach is that it presumes that these commercials are to be classified as appeals to expert opinions, or to authorities, so that we can say they are fallacious because they fail in this regard. But it is not clear that we can make such a presumption at all. They appear to be more testimonial appeals to celebrity than to expert status. Here the concept of an "authority" is being stretched pretty thin.

Winston Little, Harold Wilson, and W. Edgar Moore have a fallacy they call *misuse of authority,* but distinguish between this and two closely related fallacies, *prestige of great names* and *testimonials.* Under the former category they cite exploitation of meaning by association in the use of famous names like George Washington or Abraham Lincoln, for example in political campaigns. Under testimonials, they include the kinds of appeals, mentioned above, that are so often made use of in television commercials.

---

4. This is reminiscent of the idea of "great names" cited earlier from Creighton (1904) and Hibben (1906), in section 1, above.

> *Testimonials.* The testimonial is a favorite device of advertisers. Distinguished people or just plain citizens of no particular distinction are quoted in advertisements as using, preferring, or recommending the product being advertised. The type of person selected to make the recommendation depends upon the product. Doctors and athletes, for example, have frequently been called upon to endorse cigarettes, since there is some doubt in the public mind as to the effect of cigarette smoking on health. The purpose, presumably, is to suggest that if doctors and athletes approve of a certain brand of cigarettes, it must not be injurious to health. (1955, 28)

It is interesting and somewhat unusual that Little, Wilson, and Moore chose to treat these advertising testimonials as separate from appeals to authority.

In the case of a testimonial by a physician on the effects of cigarette smoking on health, the argument could be classified as an appeal to expert opinion. But in the case of the athlete, the appeal is likely to be not so much to expertise, but more to glamour or popularity. So there is more of a basis in this kind of use for treating the argument as separate from the appeal to authority. There is typically in these kinds of cases an appeal to popularity involved, so that, at least partly, the argument would come under the traditional heading of the *argumentum ad populum.* Yet this aspect is not the whole story either. Let us consider a common kind of case.

Case 3.5:   A famous basketball player, who is currently a leading scorer and the idol of many fans, appears in a commercial promoting a certain brand of blue jeans.

In this case, the basketball player is a sort of expert on basketball, insofar as he is a successful player. But it is not just, or primarily in virtue of his expert knowledge in basketball that is the basis of his appeal in the testimonial. The appeal is that lots of people, perhaps especially younger people who buy these jeans, want to "identify with" this person, and want others to know that they are identified with him. He is perceived as a popular and successful hero of a sort, and so many of the viewers presumably will be influenced by their positive attitude toward him as a known individual, to want to have the same kind of jeans that he professes to prefer. Whatever is going on in this kind of appeal, it is not basically an appeal to authority or expertise of any sort, at least primarily. It is better described as a type of testimonial used in advertising and promotion by using a spokesperson who is a celebrity, a widely recognized *persona* who is admired or respected at a given time by large numbers of a target audience. Such a *persona* may commonly be an authority or expert in some particular domain of knowledge or skill. But that, in itself, is not the real basis of the appeal.

However these cases are to be classified, they should not be categorized (at least primarily or exclusively) as *argumentum ad verecundiam*. However, the textbooks are right to include cases of this sort as kinds of argumentation commonly used by advertisers and promoters of causes that should be subject to careful scrutiny and critical questioning.

One does also have to be careful to note that these cases vary. If, in Case 3.5, the testimonial had been to promote a particular brand of basketball or running shoes, there would be more of a basis for categorizing it as an appeal to expertise or authority. But even here, the appeal to expertise is mixed in with the type of appeal to celebrity status described above, which seems to be inherently different as a type of argumentation.

7. Position to Know

Black made an important distinction between appeal to authority in the sense of appeal of expert opinion in a domain of knowledge, and appeal to experience or special competence of a kind that could be called "being in a position to know." Two cases presented by Black make this distinction clear, and indicate its importance (1946, 233–34).

Case 3.6:   When deciding whether to have an inflamed appendix removed, we rightly pay more attention to the advice of a licensed doctor of medicine than to that of Aunt Jane. For the possession of a legal right to practice medicine is some assurance that the doctor's skill and knowledge has been scrutinized by other competent doctors (i.e., by other authorities). And our confidence in the doctor's recommendation for an appendectomy is materially strengthened if we find that two or three other doctors independently arrive at the same judgment. Here we are applying the test of agreement of authorities.

Here the contrast is between the advice of a layperson and that of a qualified professional in a definite domain of knowledge or skilled expertise. However, in other cases we may base an opinion on experience, or on the source's being in a special position to know, even if he is not necessarily an expert in the above sense.

Case 3.7:   If we want to know what it feels like to be in battle, we are rightly inclined to pay more attention to the report of a soldier who has been in the front lines than to the account of a man, however imaginative, who has never been exposed to the shooting. For, in such a case, we feel that the personal experience of the person giving testimony is essential to the reliability of his account.

I pose an even more common type of case:

Case 3.8:   Ralph is walking down the hall at the University of Winnipeg, and asks someone passing, "Could you tell me how to get to the Dean's Office?" She replies, "Go down to the end of the hall, turn right, and then go past the escalators."

Here, the advice-giver is not an expert—she is not an architect, or cartographer, or any sort of special authority on the buildings or hallways of the University of Winnipeg. However, she is able to give Ralph good advice on how to get to the dean's office because she is familiar with these buildings and hallways, having been a student at University of Winnipeg for a couple of years. Here, Ralph operates on the presumption that her directions are correct, but if they are not, it is not a big problem. He can always ask someone else, if he does not arrive at the dean's office.

So we have now found three borderline types of argumentation—appeals to tradition, appeals to celebrity testimonials, and arguments from position to know—that are questionable on whether they ought to come under the heading of appeal to authority or *ad verecundiam* arguments. If *argumentum ad verecundiam* is defined as appeal to reverence for "great names," the first two types of arguments would seem to fall under the category of *ad verecundiam*. But if we define *argumentum ad verecundiam* as appeal to authority, it becomes questionable whether any of these three neighboring types of argumentation rightly fall under the *ad verecundiam* classification.

These borderline cases will remain open as long as the term 'authority' is not defined in any more clear or precise way. The more clearly we define the meaning of 'authority' in the phrase 'appeal to authority,' as suitable in logic for the name of a distinctive type of argumentation, the more we will be able to see just how much these neighboring types of argument come under this general category.

8. Authority and Expertise

How should we proceed, then, in order to define the *argumentum ad verecundiam* as a target of analysis in a precise enough way to enable a focus of research on a distinctive type of argument the textbooks are concerned to teach about? It would be tempting to define it as the use of appeal to expert opinion in argumentation, since such a narrower approach would make it much easier to analyze, and this focus is in fact what is mainly emphasized by the examples treated in the textbooks. However, the leading recent textbooks typically tend to define the *argumentum ad verecundiam* more broadly as appeal to authority or argument based on authority. And somehow it does seem that the notion of authority is essential to a full understanding of the fallacy. It is because the opinion of an expert has a special status as a kind of argument or evidence, reflecting a knowledge or skill that the expert has that we treat the say-so of such a source as having "authority," as being an authoritative source. Perhaps all this means, in a twentieth-century context, is that such an opinion carries a greater weight of presumption in favor of its being plausible, over that of the say-so of a layperson in the field of the opinion. 'Authority' of the cognitive type is used here in a fairly weak sense of meaning a challengeable source, open to critical questioning, but one that is given a certain standing or weight of presumption as (fallible) evidence, where direct access to knowledge (or "the facts") is not available within the practical constraints of arriving at a prudent conclusion on how to proceed in argumentation. What seems to make most sense is to take 'authority,' in a broad sense, to comprise many types of administrative and *de jure* notions, as well as the narrower sense of epistemic authority represented by expertise in a domain of knowledge or practical skill.

Stephen Toulmin, Richard Rieke, and Allan Janik construe the appeal to authority quite broadly as a type of argumentation.

> One very common type of argument comprises those based on the *authority* of particular people or institutions. Early in our lives, we see our parents as capable of supplying reliable

information and beliefs. (If Mom or Dad said it, it must be so.) At a later stage, we may see representatives of schools and churches as authorities. Others who can serve as authorities in one domain or another include respected members of our own peer groups, experts on one or another subject matter, government officials, and those holding high elective office. (1979, 155)

Among arguments based on authority, they include the say-so of the U.S. president to establish U.S. policy, the authority of a religious leader to promulgate church doctrine, and the giving of the informed opinion of a medical doctor as an expert witness on the cause of an injury in court. Once we take 'authority' in this very inclusive way, we can see how both respect for authority, i.e., "reverence," and prestige, or the "halo effect" are important aspects of the fallacy of *ad verecundiam,* construed as the misuse of the appeal to authority to unfairly or deceptively get the best of a partner in argumentation. Locke's analysis makes this fairly evident.

Ralph Johnson and J. Anthony Blair begin by characterizing appeal to authority quite broadly as a type of argumentation. "From our earliest days as children," they write, "our thoughts are influenced by the opinions of parents, teachers, and others who know more than we do" (1983, 144). However, after acknowledging this broad sense of 'authority,' Johnson and Blair narrow down the meaning of the term explicitly to the authority of expertise, insofar as their definition of appeal to authority as a type of argumentation is concerned, as treated in their analysis.

> The mere mention of the word "authority" is enough to raise the hair on some people's necks. So let's be clear at the outset what we mean here by an "authority." We do not mean a person who is in a *position* of authority (priest, politician, teacher, boss) and who is therefore able to command others to act in certain ways, or to do certain things. We mean someone whose expertise in a particular area makes her assertions reliable—more likely to be true than false. (145)

Johnson and Blair do not appear to be excluding these other types of appeal to authority entirely. But they focus their analysis centrally on appeal to expertise.

Damer does not use the words 'expertise' or 'expert opinion' explicitly in defining what he calls the "fallacy of irrelevant or questionable authority." Yet, citing Beardsley, he defines an 'authority' as essentially

an expert, qualified by training or ability to draw inferences from facts
he or she claims to know.

> An authority in a given field has been described as one who is
> in a position to have access to the facts he or she claims to know,
> is qualified by training or ability to draw appropriate inferences
> from those facts, and is free from any relevant prejudices or
> involvement that would prevent him or her from formulating
> sound judgments or communicating them truthfully and com-
> pletely. (1980, 93)

Beardsley, in his description of the fallacy of *appeal to illegitimate authority*, also does not use the term 'expert,' but his definition of 'authority'
does seem to focus on the kind normally associated with expertise.

> A person is an authority on a given field when (a) he is in a posi-
> tion to have obtained the facts he claims to know, (b) he is qual-
> ified, by training and native ability, to draw sound inferences
> from those facts, and (c) he is free from relevant bias—that is,
> from prejudices and attachments that would prevent him from
> drawing rational conclusions or from communicating them fully
> and truthfully to others. (1966, 215)

The concept of cognitive authority defined here is a special case of position to know argumentation where an expert, by training and ability,
is the one who claims to know, but whose testimony or opinion is subject to questioning, particularly on the grounds that it might be unduly
biased to one side or the other. It is on this type of cognitive or epistemic authority that the analysis of the *argumentum ad verecundiam*
should primarily focus, but keeping the broader meaning of 'authority'
in mind.

9. Terminological Choice

Broadly then, it seems best to follow the lead of the textbooks in what
to focus on as the main areas of concern expressed in their treatment
of the *ad verecundiam*. But in certain respects, their line of approach
needs some rethinking, revising, clarification, and consolidation. What
particularly needs to be questioned and revised is the tendency of so
many of the textbooks to tilt the balance of presumption in favor of

fallaciousness, i.e., to presume generally that appeal to authority (*ad verecundiam*) arguments are fallacious. If *argumentum ad verecundiam,* contrary to the literal Latin meaning, is to be taken as the generic term for appeals to authority in argumentation, and centrally, appeals to expert opinion, as these recent textbooks have proposed, it needs to be recognized, in a balanced way, that such arguments can, in many cases, or generally, be justified and reasonable, i.e., nonfallacious.

The terminological choice remains open, however. We could go back to the traditional and literal meaning of *argumentum ad verecundiam* as "argument to reverence," implying that this type of argumentation is always or generally fallacious. That is, on this way of proceeding, *ad verecundiam* becomes the name for the fallacy. Then the generic name for this type of argumentation, when it is (possibly or actually) nonfallacious, would be "appeal to authority" or "argument from authority." But in fact, a preponderance of the textbooks take *argumentum ad verecundiam* as the general name covering appeals to authority (especially expertise) in argumentation, including both the fallacious and nonfallacious uses under this heading. This is a verbal (terminological) conflict. It may not matter too much, ultimately, how we decide this terminological issue, as long as we recognize that a decision needs to be made, and that a balanced treatment of this type of argumentation is necessary, allowing (whatever we call the argument) to be nonfallacious in some cases. But for the present, the terminological differences of the definitions given or presupposed in the current textbooks are bound to be a source of confusion for students.

To take yet another example, note the difference, in this respect, between the two currently most popular textbooks.[5] Patrick Hurley (1991) treats the argument from authority (also called *argumentum ad verecundiam*), as an inductive (nonfallacious) type of argumentation "in which an arguer cites the authority or testimony of another person in support of some conclusion." However, the *appeal to authority* fallacy occurs, according to Hurley where "the cited authority or witness is not trustworthy," for various reasons (126). Copi categorizes the *argumentum ad verecundiam* as a fallacy, defining it as "the appeal to authority, that is, to the feeling of respect people have for the famous, to win assent to a conclusion." However Copi immediately conceded that "this method of argument is not always strictly fallacious," for reference to an "admitted authority in the special field of competence may carry great weight and constitute relevant evidence" (1953, 60). For Copi, the fallacy is one of relevance.

5. Copi (1953) was the most widely used logic textbook for many years, but Hurley (1991) seems to have taken the lead recently (based on anecdotal evidence only).

One interesting aspect of Copi's treatment is his comment that whether an *ad verecundiam* fallacy has been committed depends on the context (61; see also Kilgore 1968, 59).

Case 3.9:   If laymen are disputing over some question of physical science and one appeals to the testimony of Einstein on the matter, that testimony is very relevant. Although it does not prove the point, it certainly tends to confirm it. This is a relative matter, however, for if experts rather than laymen are disputing over a question in the field in which they themselves are experts, their appeal would be only to the facts and to reason, and any appeal to the authority of another expert would be completely without value as evidence.

So Copi very clearly shows to the reader how appeal to expert authority can be relevant and reasonable as an argument in one case, yet fallacious in another. But the way he defines the *argumentum ad verecundiam,* in the beginning, is as a fallacy. That is, the weight of presumption is on fallaciousness, and only later is it granted, as an exception, that it is "not always strictly fallacious." With Hurley, the burden of proof is the other way around.

10. Provisional Conclusions

Putting aside the question of determining the precise conditions under which an *ad verecundiam* argument is fallacious for later consideration, the goal of this chapter was to broadly identify it as a type of argument (a preliminary task). Should it be defined in terms of the attitude of reverence or in terms of the concept of authority (or possibly expertise)? It is clear from the Lockean analysis that both concepts should be involved. In that analysis, we have two parties arguing, and one of them cites the say-so of an authority to support her opinion or side in the argument. This seems to be basically how the argument works, as a type of argumentation structure. But Locke's account adds more than this.

According to his account, this type of argument is effective or successful because it exploits the attitude of reverence (*verecundia*) of the party who is on the receiving end of the appeal to the authoritative source. And it is this aspect that explains how the basic type of argument involved can become a fallacy or sophism. If the receiver is perhaps too respectful or "reverent" toward authority, and is therefore cowed unduly by the appeal, conceding too easily, submissively, or completely to it, instead of critically questioning it, or adding arguments of his own, he may be overlooking countervailing considerations that should be taken into account. He may be giving in too easily to a weak or inconclusive argument that ought to be questioned. This suggests that the attitude of *verecundia* is critical to explaining how, why and when the argument of this general sort becomes fallacious. Here we take 'fallacious' to refer to a persuasively deceptive type of argumentation that *seems* reasonable or acceptable when it is really not. But "reverence" is only one aspect. The concept of authority is vital too.

In the preliminary task of identifying the initial type of argument used, it is the aspect of appeal to authority (by one side to support her argument against that of the other side) that is crucial. For it is reverence to *authority,* or the prestige of authority, that is central. This suggests the course taken by the leading textbooks, of defining the basic type of argument involved as *appeal to authority.* The presumption behind this approach is that such a type of argument is not used fallaciously in every instance, that it can be justified or reasonable in some cases, and used fallaciously or incorrectly in others. Hence, the approach of defining the general type of argument as "appeal to reverence," and seeing this type of argument as generally or inherently fallacious, does not do justice to the broader picture. However, we still have a linguistic option here. We could call the fallacious type of instance the *argumentum ad verecundiam,* or argument from reverence and reserve the expression 'argument from (or appeal to) authority' as the name for the nonfallacious type of case (or the general case where it has not been determined yet whether the argument is fallacious or not).

The problem, then, is essentially one of what to do with the Latin phrase, *argumentum ad verecundiam.* Should it be taken as the generic name for the type of argument, appeal to authority, or should it be reserved for the fallacious uses of this argument? Locke seemed to be posed between acceptance and disapproval of the type of argument he labeled *argumentum ad verecundiam,* suggesting he would probably have opted for the first approach to definition. On the other hand, the expression itself, literally meaning "argument to reverence" seems to suggest a fallacy.[6]

---

6. There is a third option. One could argue that a certain degree of respect or reverence for authority is reasonable and appropriate, and that in general, one should properly be deferential or "modest" with respect to "learned" authorities. This option then is to deny that *ad verecundiam* suggests or implies fallaciousness. However, we will not adopt this approach in our usage.

At least tentatively, let us depart from the traditional assumption of the majority of the recent textbooks (and Locke). We will cease using the expression *argumentum ad verecundiam* to refer broadly to the type of argument identified with use of appeal to authority in argumentation, which could be fallacious or not (even though occasionally we may have to fall in with usage to conform to the language of the textbooks in describing their viewpoint).

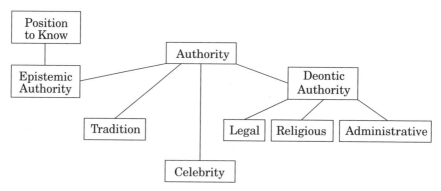

Fig. 3.1

The subclassifications of types of appeals to authority and peripherally related types of argumentation are summarized in Figure 3.1.

As noted above, it is questionable whether celebrity testimonials, of the kind so often condemned by the textbooks as committing the *ad verecundiam* fallacy, really are appeals to authority of some sort. However, we include them in Figure 3.1 on the grounds that they may partly involve some sort of appeal to authority, in some cases, mixed in with some sort of *ad populum* appeal, or other kinds of emotional appeals. In short, then, I will take as the target of analysis the concept and role of authority via consideration of the fallacies discussed in logic texts. I will use the Latin phrase *argumentum ad verecundiam* to refer only to fallacious instances of this type of argument (realizing that there is another current usage that uses this phrase for both kinds of instances). This usage will be our tentative basis for proceeding further. In the main thrust of the study, I will concentrate on the appeal to expert opinion (epistemic authority) in argumentation, as the central, clearest, and most vitally important type of appeal to authority to analyze, for our purposes.

4

FORM OF THE ARGUMENT

Now that I have roughly identified the kind of argumentation that has been broadly targeted as the area of concern with the appeal to expert opinion, the next questions to be asked are, more precisely: What type of argument is it, and does it have a general form or structure? Does it have some clearly identifiable abstract pattern or argumentation scheme that characterizes the standard correct form of its premises and conclusion? The first steps in moving toward a method of evaluating this type of argument are to identify such a form and determine whether it is a deductive, inductive, or some other recognizable type of argument.

There are two sources of hypotheses in investigating this matter. One lies in computer science, where the technology of expert systems has been remarkably successful in recent years (Waterman 1986). This now widely used technology provides many interesting structural insights on how argumentation using appeals to an expert source works as a type of reasoning that can be programmed. As we will see, however, the current computerized expert systems may not model the kinds of appeals to (mostly human) experts we are concerned with in all respects (at least very well or completely), although some of the basic concepts that define expert systems utilization as a kind of reasoning are interesting from a point of view of informal logic. The other source of clues to the forms of argument used in appeals to expertise are the few scattered remarks that have been made in the textbooks and literature on the fallacies. Not much has been ventured in these sources, but there are some clear and definite—if highly tentative—proposals that have been put forward. These suggestions are good places to begin our quest to find the form of this argument, even if they all present problems that require discussion and analysis, before much use can be made of them.

At the end of our discussion, we will see that the appeal to authority is expressed in several patterns—deductive and inductive forms— as well as presumptive arguments that cannot be assessed simply as deductive or inductive forms. In itself, this is a surprising and useful result in coming to understand the logic of the *argumentum ad verecundiam*.

1. Deductive Forms

Charles L. Hamblin, in his chapter "Formal Fallacies," briefly raised the question of whether there is any chance of a formal account of *ad verecundiam* arguments. "Precious little," he wrote, but nevertheless he seemed to think that it might be possible to construct such an account (1970, 218).

> Arguments from authority, it is true, have been rather unfairly ignored by formal logicians: starting from the undoubtedly valid
>
> Everything X says is true.
> X said that P.
> Therefore, P.
>
> We could be expected to find weaker, but still not 'fallacious,' forms of argument within which some support is given to P by premises of forms such as 'X is an authority on facts of type so-and-so.' Laplace's calculus of Testimony is probably useless; but *some* kind of calculus of Testimony must be of some use, however imponderable the factors in practical cases. Its construction will not be attempted here.

The form of argument Hamblin cites is deductively valid in virtue of the quantifier 'all' in the first premise. But of course this form of argument would only apply to an omniscient source or, at any rate, one whose assertions are always true. And notoriously, any real appeals to expert opinion fall far short of this unrealistically high standard.

This observation seems to decisively refute any possibility of finding a deductively valid type of argument from appeal to authority, and Hamblin suggests that the best way to go is to look for some weaker variant—perhaps some sort of inductive form—or, at any rate, a version with added premises that would make it an inconclusive qualified type of argumentation. To be sure, most appeals to authority are, in any practical sense, fallible and open to questioning as arguments. But even so, we may be moving away from Hamblin's idea of the deductively valid type of appeal to authority too quickly. In some cases, we assume that an expert source is definitive and has complete knowledge of a subject domain, as a premise to act on. For example, suppose we are in Leiden, on the train platform.

Case 4.1:   Looking to the train schedule posted on the platform, we see that train 12 leaves shortly, and we look to see whether train 12 stops at Haarlem, according to the schedule. The schedule says that train 12 stops at Haarlem and Amsterdam Central Station.

It is possible that train 12 is out of order or, for some reason, that the posted schedule is not right in this instance. But as an assumption, it is reasonable to act on the premise that the schedule indicates all the stops for train 12 correctly. In effect, the schedule can be treated as an authoritative source in guiding one's actions.

Where S is the domain of knowledge of railway stops of the Dutch train system, E is an expert, authoritative source, and A is a proposition, the form of argument used in the reasoning in Case 4.1 is this:

(E1)   Everything E asserts on subject S is (or may be assumed to be) true.
        E asserts that A is true.
        Therefore, A is true.

Of course, the first premise in (E1) represents a kind of ideal of accuracy of a knowledge base that may fall short of being true, in the real world of contingent events. But if it can be assumed to be true in (E1), as a premise, then (E1) would appear to be a deductive type of argument, because the whole argument has a valid form, namely: All A are B; x is an A; therefore x is a B.

A similar form of argument, but based on a negative premise, is used when we can justifiably assume that a knowledge base or expert source is complete, in the sense of containing all the knowledge in a subject domain. For example, suppose we are on the platform in Leiden again.

Case 4.2:   The posted train schedule says that train 12 stops (only) at Haarlem and Amsterdam Central Station. We want to go to Schipol. Since the schedule does not state that train 12 stops at Schipol, we can infer that it does not stop at Schipol. Conclusion: do not take train 12.

We assume in this case that the authoritative source, the posted train schedule, is complete or epistemically closed in just this sense: if there were additional stops (e.g., in Schipol), they would be posted on the schedule. Let us say that we know this because we know that it is a convention, a railway policy, to always indicate *all* stops on the posted schedules.

This form of negative reasoning by exclusion has been recognized as an important type of argumentation in computer science. Raymond Reiter defines the *closed world assumption* as the assumption that all relevant, positive information has been presented in a knowledge base, using the example of airline schedules (1987, 150).

Case 4.3:   If we look at a database for an airline flight schedule, and see that a connection between Moose Jaw and Paris is not stated, we can assume that this flight does not connect Moose Jaw with Paris.

The basic principle behind this way of presenting information, according to Reiter, is that there is far too much information to present explicitly. So nonexplicit information is presented indirectly by an inference drawn from an implicit premise of the closed world assumption, licensing the respondent to draw a conclusion by negative reasoning.

The kind of negative inference used in the last two cases is a species of the type of argumentation known in the logic textbooks as the *argumentum ad ignorantiam*. It is shown in Walton (1992a, 385–86) how this kind of argumentation has deductively valid form.

> To the extent we know a knowledge-based *K* is closed, i.e., complete, in the sense of containing all the relevant information, we can infer that if a proposition *A* is not in it, then *A* is false. This argumentation scheme for the *argumentum ad ignorantiam* has the following form.

All the true propositions in domain D of knowledge are contained in K.
A is in D.
A is not in K.
For all A in D, A is either true or false.
Therefore, A is false.

This form of inference is deductively valid. To the extent that it can be established (and not merely presumed or assumed) that K is closed, we can conclude on the basis of what is known (and not just on the basis of presumption) that A is false. Hence, in such cases (rare though they may be, in actual practice), the *argumentum ad ignorantiam* is not a merely presumptive type of argumentation, in the sense of being inconclusive, as opposed to being based on established knowledge.

However, it is also shown in Walton (1992a) and Walton (1996a) that the *argumentum ad ignorantiam* is, in many cases, a weaker type of argumentation where the knowledge base cannot be assumed to be closed.

We see, then, that there is an important connection between the *ad ignorantiam* and the *ad verecundiam* as types of arguments. We also see that there is a deductive form of the *argumentum ad verecundiam,* even though some weakened nonconclusive variant is probably more commonly used in everyday argumentation. To cover the negative appeal to authority types of cases like 4.2 and 4.3, we need to add another premise to the form of (E1) making the form of argument more explicit for this type of case.

(E2)   All the propositions in E's knowledge base K on subject S are true (*truth condition*).
All the propositions on subject S not in E's knowledge base K are false (*completeness condition*)
E is asked whether A is true.
E replies that A is not true (as far as E knows).
Therefore, A is false.

What makes this distinctive type of argument deductively valid is the completeness (closure) condition, expressed in the second premise.[1]

Thus there are two deductive forms of the *argumentum ad verecundiam*: the simpler positive form (E1) and the more complex negative form (E2).

---

1. What is called the completeness condition in (E2) seems to correspond to what Reiter (1987) calls the closed world assumption.

2. Probable Inferences from a Knowledge Base

According to Allan Collins, Eleanor Warnock, Nelleke Aiello, and Mark Miller a lack-of-knowledge inference occurs where a respondent fails to find a queried item of information (a proposition) in a knowledge base and concludes, therefore, that this proposition is (presumably) false. As an example, Collins, Warnock, Aiello, and Miller cite a geology knowledge base called SCHOLAR, whose domain includes knowledge of industries in various areas (1975, 398). SCHOLAR is asked a question on this subject, and responds as follows:

Case 4.4:   Is rubber an agricultural product of Guyana?
        RUBBER IS AN AGRICULTURAL PRODUCT OF PERU AND COLOMBIA. I KNOW ENOUGH THAT I AM INCLINED TO BELIEVE THAT RUBBER IS NOT AN AGRICULTURAL PRODUCT OF GUYANA. THE AGRICULTURAL PRODUCTS OF GUYANA ARE SUGAR AND LUMBER.

SCHOLAR does not know whether Guyana produces rubber, for neither this proposition nor its negation are in SCHOLAR's knowledge base. SCHOLAR does know that Peru and Colombia are major rubber producers, and on the basis that Guyana is not included here in its knowledge base, SCHOLAR can infer indirectly that, presumably, Guyana is not one of the major rubber producers in South America.

How does SCHOLAR arrive at such a conclusion? This nonexplicit premise appears to be a counterfactual assumption to the effect that if Guyana were a major rubber producer, this fact would most likely be in SCHOLAR's knowledge base. By *modus tollens* reasoning SCHOLAR can conclude that since it is not there, we can guess that it is probably not true.

What appears to be going on here is something like the closed world assumption, but of a probabilistic kind. SCHOLAR's knowledge base on industrial products in South America is being assumed to be complete enough to validate the presumption that if a country is a major rubber producer, SCHOLAR would know it. But not enough is known in this case to certify conclusively that the closed world assumption holds and that SCHOLAR's knowledge base is absolutely complete. Instead, as Collins, Warnock, Aiello, and Miller put it, the conclusion is "hedged" and "uncertain" (398). SCHOLAR would say "Don't know," except that there is enough of a basis to make an intelligent guess that "No" is a justifiable, qualified answer, i.e., "Not as far as I know, therefore probably not." This lack-of-knowledge inference is an instance of the probabilistic use of the *argumentum ad ignorantiam*. The greater our confidence that the expert knows all there is to know about the subject of the question asked, the greater is our confidence that this negative reasoning used to draw a probable conclusion is justified and acceptable. But on subjects where the experts disagree, the closed world assumption is not justified and the argumentation is based on presumption and burden of proof.

Allan Mazur studied cases where experts disagree on scientific and technological questions that are relevant to political issues. In particular, he studied how the experts argued, comparing two controversies: the disputes about the harmful effects of low doses of fluorine and radiation on human beings. There is no clear scientific evidence on whether these low doses are harmful or not, so experts have argued for both sides—some saying they are harmful, others saying they are not. Mazur composed a long list of "rhetorical devices" or common arguments used by the experts on both sides of the issue (1973, 244–49).

What many of these arguments had in common was that, due to the absence of hard scientific evidence on the issue, the participants used arguments designed to shift the burden of proof to the other side. In short, these argument strategies used by the experts were variants of the argument from ignorance.

> The most common rhetorical device appears to be the phrase, "There is no evidence to show that . . ." or one of its variants. This blank denial of the claims of the opponent on the ground that there is no basis for his position appears in both controversies. (248)

The experts used variations on themes like, "As far as any evidence has been brought out at the present time, there is no danger" or "The councils of the American Medical Association are unaware of any evidence that fluoridation of community water would lead to structural changes in bones" (248). All of these arguments from expert opinion are instances of the more general pattern of the *argumentum ad ignorantiam*.

If a subject, like geography, is both deep and broad in the knowledge it includes, it may be uncertain whether the closed world assumption is justified or not. The question of how confident we can be in inferring a conclusion, based on what is in that knowledge base or not, becomes more one of probability, in such a case.

3. Inductive Forms

Wesley Salmon begins his consideration of the argument from authority by considering the following form, where the variable E stands for an authority or expert source (a person, institution, or writing), and A stands for a proposition or statement.

> (F1) E asserts A.
> Therefore, A.

Salmon writes that this form is "clearly fallacious," at least "as it stands," but that it would be "sophomoric" to reject every appeal to authority as illegitimate (1963, 63). What is legitimate as an argument, according to Salmon, is an appeal to a *reliable* (honest and well-informed) authority. Hence Salmon revises his account to the following form, which he says is "correct."

> (F2) E is a reliable authority concerning A.
> E asserts A.
> Therefore, A.

This form, according to Salmon is not deductively valid, because "reliable authorities do sometimes make errors." However, a modified version of it is "inductively correct," being "a special case of the statistical syllogism" (64).

> (F3)   The vast majority of statements made by E concerning subject S are true.
> A is a statement made by E concerning subject S.
> Therefore, A is true.

This form of argument is said to represent a type of argument that is inductive, meaning that the assumed truth of the premises only gives probable, but not conclusive, grounds for the truth of the conclusion. It is said to be statistical in nature, presumably because the expression 'vast majority' in the first premise is a statistical claim that could be filled in by some numerical ratio representing a statistical finding.

When it comes to explaining how the argument from authority is misused or becomes an incorrect argument or fallacy, however, Salmon's account does not appeal to statistics but to five different factors that appear to have little to do with inductive reasoning or statistics:

1. the authority may be misquoted or misinterpreted;
2. the authority may only have "glamour, prestige or popularity" instead of "special competence in any field of learning";
3. A may be outside of the field of competence of S;
4. the opinion expressed may be a matter on which the authority could not possibly have any evidence about; and
5. equally competent authorities may disagree (64–66).

The first three factors relate to the premises of (F3): 1 relates to the second premise being false, and 2 and 3 relate to the first premise being false; 4 and 5 seem to relate to factors external to the form (F3), as additional considerations.

David Annis also sees the logic of appeal to authorities to support a proposition as inductive in nature, postulating the following form (1974, 91–92):

> (F4) E is an authority and asserts that A (makes probable).
> Therefore, A.

However, Annis sees this form of argument as "fallacious as it stands," and proposes instead:

> (F5) E is a reliable authority on the subject matter of A, and, on the basis of the total relevant evidence available, honestly asserts that A is true.
> There is no reliable authority concerning A that honestly asserts on the basis of the total relevant evidence available that A is false (make probable).
> Therefore, A.

Robert Yanal and Patrick Hurley also classify the appeal to authority as an inductive type of argument. Yanal thinks that an appeal to authority argument should be evaluated as strong if the authority is appropriate and reliable (1988, 382–87). Hurley classifies the appeal to authority as a type of inductive argument based on testimony which becomes fallacious when "the cited authority or witness is not trustworthy" (1991, 126–28).

Merrilee Salmon also sees arguments from authority as inductive in nature, because "experts or authorities are almost always, or usually, correct when they make statements about the subject in which they are experts" (1989, 71). Salmon classifies such arguments as species of statistical syllogism that are reasonable when three conditions are met (71–73):

1. The authority invoked is an expert in the area of knowledge under consideration.
2. There is agreement among experts in the area of knowledge under consideration; and
3. The statement made by the authority concerns his or her area of expertise.

When these conditions are fulfilled, the form of the argument from authority is formulated as follows:

> (F6) Most of what authority E has to say on subject matter S is correct.
> E says A about S.
> Therefore, A is correct.

According to Salmon this form of argument is a statistical syllogism, because the first premise is a "statistical generalization," and the second premise is a "particular assertion" that is a "member of the reference class of the first" (72).

4. Presumptive Forms

The first premise of Merrilee Salmon's inductive form of the argument from authority is a statistical generalization about the number of times, or percentage of times, that what the authority has said is true. This is the matter of the expert's so-called track record. But in judging the worth of an appeal to authority in everyday argumentation, most often track record is not a significant factor. It may not be known, quantifiable, or even be a relevant consideration, in most cases. Instead of track record, Salmon's cited factors seem to be the most important considerations that need to be taken into account when evaluating an appeal to authority. However, the three factors do not seem to be statistical in nature but are contextual matters that would not appear to be statistical generalizations.

The suggestion indicated by this observation is that the form of the argument from expert opinion, where the closed world assumption does not obtain in a given case, is not that of a statistical syllogism but is a weaker type of argumentation based on presumptive reasoning. Presumptive reasoning, according to the account given by Walton is based on generalizations that are not (absolutely) universal, or statistical, but on generalizations that are typically (normally) true, subject to exceptions (1992a; 1992b). Called plausible reasoning by Rescher (1976) this type of argumentation generates inferences that are provisionally acceptable, but defeasible, subject to new incoming information in a case. A much-used example in computer science is the following inference: Birds fly; Tweety is a bird; therefore Tweety flies. If we find out in a given case that Tweety is a penguin, the conclusion 'Tweety flies' is defeated. As Reiter puts it, the inference is *defeasible,* or subject to default, because the major premise says "Normally, birds fly." or "If x is a typical bird, then we can assume by default that x flies" (1987, 149). This normal presumption is defeated, however, in the case of a penguin.

A few textbooks have recognized that the appeal to authority could be a presumptive type of argumentation. Thomas Vernon and Lowell Nissen proposed that the form,

> (G1) E asserts that A.
> E is a respected authority.
>   Therefore, A is true.

may be a legitimate argument in some instances, yielding a kind of evidence that is "pertinent but not sufficient." Vernon and Nissen call it "good contributory evidence" in such a case (1968, 147).

Harry Gensler cites what he calls a correct form of appeal to authority (1989, 338).

> (G2) E holds that A is true.
> E is an authority on the subject.
>   The consensus of authorities agrees with E.
>   Therefore, there's a presumption that A is true.

Gensler thinks that this type of reasoning is not conclusive, and holds only if we have no evidence to the contrary, in a given case.

Another textbook that has portrayed the *argumentum ad verecundiam* as being a subject-based form of argument, unlike deductive and inductive forms of argument, is *Argument: The Logic of the Fallacies* by Woods and Walton (1982, 97). In this textbook, the appeal to expert opinion is seen as a form of plausible reasoning, subject to evaluation by the raising of critical questions of a kind similar to those proposed by Wesley Salmon (1963). These critical questions correspond to six adequacy conditions on the acceptability of an appeal to expertise given in an article by Woods and Walton (1974). First, the judgment put forward by the expert must actually fall within her field of competence. Second, the cited expert must be a legitimate expert, and not merely a celebrity, or someone not an expert. A third factor is the question of how authoritative an expert is, even if she is a legitimate expert in a field. Questions of specialization within fields of expertise are relevant here. Fourth, if several qualified experts have been consulted, there should be some way of resolving inconsistencies and disagreements that may arise. Fifth, if objective evidence is also available, this should be taken into account. In particular, an expert should be able to back up her opinion, if queried, by citing evidence in her field. The sixth requirement is that the expert's say-so must be correctly interpreted. This requirement may not be easy to meet, for it involves rendering the expert's exact words in clear language intelligible to a layperson.

In the Woods and Walton article, the following form of the *de facto ad verecundiam* argument is proposed (1974, 150).

> (G3) E is a reliable authority in domain S.
> A is a proposition contained in S.
> E asserts that A.
> A is coherent with relevant information obtained from other factors
> Therefore, A.

The last premise is really a composite of two distinct factors: the relevant information and where it was obtained. Hence, the form of the appeal to expert opinion as a type of presumptive argument can more perspicuously be set out as follows:

> (G4) E is a genuine expert in S.
> E asserts that A.
> A is within S.
> A is consistent with what other experts say.
> A is consistent with available objective evidence (if any is known).
> Therefore, A can be accepted as a plausible presumption.

This account of the form of the argument makes the appeal to expert opinion more complicated. We now have five different kinds of premises to be concerned about in justifying this type of argument. Perhaps it would be better to make the basic argument of the presumptive form have just the first three premises and leave the fourth and fifth premises as background considerations, to be taken into account only when the case requires one or the other matter to be brought in.

Jim Mackenzie has expressed the basic structure of the presumptive type of appeal to expert opinion succinctly (changing his notation to ours).

> We want to know the conditions under which 'E says that A' gives us reason to accept that A. This plainly depends both on the relation of E to A, and on the nature of A itself. The rule is simply this: is it the case that E, from situation, experience, background, training, or knowledge, is more able than we who are discussing the matter to judge whether or not that A? If so, the testimony of E is worth having, though not always decisive in itself. We can then go on to test E's claim that A according to ordinary methods of critical discussion: the antecedent probability that A, E's reasons for A, any conflicting testimony, the possibilities for mistakes about whether A, E's motives for care in investigation or for deceit, independent evidence, and so on. (1988, 60)

The basic rule is that if E is an expert (basically someone who is more able to judge whether the proposition A is true or false than we the layperson discussants) are, then A ought to be accepted (as "worth having"). Thus the basic pattern of the argument from expert opinion stems from E being an expert (having knowledge) and from E's giving testimony that A is true. We would add to Mackenzie's account a third premise relating to the field in which A lies and in which E is an expert.

Having now defined the basic form of the argument with these three characteristic premises, we can go on to evaluate it by raising appropriate questions in a critical discussion. Then other relevant factors can be addressed as critical questions and used to evaluate the form in context.

We have three different forms of the *ad verecundiam* argument: deductive, inductive, and presumptive. Each appears to be applicable to different situations. However, many of the expert authorities of the kind appealed to in the *ad verecundiam* arguments cited as examples in the logic textbooks are fallible human authorities venturing opinions on complex and controversial subjects. One might expect, then, that the presumptive type of argument should be the most common one used in the kinds of cases we are concerned about.

But it could be that different types of appeals to authority involve different concepts of what an expert or authoritative source is. Appealing to a railway station schedule may be different, as a form of argument, from appealing to the say-so of a computer program like SCHOLAR. And this in turn may be a different form of argument from appealing to a human expert, like asking your financial adviser what to invest in, or asking your physician for advice on a health problem.

One relatively simple model of the structure of a form of appeal to expert reasoning is that of the expert system.

5. Expert Systems

An *expert system* is a computer program that simulates the expertise of a human expert in a specific domain of knowledge. Expert systems have several distinctive characteristics. First, they work best in some specific domain of knowledge where expertise can be brought to bear and do not work well outside such a domain or if the domain is not narrowly focused. Second, expert systems are meant to work on problems requiring the experience of expert skill and judgment, not on problems where an algorithm or deductive solution exists. Third, an expert system separates the set of facts in the domain from the set of inference rules or reasoning methods used to derive conclusions from the set of propositions designated as facts. Fourth, an expert system should have the capability to give an explanation of its reasoning in a particular instance if queried.[2]

A wide variety of expert systems currently in use have been very successful in a range of applications. The expert system DENDRAL has been widely used to identify chemical structures. The geology expert system PROSPECTOR has been used to predict the location of mineral deposits. The expert system DOC can diagnose computer crashes better than human experts. The expert system PUFF diagnoses pulmonary disorders at the Pacific Medical Center in San Francisco (Denning 1986).

Rule-based expert systems can use rules of the "if . . . then" (conditional) sort in sequential form where several *modus ponens* steps, for example, can be put together in a chaining sequence using hypothetical syllogism. The resulting graph of an argument in an expert system reasoning sequence bears many important similarities to methods of diagramming complex arguments in informal logic. This technique has been formalized in Shoesmith and Smiley (1980) and Walton and Batten (1984).

A key feature of expert system reasoning however is the distinction

---

2. See Intelliware (1986) and *Introductory Readings in Expert Systems,* ed. D. Michie (New York: Gordon and Breach, 1982).

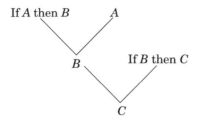

Fig. 4.1

between forward and backward chaining. The above example illustrated forward chaining to conclude C. However, given C, we could reason backwards in a backward chaining sequence, and conclude that C is based on fact A.

The reasoning structure of expert systems is also related to the study of circular argumentation in informal logic. As is shown in the software manual of Intelliware, where a hypothesis appears in a forward or backward chain which is trying to prove that very hypothesis, the expert system reasoning may "loop" forever. Consider the following type of pattern (1986, 30–31):

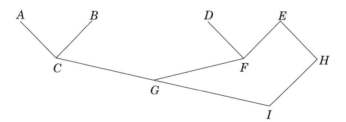

Fig. 4.2

The problem is that E has been used as a basis for inferring the conclusion G. But then the sequence of inferences "loops back" from G to E, as well. According to the Intelliware manual,[3] designers of knowledge bases for expert systems generally try to avoid using rules that could lead to circles, because circular reasoning could increase performance costs in executing expert programs. Similarly, in Douglas Walton and Lynn Batten (1984), it is shown how conditions on reasoning can be set that eliminate circular argumentation as "fallacious." However,

3. Intelliware, Inc., *Experteach* (Los Angeles, 1986).

it is argued in Walton and Batten that circular reasoning is not necessarily fallacious in all cases, but only subject to criticism in certain contexts of reasoning.

Two further characteristics of expert systems are worth noting here. One is that an expert system needs to have a method of *conflict resolution* to apply to a case where too many conclusions can be drawn from a given knowledge base by the rules of inference. This too parallels techniques used in informal logic to deal with inconsistencies when too much information is available (Woods and Walton 1982, chap. 5; Rescher 1976). In both expert systems and informal logic, different methods of conflict resolution can be employed in different contexts. Another important characteristic of an expert system is that it must have a *user interface,* meaning that a nonexpert asks the expert system questions, and the system must be able to respond in a helpful way to such questions. Also, the system must also ask questions of the user, because typically the system does not know all the facts. So the system should ask the user to input those facts which the user may know about (Bratko 1986, 315). This means then that the interaction between the system and the user takes the form of question-reply dialogue.

The system does not try to prove the facts supplied by the user but only asks the user about their truth. Even the fact that some proposition is "askable" can itself be viewed as a fact and added to the system's knowledge base. Hence, each party supplies input through dialogue that generates the reasoning that leads to the conclusion.

The importance of the dialogue interaction between the user and the system is dramatically illustrated by a tutoring expert system called GUIDON developed at Stanford University. GUIDON is a case-method tutoring expert system designed to improve a student's diagnostic ability in medicine (Clancey 1979). It was designed to teach about the domains of expertise represented in EMYCIN, a generalized diagnostic system based on an earlier system called MYCIN that is used to diagnose infectious diseases and recommend drug treatments. The inference rules of MYCIN did not correspond closely to human expert reasoning, but NEOMYCIN is more natural. GUIDON uses a NEOMYCIN knowledge base, but also uses an *overlay student model* that represents the knowledge of the student as overlaying sets of understood and misunderstood concepts. Thus GUIDON is a dialogue structure that works on interactions between the students repository of accepted propositions and the knowledge base of the tutor system. As well as *domain rules* that come from the knowledge base of the system, GUIDON has *tutorial rules* which guide discussions, rank domain rules as more or less relevant to a discourse, and rules that modify the knowledge of the student as the dialogue progresses. The precise form of these rules is given in Clancey (1979, 26–28).

The important thing about an intelligent tutoring (expert) system is that it is built on a model of reasoning as two-way interactive dialogue that takes into account modification of the student's accepted positions in the dialogue in relation to the presentation of the knowledge in the expert system to the student.

6. Informal Logic and Expert Systems

The inference engine and the user interface of an expert system make up the *expert system shell,* which can be applied to the *knowledge base,* the knowledge that is specific to a domain of application. In informal logic, the counterpart to the knowledge base is the *arguer's position,* the arguer's set of commitments, collected together as a set of propositions (Walton 1985). In informal logic, the counterpart of the expert system shell are the rules of procedure for dialogue, including rules that regulate the relationship of the participants and control the kinds of moves that can be made, the kinds of questions that can be asked, and so forth.

In many contexts of argument, the arguer's respective commitment-sets are not called "knowledge bases" because they do not necessarily contain a large enough body of well-organized propositions to correspond to some domain of expertise (Hamblin 1970; Walton 1985). In reasonable dialogue, it is not generally required in every case that the arguer's position be tightly restricted to one topic, that they be internally consistent, or that they contain conditionals (rules) that are characteristic of what is called a knowledge base in artificial intelligence. Nevertheless, the basic function of the knowledge base in AI and the arguer's position in informal logic are essentially similar. They both represent a pool of data or "accepted facts" from which the premises of the reasoner are drawn, and against which his inferences and arguments are tested.

Rules in expert systems can be in the form of plausible conditions of the form: *if* situation S *then* action A. Such rules may have a number attached to the consequent of the conditional, called the "conclusion" of the rule, which indicates the trustworthiness of the rule as applied to any particular situation. The following rule is an example of one in the MYCIN knowledge base.

IF (1) the gram stain of the organism is gram negative and (2)
the morphology of the organism is rod, and (3) the aerobicity of
the organism is anaerobic, THEN there is suggestive evidence
(0.6) that the genus of the organism is Bacteroides.

The number 0.6 given in the conclusion of the rule allows the inter-
preter of MYCIN to get an idea of how plausible the rule is in any particular case by giving an indication of the scope for possible exceptions.
In this way, the user of MYCIN can weigh the advice given by the
expert system alongside his own knowledge of the particular situation,
and arrive at his own conclusion. The conclusion advanced by MYCIN
could admit of several kinds of clear exceptions known to the user. Yet
even so, as a plausible conclusion, it could be valuable as a partial basis
for the user's diagnosis and action.

The theory that an expert's judgment should be taken as a plausible
conclusion, rather than as the output of a deductively valid or inductively
strong argument, is based on the assumption that to act on expert advice
is to act in a situation where better, more direct evidence is not available
within the constraints on reasonable action. One has to act on the best
reasons within the known information relative to the given situation.
Often, in such cases of reasoned action, the burden of proof tilts in a certain direction, given the agent's reasoned estimate of what is likely and
possible to expect in a situation of a type familiar to the agent, or familiar to an expert whom the agent has consulted. Such a data base may
be based on subjective opinion rather than empirically verified propositions. Even so, by tilting the burden of proof in one direction by plausible reasoning of a sort that may be intrinsically evidentially weak, an
inference based on reasonable expectations, and carefully assessed
expert advice, may serve as a kind of reasoned argumentation that may
carry justified weight in arriving at a conclusion on how to act.

In Chapter 5, I will show how the user reasons on the basis of an
expert opinion, using the expert opinion as one kind of premise in an
inference that applies this premise to particulars known by the user.
What is used as the method of inference is called 'practical reasoning,'
a kind of action-directed, goal-based type of reasoning that is typically
used in a situation of uncertainty and changing circumstances where
a decision needs to be made in the absence of complete knowledge. In
such cases, plausible reasoning based on burden of proof (Walton 1992c
and 1996b) is the best model of the inferences used in expert consultation dialogue.

The practical uses of expert systems suggest that a reasonable and appropriate requirement is to try for a system that has a rate of success good enough to be useful, even if it does not work very well in some cases. For example, according to Intelliware (1986, 57), a system that diagnoses computer crashes correctly in only 50 percent of cases, and says "I don't know." when it cannot predict very well, will still be of great help. Another factor is that the user can and should use his or her own judgment in interpreting the conclusions put forward by the expert system in a particular instance (as will be shown in Chapter 5). Hence the idea that an expert system only produces a conclusion that is plausible to a certain degree, rather than certain or even highly probable, is highly acceptable to designers and users of expert systems.

Expert systems apart, it makes sense from a point of view of informal logic that the logic of appeals to expertise can be modeled most perspicuously in the majority of cases by the presumptive form of argument. The proof of this is that, in many of the most common situations where the *ad verecundiam* is used, the following constraints on the argument are characteristic. Each participant in argument has his set of commitments, his position to defend. But the expert has an extensive and complex position based on his experience and learned skills in a domain of knowledge or craft. As users of this expertise, we as laypersons do not have direct access to this knowledge base. We can only extract it in usable form by a process of intelligent question-answer interaction (reasonable dialogue). Therefore, the logic of appeals to expertise as a source of reasoned argument involves a dialectical exchange where the user has to draw inferences based on presumptions.

In searching around for some account of the informal logic of arguments from expertise, Woods and Walton (1974) noted the basic observation that the basis of the expert's conclusion is not accessible to the layperson who has sought her advice. At least normally it would not be accessible in the form of a set of laws and initial conditions (principles and facts) that would exhibit an implication of the conclusion by deductive (or even inductive) steps of logical inference. Accordingly, the conjecture was raised in Woods and Walton (1974) that expert judgment may be based on intuition, a kind of reasoning derived from familiarity with a subject-matter of expertise, and susceptible to being spelled out in so many steps of logical reasoning accessible to a nonexpert. Even further, Woods and Walton (1974, 136) considered the possibility that in judgments of expertise the expert's verdict may be "based on inarticulable background elements" and so "not be amenable to total sentential representation." In other words, such judgments could be inaccessible to deductive logic or inductive inference because they may not be even expressible in the form of declarative sentences or propositions. We could call this a strong from of the *inaccessibility thesis* that expert conclusions cannot be tracked back to some set of premises and inference rules (known facts and rules) that yield the basis of the expert judgment.

One form of the inaccessibility thesis, however, continues to be advocated. According to Dreyfus and Dreyfus (1986) human expertise is intrinsically different form machine-based expert systems because human experts do not follow rules, except at the novice or beginner level. They cite the example of riding a bicycle, a skill learned from experience, but not accessible to us in the form of facts and rules. They cite the case of the boxer who recognizes the moment to attack not by following rules and facts, but by virtue of using practical know-how derived from his training in earlier, similar situations. Dreyfus and Dreyfus conclude that human expertise is based on intuition, which in turn is based on memories of similar experiences in the past (1986, 86–87). Thus according to their theory, expertise is based upon a recognition of similarity between new situations and familiar ones—a process of reasoning by analogy (Eliot 1986). Consequently, they think a clear distinction in principle must be made between "computer rationality" and human expertise.

7. The Concept of an Expert

A good deal of the problem in managing the *argumentum ad verecundiam* lies in getting used to the idea that appeals to human expert opinion in argumentation not only can, but should be challenged critically. Experts are not perfect, and they may exhibit highly variable degrees of ability to communicate their advice well, especially to an audience that is not expert in a given domain of knowledge. What do we mean by the term *expert*? Paul E. Johnson, a scientist who has studied the behavior of human experts for many years, cites the following five characteristics as skills that typify the expert:

1. Because of her training and experience, the expert can do things that the layman cannot.
2. Experts are not only proficient in their actions, but also smooth and efficient.
3. Experts not only know a lot but they have "tricks and caveats for applying what they know to problems and task."
4. Experts are good at sorting through irrelevant information to get at a basic issue.

5. Experts are good at recognizing problems they are confronted with as special cases of patterns or types of things that they are familiar with.

According to Johnson these are the characteristic skills of the expert displayed in the expert's actions, and underlying these skills is the body of knowledge called the expertise (1983, 78–79). These bodies of knowledge are divided into different fields, or domains of knowledge.

In general an expert in a particular field of knowledge is to be contrasted with a layperson in that field. The layperson may not be totally ignorant in the field, but he is a *layperson* if he only has the average level of knowledge of someone with no special training or experience. A *novice* in a field is an individual who has some training or experience, but is still at the learning stage in its initial phases. Then there may be more-or-less advanced stages of advanced learning or competence exhibited by students in a field. The expert is one who has sufficient knowledge and experience to have mastered the five types of skills above.

The characteristics of an expert above, given by Johnson, stress that someone is an expert not only because she knows a lot of facts, but because she can carry out certain actions in a skilled, smooth, and practiced manner, applying their knowledge in a clever way to specific tasks and problems. Emphasizing this practical nature of expertise, Dreyfus and Dreyfus stress that expert actions are carried out smoothly and automatically, and that an expert action is not characteristically carried out by detached or conscious decision-making or problem-solving. Dreyfus and Dreyfus distinguish five stages in the skill acquisition process of an expert: (1) novice, (2) advanced beginner, (3) competence, (4) proficiency, and (5) expertise. In the evolution through these stages to expertise, Dreyfus and Dreyfus see a refinement of intuitive skills that become so ingrained in the expert that she is hardly aware of them: "An expert's skill has become so much a part of her that she need be no more aware of it than she is of her own body" (1986, 31). According to their account, expertise is a kind of holistic, situational understanding that cannot be expressed as a calculative or conscious sequence of reasoning that proceeds by applying rules to facts. Although decisions are made in a more analytical way at the four lower stages of skill acquisition, the fifth stage of expertise is more intuitive. Curiously then, according to Dreyfus and Dreyfus, expert action is "arational," meaning that it is not carried out by calculative thought, logic, or analytical reasoning (36).

The above accounts of the meaning of the term 'expert' may be a little surprising, and also suggest some problems. They are surprising because we might have expected to characterize an expert as an individual who has a lot of knowledge in some special field or domain. We might have this expectation because we are thinking of experts, in the present context, as sources of information. However, there are also many areas of expertise where the skill involved is as much or more a matter of "knowing how" (practical reasoning) than a matter of "knowing that." The skilled specialized surgeon and the prima ballerina are experts in their different spheres, but their expertise is not so much a matter of academic knowledge as it is a matter of skilled sequences of actions which come instinctively, smoothly, and quickly after many repetitions and practice sessions over the years of training.

The foregoing accounts also suggest some problems. One is that real expertise in activities like ballet or surgery is characterized by a grace, smoothness, and economy of movement that is best evaluated or appreciated by someone who is fairly familiar with this sort of activity himself. The question of who the real experts are may be best answered by the other experts. Here is further evidence for the inaccessibility thesis. What is suggested by these remarks is that expertise tends to be a somewhat elusive quality. An expert may not understand why she does things in a certain way, but may only have an instinctive understanding that she is doing it the right way. Hence her ability to explain why she does something in a certain way may be limited.

According to Anna Hart, an expert is characterized by three features and three functions. The three features are: (1) *effectiveness*—the use of knowledge to solve problems with an acceptable rate of success, (2) *efficiency*—the expert can solve problems more quickly and efficiently, and (3) *awareness of limitations*—an expert knows and will say when she cannot solve a problem, or does not know how to answer a question. The three functions of an expert given by Hart are: (1) *a provider of information*—the expert can answer questions, (2) *a problem solver*—the expert can identify a solution, or give information that might lead to a solution, and (3) *an explainer*—the expert should be able to explain her line of reasoning in arriving at a conclusion (1986, 16–17). Hart's definition of an expert is very broad, but interesting because it includes dialectical skills, namely, awareness of limitations, and abilities to answer questions and explain the reasoning behind a conclusion. This brings out, once again, the critical nature of the dialogue between the expert and the user of expert advice in argumentation.

An expert, then, is not a perfect authority on a question or problem but is an individual with specialized skills that can be tapped for information to which she has a privileged access. The nature of the "tapping," however, may be a kind of dialogue sequence of question-reply argumentation that requires dialectical skills on both sides. Curiously, the most advanced expert in a field, who has achieved an outstanding mastery of the skills of her field, may be the least able to communicate her knowledge.

Studies in the representation of expert knowledge have shown that as an expert becomes more advanced in her mastery of efficiency and accuracy in carrying out her specialized tasks, she tends to lose awareness of the methods she uses, and therefore may not be able to communicate the knowledge she has, as a set of rules, or in a form that can be taught verbally to others. Paul Johnson calls this situation *the paradox of expertise*: "As individuals master more and more knowledge in order to do a task efficiently as well as accurately, they also lose awareness of what they know" (1983, 79). As a result, this skilled knowledge becomes a kind of "tacit" knowledge that the expert is least able to talk about, or to express in such a way that it could be used in a computer program.

Curiously, this paradox of expert knowledge had been observed in a study on the uses of expert opinions in argumentation by Woods and Walton, even before the advent of expert systems.

> It is notable that in judgments of expertise the expert's verdict may be based on inarticulable background elements and so not be amenable to total sentential representation. . . . [A]n authority may partly depend on his intuition or judgment formed from and enriched by substantial familiarity with the area in question. (1974, 136)

According to Woods and Walton, the specialized expert may be held to give a judgment from her special position to know the subject-matter of her area, based on an inner competence. By its nature however, this competence, though it is a source of knowledge in the utilization of expert advice by a nonexpert second party, tends to resist formulation as an explicit set of propositions that the expert can express.

These observations lead to the basic inaccessibility problem with the reasoned use of expert opinions or advice by a nonexpert (or less expert) second party who needs access to this type of expert knowledge. The expert in question may be the best person to give the advice, but she may not be the best person to express it clearly in some explicit form of a set of propositions that the layperson can use or communicate to other users. And the expert may also not be the best person—by herself, at any rate—to articulate the reasons that lie at the evidential roots of her opinion. Indeed, the most advanced expert, whose advice may be the most useful or most correct, may be the person least able to set out the line of reasoning—in a form accessible to the layperson, especially—that led her to use the knowledge in this field to arrive at this particular conclusion. This shielding of accessibility between the expert and the user is the basic problem of all appeals to expert opinion as a reasoned form of guidance, and it is the root of numerous other related problems and pitfalls in the use of expert advice as a form of argumentation.

Commenting on the paradox of expertise, Donald Waterman formulates the following rule of thumb for acquiring knowledge from an expert: "Don't believe everything experts say!" Waterman advises the consultant who is attempting to reconstruct an expert's reasoning not to simply go by what the expert says when she explains how she arrived at a certain conclusion (1986, 154). If this is a sound approach, it means that expert opinions are inherently fallible in many cases, and cannot generally be taken at face value. They should be regarded as subject to interpretation, questioning and clarification. The expert is a source of plausible opinions, but it should not generally be presumed that an expert opinion is beyond questioning.

8. Reliability and Bias—Subjective Factors

On account of the inaccessibility problem and the paradox of expertise, the interface between the expert source and the layperson user needs to be a complex layer of judgments, explanations, questions, and so forth. When dealing with encounters with the kinds of high-level human experts encountered in typical cases where the *argumentum ad verecundiam* might be a fallacy, there is a gap between possessing knowledge and transmitting it to a nonexpert.

When somebody appeals to the say-so of an expert authority to support their argument, what gives the expert's say-so status as evidence, as rational support of the claim made? Basically, it is that the expert is supposed to have knowledge. However, the claim to knowledge is an indirect one. The arguer who made the claim is not getting knowledge directly, as she might by say, in engaging in scientific research to support her claim. Instead, the presumption is that the expert has this kind of first-hand knowledge, and the claimant in the argument who appeals to the expert's say-so is getting access, indirectly or second-hand, to this knowledge, through the mediation of the expert. Thus the expert is a kind of testifier to the reliability of this knowledge. It is the fact that the expert has what we presume to be knowledge that makes the appeal a kind of evidence.

But what guarantee do we have that the expert is not lying, or is biased in a certain way, or is lacking in knowledge in certain areas she is weak in? In general, we cannot take it for granted that such possibilities do not exist, in a given case where an appeal to expertise has been made to support an argument. Therefore, it is best to see such arguments as inherently fallible, testimony-based appeals that are different from what Locke called *ad judicium* arguments in their structure. They are, in a sense, subjective, or source based, and depend on the reliability of the source who functions as an intermediary between knowledge and the recipient who makes the appeal to the source to support his argument. And this is basically why they have a different logic from deductive or inductive arguments.

In Chapter 3, I argued that the best way to see the source of an expert opinion cited in argumentation as an authority is as a testifier or voucher for that opinion who is presumed to be sincere and honest in certifying that that is her real opinion on the issue. This introduces a subjective element into the evaluation of such appeals that have been recognized by some of the textbook treatments of the *argumentum ad verecundiam.*

A. E. Mander stipulated four conditions that must be complied with to justify a judgment on the basis of appeal to an expert authority: (1) the speaker must be identified, (2) the speaker must be recognized as an expert authority in the particular subject by her peers, (3) the authority must generally be a living person (i.e., not an outdated source), or if not, we must be sure that no "fresh facts" have come to light since her death, and (4) the authority must be unbiased, or if there are several authorities being consulted, their biases must "cancel out." This last factor of bias is especially interesting (1936, 41–42).

While it may be possible for an expert system to have or reflect a bias of some sort, perhaps reflecting the bias of the programmer, or of the intended application of the system, the problem of bias looms much larger with human experts. This factor is made explicit in the account of the *ad verecundiam* given by Fearnside and Holther (1959), which stresses not only that the expert should be qualified, but also personally reliable as an honest or sincere source who is not biased. Fearnside and Holther do not use the expression *argumentum ad verecundiam,* but they do have "appeal to authority" or *ipse dixit* listed under the category of psychological fallacies. They see the appeal to authority as, strictly speaking, "logically irrelevant," but they suggest that as a type of argument it can be "practically justified" in some cases to suit a speech to the particular audience concerned. As they see it, it is proper in many cases, and even inevitable, that authorities should provide information to support an argument. But they add that such appeals should be given due weight only if the source is (1) personally reliable, and (2) qualified as an expert. It is apparent that for Fearnside and Holther, an appeal to authority, in the sense they are concerned with, is taken to mean an appeal to expert opinion (84–89).

Fearnside and Holther treat appeal to authority as kind of witness testimony in favor of a claim. As such, they give a number of criteria for judging the reliability of a source who testifies for a claim in a given case. An authority is *personally reliable* only if (1) there is no reason to suppose the witness is lying, (2) there is no reason to believe the witness is swayed by bias, and (3) there is reason to believe that the witness has been conscientious and attentive in gathering data. An authority is *qualified as an expert* in a field in which the opinion is cited only if (1) the authority is clearly identified, (2) the authority has professional standing with fellow experts, (3) the authority is current, (4) the authority's opinion is within her field of competence, and (5) the authority holds representative views in the field (85–86). Thus Fearnside and Holther take a balanced view of appeal to authority as a type of argumentation. They see this type of argument as proper where "the problem is technical and the expert cited is qualified and personally reliable." Otherwise, they judge the appeal to be "suspect," meaning that it should not be given due weight, because it fails to meet one or more of the requirements of personal reliability or expert qualification (87).

Fearnside and Holther (1959, 89–92) treat *appeal to tradition or faith* as a separate fallacy from appeal to authority. The traditional textbooks would partly treat this under *ad populum* group appeals to solidarity and the like. But the older textbooks would also have included much of this material, e.g., appeal to religious or academic traditions or to "great man," as coming under the heading of *ad verecundiam*. Thus Fearnside and Holther adopted a relatively narrow view of appeal to authority, seeing it primarily as an appeal to expert opinion. Yet in another sense, their account is quite broad, in that it stresses the personal reliability of the expert, in addition to the factors dealt with in the various forms of *ad verecundiam* argument considered in sections 1, 3, and 4 above.

9. Human and Machine Expertise

The deductive form of the *ad verecundiam* argument, *(E2)*, is appropriate for a closed data base that contains *all* the facts in a particular domain, and we just want to ask a simple yes-no question of the form, 'Is proposition *A* true?' In the negative case, the inference, '*A* is not in the data base, therefore *A* must be false,' is a form of *ad ignorantiam* argument. This deductive framework works well enough in relatively simple cases of appeal to an authoritative source, like Cases 4.1 and 4.2, the train schedule queries. In these cases, the truth condition and the completeness condition of (E2) seem to apply well enough to the case.

What makes (E1) and (E2) deductive is the use of the word 'all' (the quantifier) to denote a universal generalization that is completely general, in the sense that one counterinstance refutes the generalization. Of course, this is not realistically applicable to most cases of appeal to authority typically dealt with by informal logic. Where the 'all' represents a statistical, or some other sort of inductive generalization, then an inductive form of the *argumentum ad verecundiam* like (F3) is applicable.

However, our analysis of the concept of an expert in this chapter tended to indicate that quantifying the propositions in an expert's knowledge base, in any absolute, or even statistical way, is very often not an appropriate way to proceed. The if-then propositions (called "conditionals" in logic and "rules" in AI) are very often not of a deductive or inductive type. Instead, they are presumptive and defeasible in nature, subject to qualifications and exceptions that could not be very well predicted statistically, by all indications so far. What is suggested as appropriate for these cases is a presumptive form of the *argumentum ad verecundiam* like (G4). Of course (G4) is not the final formulation yet of this form of argumentation. But it is a basis for further exploration of how presumptive *ad verecundiam* appeals are used in argumentation.

Even expert systems use presumptive, defeasible rules, but there are important differences between how expert systems work, at least as developed to the current state of the art, and how appeals to human experts (at least the kinds of appeals most frequently of concern in informal logic) work. Human experts may not always arrive at conclusions by the use of rules, and if this is true, human experts may use intuition, or some other form of information processing that is dissimilar to the machine-reasoning structures used by expert system programs. Whether this is so or not, expert systems are highly interesting to the student of informal logic, because the analysis of *ad verecundiam* argumentation is parallel to studies of the uses of expert systems in many important respects. But how do we define 'expert'? An expert system shell can be applied to any knowledge base. What rule-based program then is not an expert system?

Roger Schank compares the way an expert stores knowledge about her field to the way a library catalogue does the same job. What is the essential difference? According to Schank, one key difference is that in order to be updated, the library catalogue requires outside intervention, whereas the expert can alter her knowledge as her field or her interests may change. Thus the expert is a self-conscious entity—she knows when she knows something and can change things when she observes something. According to Schank, then, an expert is a dynamic processor of information that has an awareness of its own internal states and can learn and improve its knowledge internally, by its own internal operations (1982, 1).

But what does "awareness of its own internal states" mean? A program can continually update itself. For example, a financial expert system can modify its conclusions continually as it obtains incoming information on stock quotes. A higher-order hierarchical system can have feedback. It can modify its own internal states, for example, by correcting contradictions in its knowledge base (Wilensky 1983). Does this count as "awareness" or "dynamic information-processing"? Given these questions, it seems difficult to determine exactly what is the difference, in principle, between a human expert and a machine-based expert system. Instead, it seems that there are many practical differences of degree that vaguely mark off constantly changing differences between human expertise and machine expert reasoning.

Another difference is that we expect a human, professional expert who gives us advice on how to proceed with a possible course of action (that may have harmful consequences) to use judgment, and even what some might call "wisdom" or "common sense." But much may depend on what kind of question the expert is asked. If it is a purely factual question about railroad schedules or industries in South America, a relatively straightforward answer can be given as to whether a proposition is in a knowledge base or not. But if, for example, you go to your lawyer, your physician, or your financial adviser for practical advice on a course of action, e.g., "Should I plead guilty?" or "Should I take medication X?", the question is of a different sort. It is a practical question about the prudence or practical wisdom of a course of action. Here we expect careful, judicious advice, as well as a factual, informed approach.

The difference here, in medicine, might be comparable to the difference between a diagnostic system, like PUFF, and a physician's recommendation on treatment, where dangerous side effects of one possible course of treatment are a risk. Here, judgment of some sort may be needed to assess, in a given case, which treatment should be recommended. It is here that a human expert seems to be needed, to supplant whatever assistance might be given by using an expert system. However, current research is attempting to program expert systems with heuristic considerations that constitute "strategic common sense" in just this kind of case (Mussi 1993, 380). This is done by inserting rules used to manage "trade-off" problems into the system. But the extent to which such a system can practically be used to replace human judgment on serious cases of expert advice, like medical treatment decisions, is still an open area.

Both human experts who are consulted to give advice on how to act or make a decision to act in a real situation, and also robotic programs that are designed to carry out practical tasks, used the same kind of knowledge-based, goal-directed reasoning traditionally called practical reasoning (Aristotle called it *phronesis*) in philosophy. To study any kind of advice-giving transaction of this sort, whether by machine or human expert, practical reasoning is the form of argumentation that needs to be studied. Practical reasoning is a kind of goal-directed reasoning of the following general form. A and B are *states of affairs*, or propositions that represent the possible outcomes of actions, and a is an *agent*, an entity that can carry out informed actions on the basis of information known about its circumstances (a knowledge base).

> (H1)   It is a's goal to bring about A.
> As a sees the situation, B is the means of bringing about A.
> Therefore, a ought (practically speaking) to bring about B.

The above form (H1) is simplified in several respects. First, there may be many steps of action required in a complex (hierarchical) act-sequence. Second, there may be alternative necessary or sufficient steps to consider throughout the sequence. Third, there may be compound goals (with varying priorities). Fourth, there may be side effects (possible future known consequences of actions) to consider. Fifth, if B is not possible to carry out, in the situation, other means or intentions may be open to consideration (Walton 1990b).

Practical reasoning has been most notably studied by von Wright (1983), Clarke (1985), Audi (1989), and Walton (1990). The uses of practical reasoning in informal logic have been studied in Walton (1992a; 1992b). And the theory of rational planning studied by Wilensky (1983) in AI is the natural setting for future studies of practical reasoning.

We could sum up our provisional findings as follows. Both the study of the reasoned use of expertise in informal logic and AI require a reorientation toward the study of practical reasoning as a form of goal-directed plausible reasoning in question-answer two-person dialogue. Practical reasoning is a kind of inference that leads to action in a particular situation and is based on what the agent knows (knowledge base) in a situation as he (she, or it) sees the situation, which may be fluid and uncertain (in common realistic cases of acting on the basis of expert advice). Therefore, although practical reasoning can be expressed in deductive or inductive forms, typically it is used as a species of presumptive, defeasible reasoning, subject to revision as a knowledge base is updated. Therefore, it is primarily the presumptive form of the *argumentum ad verecundiam* that should be the primary focus of our investigation of the kind of advice-giving argumentation that is given from an expert source to a layperson user (of the kind we are concerned to analyze). Case 4.4 showed, however, that even in the more purely factual type of exchange of information, the presumptive form of argument most accurately represents the form of the reasoning.

What we need to investigate next is how (H1) fits in with (G4), for it seems that these two forms of reasoning are combined in the *argumentum ad verecundiam*. To do this, we need to focus less narrowly on the forms of argument *per se*, and to study how they are used in a context of argumentation where one party tries to support his argument, to persuade the other that his argument is justified, based on the say-so of a third-party expert source.

10. Evaluating the Form in a Context of Dialogue

The most potentially useful account of the form of the *ad verecundiam* we came up with in this chapter, to model what seems to be the characteristic argument of this type identified in Chapter 1, was (G4). The key concept in this form is that of 'genuine expert,' contained in the first premise. An expert is defined as a repository of knowledge or skill, so that the form (G4) is a kind of knowledge-based inference, of the kind studied in expert systems.

What gives (G4) its presumptive weight as a knowledge-based type of argumentation, is its first three premises. S is a knowledge base, and because E possesses the knowledge in S, when E asserts A (as true, or known to be true), this licenses the inference to the conclusion that there is a weight of presumption in favor of the hypothesis that A is true. This presumption depends on the assumptions, however, that A is consistent with the available objective evidence, and that E is telling the truth (as known to E).

The argument from expert opinion typically flows from human testimony of a kind that cannot be verified directly (in any conclusive way), so it is a subjective kind of argument. From what we have seen in this chapter, it tends, in practice, not to be a deductive type of argument, nor is it an inductive type of argument, at least of the kind based on statistical probability. We leave open whether it could be analyzed as some species of subjective probability, of the kind studied in statistics.

We prefer to analyze it as a species of presumptive argument which carries provisional weight, as a basis for practical reasoning, even though it tends to be tricky and unreliable in many cases. We will deal with this trickiness and unreliability factor by introducing separate consideration of several requirements (critical questions) that need to be taken into account. The central notion in this type of argumentation turned out to be that of cognitive authority (expertise). Generally, *cognitive authority,* we found in Chapter 2, is distinct from *administrative authority.* In cognitive authority, the opinion of an expert in a domain of knowledge carries weight or plausibility within that domain. This distinction will make our version of the argumentation schemes for arguments from authority inherently more complex than the scheme proposed by Hastings (1962, 131). An *expert,* as we defined this concept, is an individual who exhibits a high level of skill or mastery of a particular field of practice or knowledge, and who is acknowledged by other experts in that field.

The expert consultation type of dialogue, in which the appeal to cognitive authority occurs as a type of argumentation, can be a species of advice-seeking and advice-offering dialogue between a layperson and an expert. The goal is for the layperson to get relevant advice from the expert. The initial situation is a need for expert advice. An important benefit of expert consultation is informed (intelligent) action. But in other cases, it can simply be a type of information-seeking dialogue where the inquirer is trying to get the opinion of a scientist or expert on whether a particular proposition in her field is true or not.

Characteristically, however, the *argumentum ad verecundiam* involves a dual context of dialogue. The most usual primary context is that of a persuasion dialogue (critical discussion), where one party is trying to use an appeal to expert opinion to convince (persuade) the other party that the first party's point of view is right. But this primary dialogue presupposes a secondary dialogue between the proponent of the appeal in the primary dialogue and a third-party expert whose opinion is being used to back up the proponent's argument. This secondary, advice-seeking or information-seeking dialogue may not have actually taken place, as a verbal or written exchange we have actual evidence of, in a given case. But normatively, in order to evaluate any instance of an *argumentum ad verecundiam* as weak, strong, fallacious, etc., we must presume that the argument is based on the existence of this secondary dialogue. We mean by 'dialogue' here a normative structure of conversation, with rules and appropriate sequences of questions and replies (Walton 1995, chap. 4). The six main types of dialogue defined in Walton (1995, chap. 4) and Walton and Krabbe (1996, 80; see also Fig. 1.1) are outlined, with respect to their main characteristics, in Figure 4.3.

In a persuasion dialogue (Walton 1989a, 5–7) each party tries to prove his thesis from premises that are commitments of the other party. There are two basic types of persuasion dialogue. One is the symmetrical type of persuasion dialogue, where both parties have a designated thesis to be proved, and the goal of each party is to prove that thesis using only premises that are commitments of the other side. The other is the asymmetrical type, where the one party, the proponent, has the positive burden of proof described above, while the respondent has the weaker burden of asking critical questions that throw sufficient doubt on the proponent's attempt to prove her thesis so that she fails to meet the burden of proof.

An example of the symmetrical persuasion dialogue would be the dispute between the theist (who claims that God exists) and the atheist (who claims that God does not exist). An example of the asymmetrical type would be the dispute between the theist (who claims that God exists) and the agnostic (who merely doubts that God exists).

The goal of the inquiry is to prove something, implying a high burden of proof. Proof, as required in this sense, means definitely establishing a conclusion by careful inferences from premises that are known to be true. In an inquiry, the goal is to assemble all the available relevant evidence, and then to only infer conclusions that can be inferred by high standards of reasoning from this evidence. The distinguishing characteristic of the inquiry as a type of dialogue is that it is *cumulative,* meaning that the line of argument is always meant to move forward from premises that are well established, to conclusions that are derived carefully, so that retractions will never need to be made. The ideal of cumulativeness is that retractions will never be necessary. But in reality, ultimately retractions will probably have to be made, at some point in the future.

The collective goal of the negotiation type of dialogue is "to make a

TYPE OF DIALOGUE	INITIAL SITUATION	INDIVIDUAL GOALS OF PARTICIPANTS	COLLECTIVE GOAL OF DIALOGUE	BENEFITS
Persuasion	Difference of Opinion	Persuade Other Party	Understand Positions Better	Reveal New Arguments on an Issue
Inquiry	Lack of Proof	Contribute Findings	Prove or Disprove Conjecture	Obtain Knowledge
Deliberation	Contemplation of Future Consequences	Promote Personal Goals	Act on a Thoughtful Basis	Formulate Personal Priorities
Negotiation	Conflicts of Interests	Get What You Want Most (Self-Interest)	Tolerable Settlement	Harmony in Moving Ahead
Information-seeking	One Party Lacks Information	Obtain Information	Transfer of Knowledge	Help in Goal Activity
Quarrel (Eristic)	Personal Conflict Sparked	Verbally Hit Out and Humiliate Opponent	Reveal Deeper Conflict	Vent Disruptive Emotions and Deep Feelings

Fig. 4.3. The Six Main Types of Dialogue

deal." The initial situation in which negotiation begins is that there is some set of goods or services that the participants cannot have as much as they want of. They have to bargain (negotiate), in the form of arguing by making offers and concessions to the other party, in order to try to get what they most want from the given set of goods and services. According to the account given in Walton (1995, 104), the goal of the negotiation type of dialogue is to reach an agreement that both parties can live with, even if it involves compromises. According to this theory, a negotiation dialogue is successful if both sides get enough of what matters to them most so they can feel satisfied that they have reached an outcome that is tolerably acceptable.

The goal of information-seeking dialogue is the transfer of information from one party to another. The beginning situation of an information-seeking dialogue is a set of circumstances where one party has some information that the other party wants to find out about. An example of information-seeking dialogue would be someone who asks a passerby on the street where a certain building is located. Another example would be a celebrity interview, where the interviewer wants to find out certain information about the private life of the celebrity that would be of interest to a public audience. The expert consultation dialogue is a subtype of information-seeking dialogue where the user needs an expert opinion or advice for some purpose; for example, he may need it to take intelligent action in a deliberation, or he may need it to support his argument used in a persuasion dialogue.

Deliberation is a type of dialogue where a person or group confronting a practical problem needs to act on a thoughtful basis. The participants in a deliberation type of dialogue—in many cases, it is one person looking at the pros and cons of a possible future line of action—use goal-directed (practical) reasoning to try to determine a prudent line of action in a given situation.

In the quarrel type of dialogue, the purpose is for the two participants to reveal hidden grievances or grudges of a kind that would not normally be expressed in polite public conversations, in order to articulate these grievances to another party. In a successful quarrel, the two parties make up and resolve to be more sensitive about these things that have now been articulated, and the hope is that this dialogue will help to make for a better relationship between them. A benefit of the quarrel is a kind of cathartic effect where these hidden conflicts or antagonisms are brought to the surface. The quarrel is generally held to be a negative type of dialogue, and it seems strange at first to think of it as a normative model of dialogue in which arguments can be judged both positively and negatively. And to be sure, the quarrel usually generates more heat than light, and is not much of a friend of logic at all. One problem is that, in a quarrel, the participants tend to skip from the original issue to other issues that are completely unrelated to the original issue (except that the arguer has a deep grievance about each issue). But even so, the quarrel can be beneficial in some cases. From a logical point of view, however, it is important to watch carefully for signs of a shift to the quarrel from another type of dialogue. Such shifts to the quarrel can be highly counterproductive, and are often associated with fallacies.

We found in this chapter that the appeal to expert opinion has a definite form as a presumptive type of argument, but to evaluate whether this form of argument has been used correctly or not in a given case, we need to judge it in light of the context of dialogue appropriate for that case. Such an argument is weak or faulty if certain requirements are not met. For example an instance of the faulty use of *ad verecundiam* argument would occur where the authority whose opinion was solicited was badly outdated in her knowledge of her special field, given that recent knowledge has changed the field on the topic.

Moreover, it will be a contention of this chapter that an erroneous appeal to expert opinion in argumentation is not necessarily a fallacious *ad verecundiam*. An appeal to expert opinion will be said to be weak or inadequately supported where the requirements of the argumentation scheme for the appeal have not been met. Such an appeal will only be ruled fallacious where the technique of arguing from expert opinion in a dialogue has been seriously abused, in a way that goes against the goals of the dialogue. In Chapter 8, the question of whether this may be said to occur is taken up.

Hamblin writes that arguments from authority have been particularly disliked at various historical periods (1970, 43). And indeed, the rise of scientific method could be seen, to a significant extent, as a reaction against the important role that respect for authority played as a form of argumentation in medieval scholarship. While it is true that the *argumentum ad verecundiam* is found in the "fallacies" sections of the modern logic textbooks, these accounts often stress that arguing on the basis of expertise can be nonfallacious in some instances. Copi writes, as noted above, that being guided by the "best judgment of an expert authority" is "in many cases perfectly legitimate" as a method of argument (1986, 98). In Chapter 7, I will argue that the difference between the reasonable appeal to expert opinion in argumentation and the fallacious *argumentum ad verecundiam* is a question of how this technique of argumentation is used properly or abused in a context of dialogue.

5

DIALECTICAL ASPECTS

So far, I have been able to show that appeal to expert opinion has an identifiable form (or several forms) of argument. Instances of this form can be reasonable arguments of a familiar kind that we commonly rely on in everyday argumentation. Use of such a form of argumentation, I have argued, is justified on the basis of the presumption that expert sources contain knowledge. And I defined in Chapter 4, section 7 (without yet examining the many, contestable borderline cases) what an expert is. So far, so good. But as Wesley Salmon's analysis has already indicated (Chapter 4, section 3) there are critical questions that seem to be important to evaluating *ad verecundiam* arguments, over and above the question of whether the logical form is satisfied in a case.

When we begin to examine some realistic longer cases where the *ad verecundiam* form of argument is used in everyday argumentation, quite a number of contextual factors begin to surface; that is, critical questions emerge on how we should judge an argument fallacious or nonfallacious in a given case. These complexities seem to outrange the capacity of the forms of argument given in Chapter 3 to function as an exclusive basis for arriving at evaluations of appeals to authority.

1. The Case of the Deadly Radar Gun

We begin by presenting a case from the news media where the *argumentum ad verecundiam* was an important part of the argumentation. What follows, the case of the deadly radar gun, is an account of a controversy described in the news report "Zapped!" broadcast on June 21, 1992, by *60 Minutes*. In this case, you will notice that there are several appeals to expert opinion used where the source is a genuine expert and his or her opinion is within his or her field of expertise. Yet we definitely evaluate these appeals as convincing in the one instance and not convincing in the other. What then is the basis for these evaluations? It seems that the broader context of use—the sequence of dialogue in the case—has to be taken into account in order to answer this controversial question.

The program begins with interviews of two police officers who had used handheld radar units for many years in their police cars to clock speeders. Both said they had the habit of resting the radar gun between their legs. Both officers were diagnosed with testicular cancer and felt that the cause was the radiation from the radar gun. Another officer interviewed, Ohio State Trooper Gary Poynter, had investigated links between radar guns and cancer for two years and wrote an article that concluded that there are serious hazards from long-term exposure to police radar devices. Officer Poynter contacted twenty-two police officers who had testicular cancer and reported that twenty of them had used handheld radar units that they had rested in their laps.

Two other police officers interviewed by Morley Safer, the *60 Minutes* interviewer, reported that they had used radar units in different places in the police car. One mounted it on his shoulder for twelve years, and now had a rare tumor in his shoulder joint. The other mounted it behind his head for fourteen years. He was diagnosed with skin cancer that had spread to his eye and brain.

Next, the program showed an interview with Eleanor Adair, identified as "a lecturer at Yale University" who "studies biological effects of microwave radiation," and who "led the group which recommended the safety standard for microwave radiation," including "the kind emitted by radar guns."

> ADAIR: These devices are held to be safe by the FDA, by the FCC, by OSHA and they are regarded as safe by the Institute of Electrical and Electronics Engineers—standard-setting

groups—and their Committee on Man and
Radiation. And all of these opinions are based
on the science that has been done over the
years (*60 Minutes* 1992, 5).

Next, the program interviewed Dale Smith, who had manufactured
traffic radar units in the 1970s and who invented the Fuzzbuster radar
detector. Smith expressed serious doubts about the safety of these
units.

DALE SMITH: *(Manufactured Radar Units in 1970s):* The
radar units were designed to be used outside
of the vehicle at all times. As a matter of fact,
the brackets were even designed in such a way
that they could not be used inside the vehicle.

(Footage of Smith)

SAFER: *(Voice-over)* And why were the radar units
designed to be used outside the vehicle?
SMITH: The people in the industry, myself included,
you know, were advised that there was a—a
possible hazard because of the radiation levels
that—transmitted by the radar.

(Warning label shown)

SAFER: *(Voice-over)* The microwave transmitters that
were to be installed in the radars arrived from
his supplier with a warning label urging
caution during any exposure to radio frequency
radiation. Smith then placed the warning tag
on the units he was shipping out to police
departments.
SMITH: I ran into some very serious political problems
with some of the higher-level police officials
that said, 'We don't want these tickets on here
because they're scaring our officers.' So over a
period of time, the practice of—of sending the
hazard stickers with the units went away,
although during the time I built them, I
always put them on.

(Cover of an operator's manual for a radar gun shown)

> SAFER: *(Voice-over)* Not only were there no warnings
>   on the radar guns, operation manuals like this
>   one from Kustom Signals, the biggest supplier
>   of radar units, said, "microwave energy emis-
>   sions meet the industry standard and need not
>   be a concern." (6)

Footage of Eleanor Adair was then shown. She was asked if the manu-
facturers had shown her any studies that the radar units were safe,
and she replied: "They have certainly made measurements of the output powers of their units, as have many other people, and the power
outputs are extremely low" (7). The implications of Adair's answer seem
to clash with the advice of Smith that certain uses of these units pose
a possible hazard.

Next, the program showed an interview with Louis Slesin, editor of
the *Microwave News,* and is described as having been "reporting research
on electromagnetic radiation, including possible links to cancer" for
twelve years.

> SLESIN: The standards that people are talking about
>   were written by the military, by industry to
>   serve their interests, not to serve the interests
>   of public health, not to serve the interests of
>   occupational health. There have been practi-
>   cally no studies that are relevant to this
>   situation.
> SAFER: One hears the argument that the—the level of
>   emission is about the same as a garage door
>   opener, a little more, a little less.
> SLESIN: You know, we're talking of low levels, there's
>   no doubt, but how low is low enough? You
>   know, there are hundreds of studies out there,
>   but most of them are high dose, short time.
>   What we're talking here is low dose, long time.
>   And this is the difference between an acute
>   hazard and a chronic hazard. We're talking
>   about police officers who are exposed every
>   day on their shift for years at a time. (7)

Next, the program showed footage of Morley Safer talking to two other

officers who had used handheld radar units (for fifteen and seventeen
years, respectively), and who both got testicular cancer. When these two
officers both reported that they had rested the unit between their legs
when it was not in use, Eleanor Adair was reported as replying, "the
power output of the unit would be insufficient to create any biological
damage to the testicles." Here again, there is a conflict of opinions
between the two sources.

The follow-up interview sequence with Slesin leads the viewer to one
side in this conflict.

> SAFER: So this is—what?—coincidence?
> ADAIR: It's coincidence.
>
> *(Footage of the Wyoming Police Justice Building)*
>
> SAFER: *(Voice-over)* Coincidence? Maybe. But scientists
> have calculated the incidence of testicular
> cancer in those two departments to be at least
> seven times the expected rate.
> SLESIN: We also have animal studies that show that
> animals exposed to this radiation do develop
> cancer at an abnormal rate. We have studies of
> human beings in the military who were
> exposed to this radiation also developing
> cancer up to seven times the expected rate. So,
> you know, you have three—three levels of
> argument here—the anecdotal, the scientific
> and the—you know, the policy, if you will. And
> all of them say, 'Study this, please.' (8)

Following this exchange, Safer reports that a number of police departments in other states have banned handheld radar, including Connecticut,
where the units were mounted on a bracket outside the car. Eleanor
Adair replied, however, "Why put it outside when there's no evidence
that the—it's not doing any harm inside." When asked whether she
would "happily sit with a radar gun in [her] lap or beside [her] for 40
hours a week," Ms. Adair replied, "Absolutely, no problem" (9). The program concludes with Officer Poynter remarking that the problem he
has had in his research in the last three years is that he cannot talk to so
many of the police officers on his list any more because they are now dead.

In this case, there are two main appeals to expert opinion that are
centrally important to the argument as a whole—the appeal to Adair's
opinion that the radar devices are safe, and the appeal to Smith's
opinion (backed up by the other sources interviewed) that the devices are

hazardous. If you were to look at each appeal in the absence of the context of the dialogue of the rest of the case, it would appear to be a reasonable and credible argument from authority of expert opinion. But when you look at each of them in context, the evaluation is quite different.

When you look at these two arguments in context, the first thing to notice is that one has the opposite conclusion of the other—the two arguments are opposed. The second thing to notice is that the physical evidence presented—the cases of the police officers who used these units in their cars and then got cancer—is opposed to the conclusion of Adair's argument. The testimony of the police officers does not, by and large, appear to rest on appeal to expert opinion or to be a convincing argumentation that rests on the police officers' personal experiences in using these radar units. However, there are some elements of appeal to expert opinion involved, as well. Both officers Malcolm and Nelson used the handheld radar units over a long period and both had testicular cancer. Their relating of their personal experiences is a factual kind of evidence, not (at least, significantly) based on their being experts, either on these radar units or on police work generally.

The case of Officer Poynter is more complex because he is said to have "been looking into possible links between radar and cancer" for three years. This way of putting it does imply a knowledge of the subject. However, he is not an expert in the sense that an engineer or someone who designed or built the radar units would be said to be an expert on it. Nevertheless, there is an element of appeal to expert opinion here. However, in all the other cases, including those of the testimony of officers Rachele and Vessels, what is primarily important is their account of what happened to them personally. This is more of a personal testimony of "what happened to me," a kind of anecdotal evidence, not resting for its value as evidence on any particular claim of scientific expertise. Poynter is said to have heard from ninety other officers who used other radar units and got cancer. This report carries more weight as evidence, apart from any expertise we may attribute to Poynter as a police officer or as someone who has looked into the matter and collected data on it. Even though this collection of data from cases does not meet standards for scientific evidence, of the kind that would be necessary in a clinical trial or epidemiological study, it does suggest a plausible hypothesis.

In the program, when all the plausible physical evidence is presented first, Adair's argument appears very dubious. In fact, we (as viewers) reject Adair's *ad verecundiam* argument. The typical viewer would definitely think that Adair's argument is not plausible and would be strongly inclined to doubt it. Adair, we are told, is a lecturer at Yale who studies "biological effects of microwave radiation." We are not told what her credentials are, beyond that, or even what her field of expertise (discipline) is. We are told, however, that she has led a group "which recommended the safety standard for microwave radiation." Thus it would appear that she has been recognized as an authority in this area, and it would appear reasonable to presume that the appeal to her expert opinion on it should carry weight. In other words, the appeal to her as an expert source of knowledge meets many of the requirements of the form of the argument from expert opinion. She backs up her opinion by citing recommendations of other expert standard-setting groups. This might seem questionable—in law it would be regarded as "hearsay" (Imwinkelried 1991, 11–16). But as a presumptive type of argumentation in the contexts of the *60 Minutes* dialogue (1992), it seems a reasonable enough kind of argument, giving her opinion some more weight than it might otherwise have.

Adair's expert opinion then does, in principle, at least initially carry weight. But placed in the context of the previous testimony by the police officers (which contradicts her opinion), the plausibility of her argument is brought sharply into question. Then, given the subsequent expert testimony of Smith and Slesin, which again leads to the opposite conclusion to that of Adair, her argument is made to seem not very plausible.

Smith and Slesin are not high-level experts. Neither one, so far as I know is an engineer nor an academic expert on microwave physics. But both have a certain status as skilled craftsmen who have practical knowledge on how these units work, and on aspects of their safety. Slesin has conducted research in the field of electromagnetic radiation and its possible links to cancer. Hence, an appeal to him as someone who has expert knowledge is reasonable, in this context. And he does, when questioned, back up his opinion by citing animal studies and studies of human beings in the military. His opinion also fits in very well with the evidence given by the policemen, to the effect that this kind of microwave radiation is hazardous. Slesin also contradicts Adair's opinion, when he claims that the safety standards she defends "are not relevant to this situation" of handheld radar units being held in such close proximity by humans over such a prolonged period (9). All this cumulative body of evidence, amassed in the *60 Minutes* dialogue (1992), tends to give a strong basis for rejecting the appeal to the expert opinion of Adair, or casting serious doubt on it.

Following Adair's argument in the case, Smith's argument is presented. As a former manufacturer of these radar units, his opinion as an expert witness would probably be found credible by the public, because of his practical experience with how these devices were made. Thus when his very persuasive presentation of his opinion is put forward, backing up the previous quite convincing physical evidence, it has the effect of tilting the weight of presumption very much to the one side. We are convinced that these radar units are hazardous and are probably what caused the cancer in the cases of the police officers cited. Smith's *ad verecundiam* argument is convincing.

The *60 Minutes* program (1992) took a fair-minded, nonbiased approach to the issue by citing the opinions of experts on both sides. Yet the viewer is definitely moved toward the plausible conclusion that there is a strong weight of evidence on the one side. In context then, the one *argumentum ad verecundiam* comes out as credible and persuasive, the other does not. The program has a definite "spin" by posing the conflict of opinions and presenting a much more convincing weight of evidence on one side than the other. The kinds of examples of *ad verecundiam* arguments cited in the logic textbooks, as Chapter 3 indicates, tend to be short examples that are taken out of context, i.e., little explicit contextual information is given on how the argument was used in a case. Typically, the reader is left to make presumptions on the basis of general knowledge.

When examples of the *ad verecundiam* argument are presented in a context like that of the case above, however, our basis for evaluating the argument may be quite different from simply looking at its logical form. We need to see how that type of argument is being used in a broader context of dialogue, to get a proper evaluation of it. In this case, we see that the interviewer, Morley Safer, is asking questions of the experts. This footage of the interviewing is edited, and then fitted into the *60 Minutes* presentation format, along with other reported facts and interviews of other sources. Thus the subdialogues between Safer and the two key experts are fitted into a larger context of dialogue that is the *60 Minutes* report as televised.

Neither *ad verecundiam* argument is fallacious nor are they absolutely conclusive. Instead, each of them (by itself) shifts a weight of presumption one way or the other, each being a small (but important) part of the larger body of evidence that the viewer uses to arrive at a conclusion in the case.

This factor of nonconclusiveness is typical of how *ad verecundiam* arguments work in argumentation in everyday conversation, where it is a type of argument that is very commonly used. By itself, such an argument is generally not conclusive. Instead, it fits into a larger evidential picture that includes nonexpert sources of testimony as well as other appeals to expert opinion. The function of the *ad verecundiam* is to carry a weight of presumption to shift a burden of proof from one side toward the other on an issue where two conflicting viewpoints, supported by appeals to expert opinions, are divided. In the radar guns case, much of the evidence on the one side was "anecdotal" (as a scientist in a field of knowledge would call it), a kind of evidence based on testimony or the collection of facts in individual cases that does not meet the standards of data processing and proof required for a scientific field of expertise.

In the next major case study, the conflict at issue was between expert opinion based on scientific research in a domain of knowledge and anecdotal evidence used to guide two individuals in their search for a way of solving a problem they faced, where expert opinion was not of much help, without a big push.

2. The Case of Lorenzo's Oil

Lorenzo's Oil is a Hollywood movie based on the real-life efforts of Augusto and Michaela Odone's efforts to find a cure for their five-year-old boy, Lorenzo, who was diagnosed in 1984 as having a rare and incurable disease, adrenoleukodystrophy (ALD). The disease is caused by a genetic defect that shows up only in boys (but is carried by girls). Blood in affected individuals has unusually high levels of "very long chain" fatty acids (VLCFAs). The disease is caused by the VLCFAs improper elimination by the body, which sets up a process that destroys brain tissue and causes the destruction of the myelin sheafs that cover nerves. At one stage, the Odones agreed to have Lorenzo take part in a clinical trial directed by a neurologist, Dr. Hugo Moser (played by Peter Ustinov in the film), which puts the patients on a special diet that eliminates VLCFAs from the diet. But this trial failed to slow the progress of the disease in Lorenzo. Frustrated, the Odones began to read the medical literature on ALD themselves. They came up with the original idea that it might be possible to prevent a patient from producing an excess of saturated VLCFAs by feeding him unsaturated VLCFAs. To test their theory they persuaded a retired chemist to make an edible form of the required oil (Lorenzo's Oil), and when Lorenzo tried it, the level of saturated VLCFAs in his blood dropped to the normal level, stopping the progress of the disease. Lorenzo's condition, which had gotten very bad by that point, stabilized. Although his brain had deteriorated badly by then, he went on to survive past the point where he would normally have died as an ALD sufferer.

It remains controversial whether or not Lorenzo's Oil is a cure for ALD. According to Coleman and Concar (1993, 24), researchers were initially optimistic but now feel that the film claimed too much. Dr. Moser (Coleman and Concar 1993, 24) stated that the oil does not have a discernible effect on the progress of the disease and, although it does reduce the level of VLCFAs in the blood, that reduction is useless once demyelination has begun. Further experimentation is underway to test whether the oil can prevent the onset of ALD.

A theme of the film is the struggle of the Odones, who are not themselves physicians, to get the medical establishment to take their questioning of the accepted ways of treating ALD patients seriously and support their efforts to inquire into ways of treating the disease. Not only the physicians but the support groups and other health care workers kept brushing aside the Odones' questions and arguments as beneath serious consideration. The particular segment of dialogue in the film chosen as a case study to illustrate a context of use of argument from expert opinion is an ALD family conference, chaired by a husband and wife who themselves have two ALD children. Those in attendance at the meeting are members of a support group to help the parents of children with ALD. The dialogue below was transcribed (by the author) from the film.

SPEAKER: Twenty-six people have sent in recipes for the newsletter. We still need ideas for snack foods and breakfast treats. Now remember, all foods should be low-fat—the only food allowed on the Institute Diet.

MRS. ODONE: Excuse me. Our son has complied with this diet, and yet his levels of saturated VLCFAs have risen for two months.

OTHER MOTHER: That's exactly what happened to [our son].

MRS. ODONE: Well perhaps before we talk about publishing cookbooks, we should ask ourselves if the diet is working at all. Shouldn't we?

OTHER MOTHER: Damn right we should!

CHAIRPERSON (HUSBAND): This is not the way we do things here.

MR. ODONE: Excuse me, there are two families here with this paradox. Maybe there are more.

MRS. ODONE: Shouldn't we open for discussion?

ANOTHER PARENT: My boy's levels are rising.

MR. ODONE: Well now there are three families. So maybe we should, could we, have a show of hands?

And maybe we'll see how many families there
are.

CHAIRPERSON (HUSBAND): You don't understand. This is a
formal pilot study. It has to run the full six
months. We are not scientists. We don't take it
upon ourselves to interpret experiments.
That's the solemn responsibility of the doctors.

OTHER MOTHER: Come on Allard! Let's at least have a show of
hands.

CHAIRPERSON (WIFE):   It wouldn't have any meaning.

THIRD CHAIRPERSON (WOMAN): Excuse me. May I say something?
The only way that the doctors can get useful
results is with a strict protocol, and statistical
samples in a control group.

CHAIRPERSON (HUSBAND): And a proper time frame. Doctors
have to be very careful. Clinical trials must
withstand a tremendous amount of scrutiny.

CHAIRPERSON (WIFE): This is the way that medical science
works. That's the only way scientists can get
the information that they need.

MRS. ODONE: So what we're saying is that our children are
in the service of medical science How very
foolish of me. I always assumed that medical
science was in the service of the sufferers.

CHAIRPERSON (WIFE): Yes. Thank you. Now I think it's time
we get back to our agenda.

MRS. ODONE: Why? So we can discuss further salvaging our
marriages and managing our grief. No one here
is discussing the children.

CHAIRPERSON (WIFE): Now if Mary has nothing further to
add, I would like to introduce Dr. Chappell
who will talk about the nasogastric tube and
suction machine. Would you all join me in
giving him a warm welcome [Doctor starts his
speech].

Although this dialogue is a fictional re-creation, it represents an easily
recognizable profile of a kind of case where asking critical questions
about technical matters in the province of scientific experts—"that is
the solemn responsibility of the doctors"—is being brushed aside as
inappropriate. When the Odones ask for a show of hands as a basis for
collecting evidence, the chairperson (wife) says, "It wouldn't have any

meaning," and that the "medical folks" call this kind of evidence "anec-dotal." The conflict represented here is that the husband and wife chairpersons see the issue as one that must only be investigated by medical science "with a strict protocol, and statistical samples in con-trol group." They see the clinical trial as the only proper form of inquiry within which to test hypotheses and collect clinical evidence about the treatment of ALD. The Odones, however, have the purpose of trying to save their son's life, even though they are not physicians. In this case, the pursuit of these two aims reveals a conflict, and two sides (points of view) in the argumentation emerge from the dialogue.

The dialogue in this case provides an interesting example for study, because the appeal to expert opinion is used in a contextual framework where arguments and critical questions are brushed aside, or deemed inappropriate, in relation to a type of dialogue that the argumentation is supposed to be part of. The argumentation sequence in the case is reminiscent of Locke's account of *ad verecundiam*, where an arguer who fails to respectfully submit to the authority of a "learned doctor" is portrayed as impudent, or failing to show proper respect for the estab-lished learning (Chapter 2, section 7).

3. Reported Controversies

In the two major case studies above, at least the experts were identi-fied by name. But in many other cases the appeal to expert opinion is more vague. Many of the most common cases of *ad verecundiam* one notices in everyday experiences are brief media reports of controversial subjects, often matters relating to public policy decisions. Experts, often social scientists or other academics, will be cited as sources supporting some opinion related to the issue, but these experts may not be identi-fied very specifically (Walton 1989a, chap. 7). Sometimes the name or academic affiliation of the expert will be given; in many cases, it is not. Phrases are used like "according to leading experts," or "experts in field *S* say . . . ." without any further documentation being given.

How are experts selected to give input into the media and public affairs? Clearly it helps to have academic or professional qualifications, but other factors are also important. One step now is to get listed in *The 1995 Yearbook of Experts, Authorities and Spokespersons.* According to Robert Samuelson, it costs $375 to get yourself listed, though you can pay more for a larger space.

> The Yearbook amasses more than 900 pages of experts on
> everything from "addictions/Boredom" (The Boring Institute) to
> "Bird Baths" (The National Bird Feeding Society) to "Health
> Fraud/Quackery" (The American Preventive Medical Association)
> to "Legal Issues/Hypnosis" (The American Council of Hypnotist
> Examiners) to "Relationships/Couples" (The Institute for Creative
> Solutions). (1995, 49)

The book is sent out free to newspapers, radio and TV stations, and
magazines. Samuelson comments that there seems to be a free market
policy in America. The experts are self-selected, and promote themselves by being constantly camera-ready. Thus the expert that you hear
quoted in a media report on some issue of public affairs is likely to be
selected out because she promotes herself to the media as an expert.

   In debates on issues that are deeply controversial, typically expert
opinions on various points relevant to the controversy can be cited on
both sides. Very often such appeals, made in the context of the argument, are not conclusive and may be documented or backed up in a
weak and incomplete way. In some cases, appeals to expert authorities
in different fields are peppered through the text of discourse and the
outcome of the dispute appears largely to rest on these appeals, making the ultimate resolution of the argument inconclusive.

Case 5.1:   A *Newsweek* article, reporting on the debate on corporal
            punishment (paddling) in the classroom cites split opinions
            in state legislatures and among various advocacy and pro-
            fessional groups who have taken a position on the issue
            (James N. Baker, with Daniel Shapiro, Pat Wingent and
            Nadine Joseph, 'Paddling: Still a Sore Point,' *Newsweek*,
            June 22, 1987, p. 61). Don F. Wilson, president of the Ohio
            Education Association, is quoted in support of the claim
            made by paddling advocates that corporal punishment is
            necessary for classroom discipline: "A lot of child-develop-
            ment experts might change their minds if they were in a
            classroom." Immediately following this quotation, Univer-
            sity of Kansas child-development Professor Donald M. Baer
            is quoted as concurring: "Corporal punishment can be effec-
            tive in changing behavior." Immediately following this
            citation, the article states: "Most experts, and many par-
            ents, vehemently disagree." After citing a number of other
            studies by psychologists and university research centers on
            problems related to the issue, the article concludes with the

statement that "experts say there may be no consensus to end the practice" of paddling as long as adults feel that what was right for them may also be right for their children.

This article is a balanced presentation which gives many arguments and opinions on both sides of the debate, supported by expert opinions in various relevant fields. Curiously, the article even concludes with the statement that "experts say there may be no consensus" to resolve the issue of whether the practice will be continued or not.

Looking over the individual appeals to expert authority cited in Case 5.1, it could be said that none of them is wholly unreasonable but all of them are relatively weak and brief. In the very last appeal, for example, the claim is made that "experts say" such-and-such, without even any attempt or effort to name the experts or their fields of expertise, or otherwise document the appeal. This type of citation is, indeed, the weakest type of appeal to expert authority. But even so, the statement is not wholly unreasonable or fallacious, although it is certainly subject to challenge and to requests for further support, explicitization, and documentation.

The first two appeals to expert authority are on much stronger ground because they give direct quotes of named individuals whose qualifications and fields of expertise are cited. However, the one expert quoted himself cites "[a] lot of child-development experts" without further backing or documentation of the claim, and that is a weak form of appeal to expert opinion. Similarly, the article goes on to cite "most experts and many parents," which is once again, a very weak and vague form of argument.

Despite these gaps, however, the over-all line of argumentation is fairly reasonable, because it balances out the assemblage of the various appeals to expert authority on both sides of the issue. The local arguments, although individually weak and brief, are not used to try to browbeat the reader with appeals to expert authorities in an attempt to force the issue on one side of the argument. The appeals to authority are not so bad that they qualify as fallacious. But they are not so good that they carry much weight, either. The key to understanding this common kind of case is to examine the context of conversation in which the appeals to expertise are being used to support arguments. There are several layers. The journalists are reporting on a public policy issue, paddling in the schools. Public opinion is divided, and the issue is one of values or ethics, as well as an educational issue. It is unclear who the real "experts" are on this issue. It seems that there may be different fields of expertise that are relevant to various aspects of the issue.

We could say that the case presumes a background of a persuasion dialogue, or critical discussion, where there is a conflict of opinions on the subject of paddling and the views of both sides are open to discussion. The *Newsweek* article is reporting on this controversy. What is reported is that in the controversy each side has its cited expert opinions that they use to support their respective points of view. The *Newsweek* article is a summary of the highlights of this exchange of viewpoints. It may be very tempting for a logic student who has just learned about the *ad verecundiam* fallacy to cite this case as an instance of it, using the forms of arguments in Chapter 3 as the criterion. For the experts disagree in this case, and therefore the appeal to expert opinion is inconclusive. Also citing the say-so of "most experts" or the statement "experts say" is too vague, and does not, therefore, meet the requirements of a valid appeal to expert opinion as a type of argument.

This, however, is a simplistic evaluation. The *Newsweek* article is only summarizing the highlights of the controversy for its readers. The purpose of the report is not to make the appeal to expert opinion, on either side, as strong or conclusive as possible. To see it this way is to confuse the two conversational layers in the context of the case.

4. Appeal to Expert Opinion in Political Debate

In a parliamentary or congressional debate, there may be severe constraints on how much time can be spent on backing up a claim or giving extensive documentation to support the backing of an argument. The degree and nature of the backing that is appropriate in a particular case depends on the context of dialogue. In particular, it depends on the prior question of the dialogue that the argument under study is designed to be a reply to. Thus in such a context of debate, an appeal to the authority of expert opinion may not be backed up fully or completely because of the constraints on the debate.

The Oral Question Period in the Canadian House of Commons *Debates* allows the opposition members to ask relatively brief (single) questions to seek information or press for action from the government ministers in the various departments. According to the rules of parliamentary debate stated in *Beauchesne,* the replies (like the questions) are supposed to be relatively brief and to the point and, in particular, they are not supposed to be a lengthy speech or other form of political tirade. Accordingly, in both questions and answers in the dialogue in Question Period, there are constraints on the length of a move, which can be enforced by the speaker of the house, if he feels that one party is speaking too long, or going into details that are too lengthy.

The following dialogue from the Oral Question Period of the *Debates of the House of Commons of Canada (Hansard,* vol. 128, February 5, 1986, p. 10467) is a case where the speaker intervened in order to try to shorten a question and a reply. In this exchange, John Turner (the leader of the opposition) opened with a question that was not only complex and long but also aggressively loaded. The minister of finance (MichaelWilson) responded to this attack by trying to summarize government economic policies. Rightly, the speaker of the house intervened, causing the subsequent question by Turner and reply by Wilson to be shorter and more specific.

Case 5.2:   THE ECONOMY
                          EXCHANGE VALUE OF DOLLAR

> *Right Hon. John N. Turner (Leader of the Opposition)*: Mr. Speaker, my question is directed to the Minister of Finance. He will know that although the Canadian dollar was up marginally this morning, the crisis is far from over. While he has adopted in this House the attitude of blaming everyone else for his problem, he must recognize that he, as the fiscal adviser to the Government, has the sole responsibility of dealing with this matter. Will he today, Wednesday, February 5, tell this House what he is going to do to solve the dollar crisis?
>
> *Hon. Michael Wilson (Minister of Finance)*: Mr. Speaker, this Government takes full responsibility for the economic policies we brought in. We are proud of them and we think they are doing the job. I will tell the Hon. Member the sort of things we have been doing which are contributing to our economic strength. This is clearly evidenced by the fact that 1,000 jobs have been created every day since we came into office.
>
> We initiated our program with the November economic statement. This set out in a very clear way the sum total of our economic policies. We brought in policies to increase investment, both foreign and domestic. We brought in policies to invigorate the energy sector and the small business community. We have followed a—
>
> *Mr. Speaker*: Order, please. I hope questions and answers will be shorter than yesterday.

MINISTER'S POSITION

Right Hon. John N. Turner (Leader of the Opposition): I
have a supplementary question, Mr. Speaker. The answer
does not relate to the question, so I will rephrase it, in
French this time.
The Minister of Finance has the authority to solve the
problem. What concrete step will he take to put an end to
the Canadian dollar crisis?
Hon. Michael Wilson (Minister of Finance): Mr. Speaker, the
Hon. Member, a former Minister of Finance, says, to use his
words, that my response was not relevant to the question.
He asked what we are going to do to introduce a degree of
stability into the Canadian dollar as well as strengthen the
Canadian economy. For him to say that shows that he fails
to understand the effect of the policies we have brought in
and their impact on job creation, investment, housing starts,
and inflation. All of these things are very, very clear.

If he cares to read not what I say but what expert economists have to say, he will see that they say the economy is
strong and on the right track. They say they do not understand why there is a weakness in the dollar in the face of
the strength in our economy and the fact we are taking
action on the deficit, something which is long overdue after
10 years of mismanagement—

When Turner reformulates his question, it is a compact version of the
same question posed in a more lengthy fashion in the previous round.
Wilson replies that the question shows that Turner does not understand
government economy policies, and then backs up this reply with what
seems to be a weak appeal to the authority of expertise. Wilson claims
that if his questioner would care to read "what expert economists have
to say," he will see that the government policies on the economy are "on
the right track." Although Turner's reformulated question is notably
succinct, Wilson's reply is still somewhat long by comparison. Clearly
Wilson's reply can be seen to be struggling to be as brief and pointed as
possible, under the constraints imposed by the prior context of dialogue.

From the point of view of the conventional wisdom on the *ad verecundiam* fallacy, it would be strongly tempting in evaluating this case
to criticize Wilson's appeal to the authority of expert opinion as fallacious. Wilson does not name any of these experts he supposedly cites,

does not give their detailed individual qualifications, and does not quote their exact opinions in a way that can be verified or checked for accuracy of interpretation. The only reference he offers is to unnamed "expert economists," and it is precisely this sort of vague, hand-waving type of appeal that the textbooks would censure as a fallacious *argumentum ad verecundiam*.

However, the point in this particular case is that the context of dialogue indicates that there are severe practical constraints on the length of the reply allowed. Therefore, a detailed citing of sources or references, or a reading of exact quotations from sources cited in order to back up the reply, might be (quite justifiably) regarded as inappropriate and out of place, by the speaker of the house. Hence a critic should not be too quick in evaluating this case, to jump on Wilson's appeal to expert opinion as an instance of the notorious *ad verecundiam* fallacy. While it is certainly true that Wilson's appeal to expert opinion in this case is a relatively weak and incomplete argument—lacking essential backing required to support it as a strong argument—it is quite another thing to dismiss it as fallacious or worthless, an erroneously misleading or sophistical trick that should be completely refuted or rejected as fallacious. The leap from criticism to refutation, in this case, is too hasty.

As a form of plausible reasoning, an argument based on an appeal to expert opinion can be used to shift a burden of proof from one side of an argument on a controversial issue to the other. Such uses of the appeal to expert opinion do not require the argument to be absolutely authoritative with complete documentation and all supporting evidence furnished at one move in the dialogue. Instead, characteristically, such arguments from expertise should be thought of as subject to critical questioning in the course of the dialogue, which can serve to support or undermine the claim made by the appeal.

As a corollary to viewing appeals to expert opinion in this way, a clear distinction should be made between an argument of the *ad verecundiam* type that is weak or inadequately documented (subject to critical questioning) and one that is based on an underlying systematic error or strategy of deception to the extent we can justifiably classify it as fallacious (subject to refutation). Thus the appeal to expertise can have legitimate uses, in a particular case, that are nevertheless rightly evaluated as weak in certain respects, or open to specific critical questions.

An appeal to expert opinion can be incomplete in argument, but whether it is fallacious may depend on how it stands up to critical scrutiny when challenged. If critical questions can be answered that fill in the gaps required by the premises of the forms of the argument, as outlined in Chapter 3, the appeal to expert opinion may be judged nonfallacious. But if, instead of answering such questions, the proponent tries to badger the respondent into uncritically accepting the authority of the expert source cited, the argument may be judged fallacious.

In making such a judgment, the context of use of the argument in a dialogue exchange is an important factor. In political debate, politicians routinely consult experts, such as economists, to support their policies. The primary dialogue is a kind of deliberation in guiding the affairs of state or in questioning of policies by the opposition. But both sides in such a debate use *ad verecundiam* arguments to support their views and proposals. This use of argument implicitly presupposes a secondary context of dialogue involving an exchange of views with the experts cited.

5. The Context of Dialogue

The evaluation of the *argumentum ad verecundiam,* as a problem of logic, characteristically arises where two laypersons are in argumentative dialogue with each other and one of them backs up his side of the argument by citing the opinion or authority of an alleged expert on the topic of the discussion. By its nature, however, this type of problem requires for its resolution the addressing of a second type of problem posed by the following question: How did the user of expert opinion extract this support of his argument from what the expert allegedly said? Putting it in terms of the expert systems framework outlined in Chapter 3, this second problem is that of the user interface dialogue between the expert advice-giver and the knowledge-user. The two problems are linked, because the user can only justify his use of expert advice to support his argument as reasonable if he can supply evidence that the expert's advice does really in fact support his argument. So the problem of *ad verecundiam* leads to the problem of the user interface.

This is not the end of the sequence, however, because the problem of the user interface leads us back to a third problem: By what process of reasoning did the expert arrive at the conclusion he offered to the layperson? This third problem is that of the nature of the internal reasoning process of the expert as a kind of argumentation. How can the expert justify or explain the process of reasoning used to arrive at her opinion? In practice, we do not always need to go this far in adjudicating on *ad verecundiam* appeals in dialogue. But if the appeal is strongly challenged, this third problem may need to be examined in order for one who cites expert authority in argument to respond successfully to the challenge and thereby back up his argument. Thus there are three distinct kinds of problems in the use of expert opinion in argumentation. The basic problem tends to lead, in turn, to two equally serious problems inherent in the deployment of expert testimony in dialogue.

Separating out the sequence of three problems in this way brings out another, underlying problem. The initial problem arises characteristically from a critical discussion between two participants, where one arguer is trying to persuade the other by means of an appeal to expert opinion. But now a third party has entered the picture: the expert. How did the participant in the critical discussion obtain the expert's opinion? Presumably, through a secondary sequence of dialogue between this layperson and the expert whose advice was solicited. The expert consultation dialogue can be a subspecies of the information-seeking or deliberation type of dialogue; or more typically, it is a mixture of both these types of dialogue.

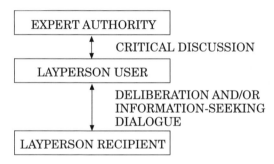

Fig. 5.1. Shifts in the Context of Dialogue

The expert consultation is different from the type of dialogue called the inquiry (Walton 1992a and 1992b). The inquiry is proof-seeking and both (or all) parties to the inquiry are (relatively) ignorant. In the expert consultation one party is ignorant, called the "layperson," and the other party is an expert in a certain discipline or topic area. The goal is for the nonexpert party to get pertinent advice from the expert. The initial situation is a need for expert advice, and informed (intelligent) action is a benefit or potential outcome of the expert consultation.

The expert consultation is a form of information-seeking question-reply dialogue where different kinds of questions may be asked by both parties. But the layperson who seeks information from the expert needs especially to ask probing questions. Particularly important, from the point of view of the layperson, are yes and no questions, which ask for opinions, and why questions, which are requests for the expert to justify his opinion by citing sequences of facts and rules. In the expert consultation, a why question is a kind of challenge to prove, or at least to back up an opinion that is queried.

The problem could be expressed in terms of the Aristotelian framework of Chapter 2, section 3, by saying that what is needed is a peirastic interval in the information-giving dialogue where the expert presents "the facts" to the layperson. During this peirastic interval, or subdialogue, the layperson must use probing dialectical arguments and ask critical questions to test out the opinions of the expert. On the other side, the expert must be tolerant and open-minded in allowing this peirastic interlude to proceed in a productive manner that is helpful to the layperson. The expert must not brush aside peirastic critical questioning by treating the questioner as impudent (as Locke put it), or by treating the questioning as inappropriate (as illustrated in the Lorenzo's Oil case). These complications suggest that the analysis of the form of the *argumentum ad verecundiam* given in Chapter 3 needs to be supplemented by a dialectical analysis that is sensitive to shifts in the context of dialogue when an appeal to expertise is used in argumentation.

The two case studies cited above, the Radar Guns case and the Lorenzo's Oil case, support the need for a dialectical framework, over and above the analysis of forms given in Chapter 3, in any adequate analysis of the *argumentum ad verecundiam* as a fallacy. These cases show that, over and above the argumentation forms, matters of how these forms are used in a given context are very important. The needed dialectical framework can be introduced by outlining the basic components of the typical dialogue context of the use of appeal to expert opinion below.

The characteristic *ad verecundiam* argument involves several dialectical shifts from one context of dialogue to another. Typically, two participants—let us call them Black and White—are engaged in persuasion dialogue, when one of them attempts to back up his side of the argument by citing the opinion of an expert authority. Let us say, for example, that White backs up one of his arguments by claiming that an expert—whom we may call Green—has vouched for the very same proposition that he, White, is now maintaining in his argument. This move in the persuasion dialogue between Black and White, then, has been advanced by White with the objective of persuading Black, or at any rate of backing up White's argument strongly so that it will be persuasive or even overwhelming against Black's side of the argument. However, once such a move has been made, it implies the existence of a secondary dialogue interchange between White and the expert Green, whose advice or opinion has been used by White. This implication holds because every *ad verecundiam* argument from expert authority involves a dialogue between the expert and the user of the expert's opinion.

Then during the dialogue between the expert, Green, and the layperson user, White, there will be peirastic intervals where White needs to ask probing questions that critically question and test out the opinions that Green has put forward, where it is not clear to White why Green accepts a particular view. During this peirastic interval, Green has an obligation to take these questions seriously and answer them as clearly, honestly, and judiciously as possible, given the constraints on posing an issue in laypersons' terminology. White may also raise objections and counter-arguments based on how he sees the situation from a "common sense" (nonexpert) viewpoint. When the peirastic subdialogue closes off, the results are then used constructively in the main dialogue.

The context of dialogue required for the analysis of this type of argumentation is even more complex than so far outlined. In many cases, the context of dialogue is really a three-layered dialogue framework, with four participants involved. According to the Lockean conception of the fallacy outlined in Chapter 2, the respondent to whom the expert opinion has been directed in argumentative discussion is accused by the proponent of being "immodest" because the latter refuses to bow to the opinion of an authority with a "reputation of dignity," requiring submission and respect. This profile of the tactic implies that the proponent is seeking to impress some audience or third party, that the respondent is not sufficiently respectful, and therefore that he is responding inappropriately to an appeal to expert opinion and his point of view should be rejected. This Lockean framework implies the existence of a third party in the context of dialogue (a fourth party, if you count the expert). Hence the dialogue structure of the kind of argumentation involved is even more complex than has been acknowledged so far. These complications are considered in the analysis of the structure of the *ad verecundiam* argument represented in Figure 5.2.

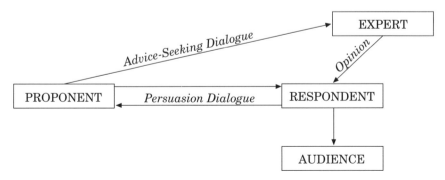

Fig. 5.2. Third Layer of *Ad Verecundiam* Dialogue

Let us call this fourth party in Figure 5.2 the "audience," even though it need not be a group of people, and it could be any participant in a dialogue situation. Even though the proponent's argumentation initially appears to be primarily aimed at convincing a respondent in a persuasion dialogue, his real aim underlying the discussion may be to convince this fourth party. He does this by appealing to a respected expert, and then when the proponent fails to be impressed or to submit to the appeal, uses this refusal to portray the respondent as insufficiently receptive to the learned opinion of a respected expert on the subject (according to Locke's analysis). Thus the respondent can be portrayed as irrational because he fails to listen to the opinion of an expert who should command the respect of every rational person. The respondent, according to Locke's account, is portrayed as "immodest," and his side of the argument is thereby made to look bad. Because the respondent has reacted inappropriately then (or, so the proponent alleges), the audience is persuaded to reject his point of view, and accept the point of view of the proponent.

The kind of case that would fit this profile of dialogue would be a political discussion where one side of the debated issue uses an appeal to expert opinion in support of his side of the argument. As a sophistical tactic to forestall legitimate critical questioning of the appeal, the proponent can press against the respondent by implying that if he does not accept it, he will look bad in the eyes of any audience who respects the opinion of an expert who is held high in the common esteem. This third layer of analysis of the context of dialogue for the argumentative use of appeal to expert opinion brings out more fully the contours and depth of the *argumentum ad verecundiam* as a dialectical tactic of argumentation of the type described by Locke. One can easily see how this complex strategic technique of argumentation can be used with such powerful effect as a tool of persuasion on an audience.

In the Radar Guns case, there is a series of dialogue exchanges between the interviewer, Morley Safer, and several experts. On one side, the appeal to the expert opinion of Adair leads to the conclusion that the use of radar guns inside the police cars is safe. On the other side, the appeal to the expert opinions of Smith and Slesin, backed up by the testimony of the police officers who used the guns, leads to the conclusion that they are not safe. The one conclusion is the opposite (negation) of the other, and it is up to the viewers of the program to decide who is more likely to be right. Although the program presents both sides, it is clear that the arguments on the unsafe side are much more convincing. On balance, the viewers will be persuaded by the appeal to expert opinion on that side as being stronger. In this case, the dialogue is one of a conflict between appeals to expert opinion, where the viewers must judge each side by the questions and replies in the subdialogues where the experts are questioned.

In the Lorenzo's Oil case of the ALD family conference dialogue exchange, there seems to be a conflict between two types of dialogue. The Odones are concerned about their son's life and are trying by any means to help him. They keep trying to ask critical questions that might move their aims forward. On the other hand, the husband and wife who are chairing the conference keep insisting that the only proper way to investigate ALD is by the kind of scientific inquiry that uses a "strict protocol" and "statistical samples in a control group." Such a clinical trial is "the solemn responsibility of the doctors," and therefore the Odones' attempts to raise questions about how well the present treatments are working are brushed aside as inappropriate for discussion in the meeting, as not on the agenda. Each time the Odones raise a question or put forward an argument, their move is said to be inappropriate and even misguided and impertinent in relation to the kind of dialogue that is supposed to be taking place in the support group meeting, which is supposed to be supporting the efforts of the physicians, the experts in the scientific methods of scientific investigation and clinical proof, who are the only ones who can properly undertake the research into the causes and cure of ALD. The issue is portrayed by them as one of "clinical trials" in scientific research, as opposed to one of saving an individual person.

In this case, then, the appeal to authority is not only a single localized argument. It is a series of them, showing a consistent pattern of use in the extended dialogue in the case. Whatever the Odones say is doomed to be brushed aside as inappropriate for the type of dialogue the participants are (allegedly) supposed to be engaging in.

6. Style of Presentation

In many cases where appeal to expert opinion is the basis of an argument, the expert is not just being quoted or her opinion being reported. Instead, the argument user is dealing face to face with the expert, and there is a real dialogue between the two parties. For example, if you are deciding on a medical treatment, your discussion with your physician and the chance to ask questions in this exchange is normally an important part of your decision-making process (Walton 1985a).

This kind of face-to-face dialogue with experts whose opinions are being weighed in argumentation is common in legal trials, where expert opinion is regarded as an important type of evidence (see Chapter 6). In such cases, the qualifications of an expert are very important in making his testimony credible to a jury, but the style of how the presentation is made by the expert can also be important. Bailey gives the following example of an expert witness whose style of presentation was a significant factor in persuading the jury to find his views acceptable (1993, 67):

Case 5.3:   For example, in an asbestos case, my medical expert, Dr. G. S., met the jurors' expectations of what a credible physician/expert should look like. He was tall and good-looking with a full mane of white hair and a British accent. He also had a dry, self-deprecating wit that endeared him further to the jurors. He did not place himself above them.

The defense lawyer went after this doctor hammer and tongs in cross-examination with a five-foot stack of medical textbooks, but none of this made any impression on the jurors. They liked this witness and judged what he was saying to be credible, even though the defense made a spirited attempt to discredit his views.

Here, appearances are a significant factor, but perhaps even more important is the ability to relate to a jury on a human level. What is involved is the communication skill of being able to communicate expert knowledge in a way that is clear and not condescending.

Trust is also an important factor. If the audience judges that the speaker has a good character, then an *ethos* is established—the speaker's perceived good character creates a positive ambiance that makes what he says more credible. Brooks gives an example in which a witness different from the typical expert was used very effectively in a case of alleged mistaken identity where it was argued that the lighting was insufficient for eyewitness identification of the perpetrator (1993, 42).

Case 5.4:   "Louie" from General Electric takes the witness stand in his overalls, with a name tag on his chest. He testifies that he has made light bulbs for 20 years and that he is an expert on bulb wattage. He testifies not only on how much the bulbs illuminate but also on what one can see within the arc of illumination.

Then Louie produces a chart showing concentric circles. The innermost circle is bright yellow; beyond it, additional circles fade to deep orange and finally to black. Louie explains how the arcs of illumination become dimmer the farther one is from the source of light. Then he places the victim in the area that is dark blue fading into black. He tells the jurors that in his expert opinion, the victim would not have been able to see the features of her attacker. How can the jury doubt a man General Electric has trusted for 20 years?

In this type of case, what is important is how the expert responds to cross-examination, and in particular, whether the manner of responding seems to convey a character that the audience likes and will trust. What is tested is the expert's reliability and judgment: Is this a person you can rely on to be honest, and to be a sensible, practical sort of person who has good judgment? Or, at least, does the expert exhibit this kind of credibility by the message he gives out, as revealed by the way he performs in the dialogue?

These matters of style of presentation can cut both ways. They can help us to deal with expert opinions on questions where we lack the technical background to make an objective judgment. But they can also lead us astray, by making weak or fallacious appeals to expert opinion appear to be much more convincing.

In a study of speech patterns in courtroom trials, Erickson, Lind, Johnson, and O'Barr (1978) showed that style of delivery is very important in influencing the perceived credibility of the testimony of a witness. A "powerful" style of delivery, as contrasted with a "powerless" style, resulted in greater attraction of the hearers to the witness, and also to greater perceived credibility. The *powerless* style, associated with witnesses of low social power and status, made frequent use of seven linguistic features:

1. Frequent use of *intensifiers* like "very" or "surely,"
2. Use of *hedges* like "kinda" or "I guess,"
3. Use of *formal grammar* or "bookish" language,
4. *Hesitation* forms like "You know" or "uh,"
5. *Gestures,* used with expressions like "over there,"
6. Use of *questioning forms* and rising intonation in declarative contexts, and
7. Use of *polite forms,* e.g., "please."

The powerful speech style, used by physicians, parole officers, or other witnesses of higher social power in court, was characterized by a straightforward manner of speaking that made infrequent use of the "powerless" features. The dialogue segment below illustrates the difference between the two styles. It is part of a pair of tapes produced in the two styles and used by Erickson et al. in their experiments (1978, 270).

Case 5.5:   Q: Then you went next door?
            A: (Powerless): And then I went immediately next door, yes.
               (Powerful): Yes.

Case 5.6:   Q: Approximately how long did you stay there before the ambulance arrived?
            A: (Powerless): Oh, it seems like it was about uh, twenty minutes. Just long enough to help my friend Mrs. Davis you know, get straightened out.
               (Powerful): Twenty minutes. Long enough to help get Mrs. Davis straightened out.

Case 5.7:   Q: Now how long have you lived in Durham?
            A: (Powerless): All my life, really.
               (Powerful): All my life.

Case 5.8:   Q: You're familiar with the streets?
            A: (Powerless): Oh yes.
               (Powerful): Yes.

Case 5.9:   Q: You know your way around?
            A: (Powerless): Yes, I guess I do.
               (Powerful): Yes.

The investigators found generally that the speech delivered in the powerful style was more persuasive than the same speech delivered in the powerless style.

   The famous Doctor Fox Lecture experiment indicated that even a highly sophisticated audience may be more highly influenced by the "halo effect" of a speaker's distinguished personal appearance, apparent professional expertise, and impressive delivery style than by an objective evaluation of the content of his speech. In this experiment, the investigators chose a professional actor who "looked distinguished and sounded authoritative," and presented him to three groups of educators as a speaker with an impressive (but fictitious) *curriculum vitae* to give a lecture entitled "Mathematical Game Theory as Applied to Physical

Education." The speaker was coached to give a lecture, made up of meaningless content and references to unrelated topics, and afterward conduct a question-answer session, with "an excessive use of double talk, neologisms, *non sequiturs,* and contradictory statements" (Naftulin, Ware, and Donnelly 1973, 631). The three audiences for presentations of the lecture were composed of psychiatrists, social workers, psychologists, educators, and educational administrators, many of whom held advanced degrees.

After each session, an "authentic looking" questionnaire for evaluating the lecture was given to the audience. None of the respondents saw through the lecture as a hoax and all three of the audiences had more favorable than unfavorable responses. In one group the favorable responses "far out-weighed" the unfavorable (Naftulin, Ware, and Donnelly 1973, 632), and the respondents' written reports indicated that they took the lecture quite seriously and even learned something from it, to the extent that they were interested enough to want to find out more about the subject-matter of the lecture. Apparently, the lecturer's authoritative and witty style of presentation persuaded even these sophisticated audiences of professional educators that they had "learned something" from his presentation.

When evaluating an appeal to expert opinion, then, it is necessary to examine connected sequences of questions and replies to get an assessment of the speaking styles of the participants. If the expert uses a powerful style of presentation and the layperson uses a powerless style, failing in his attempts to critically question and probe the expert's arguments, then the layperson may be overwhelmed and the dialogue may be one-sided. The possibility of a successful peirastic subdialogue may fail in such cases because the layperson is hopelessly intimidated by the all-controlling expert, who brushes aside the worth or even the meaningfulness of any arguments or evidence that could be brought forward by a nonexpert.

7. The Secondary Level of Dialogue

What seems to be a very important factor in evaluating real cases of *argumentum ad verecundiam* is the way the expert presents his opinion to the respondent who uses that opinion to support his argument. This dialectical factor is a subtlety that appears to be overlooked by the rather simplistic accounts of the logical form of the *argumentum ad verecundiam* presented in Chapter 4.

Many of the textbook accounts of the *ad verecundiam* fallacy, it is true, tend to stress the simple factors of violations of one or more of the kinds of premises outlined in the forms of argument in Chapter 4. Many of the textbooks, for example, define the fallacy as occurring where the expert cited is in the wrong field or where the supposed expert is really no expert at all (see Chapter 3). Creighton, for example, cites the particular species of fallacious appeal to authority that occurs where the proposition cited is not in the expert's field.

> A man who is distinguished for his knowledge and attainments in some particular field, is often quoted as an authority upon questions with which he has no special acquaintance. The prestige of a great name is thus irrelevantly invoked when no significance properly attaches to it. Thus, for example, a successful general is supposed to speak with authority upon problems of statescraft, and the opinions of prominent clergymen are quoted regarding the latest scientific theories. (1904, 170)

Other textbooks, as noted in Chapter 3, stress the kind of case where the "authority" cited is no real expert at all, but only a celebrity, or popular trend-setter.

These failures can easily be analyzed as cases where one of the requirements for the proper form of the *ad verecundiam* argument from expert opinion, as outlined in Chapter 4, is not met. It seems here, then, that the formalistic approach, using the logical form of the *ad verecundiam* argument as a normative basis for evaluation, works fairly well.

But what about other cases of the kind considered above, where the person whose opinion is solicited really is an expert in the appropriate field for the opinion in question? These would seem to be instances of the *ad verecundiam* fallacy as well. But they seem to transcend matters of the logical form of this type of argumentation, at least so far as is indicated by the accounts of logical form given in Chapter 4. Instead, they pertain to the manner in which the expert opinion was brought forward.

Several potential difficulties in this bringing forward of expert opinions stem from the fact that the expert opinion is often quoted or reported from some written or second-hand source, and experts often use technical jargon that is hard to translate into common language. As we noted in Chapter 4, section 7, real experts who have mastery of a field may not be able to express their intuitive grasp of an issue in simplified terms.

In evaluating the role of the premises of the argumentation schemes or forms studied in Chapter 4, therefore, there is an additional set of critical questions concerning the consultation dialogue between the expert and the respondent (who is using that expert advice to make a point in a critical discussion) that needs to be taken into account. These four additional critical questions were originally noted by DeMorgan (1847, 281), and are noted in Woods and Walton (1982, 88) and Walton (1989a, 190).

1. Is the expert's pronouncement directly quoted? If not, is a reference to the original source given? Can it be checked?
2. If the expert advice is not quoted, does it look like important information or qualifications may have been left out?
3. If more than one expert source has been cited, is each authority quoted separately? Was the opinion drawn by inference based on a premise from the one authority, and another premise from the other? Could there be disagreements among the cited authorities? If answers to the last two questions are 'yes,' then we have a problem.
4. Is what the authority said clear? Are there technical terms used that are not explained clearly? If the advice is in layman's terms, could this be an indication that it has been rephrased from some other form of expression given by the expert? If so, is the rephrasing accurate?

The above set of four critical questions take us back to the secondary level of dialogue. The proponent can only justify his use of expert opinion to support his argument in persuasion dialogue if he can supply evidence (upon the other party's request) that the expert's advice does really support his side of the argument. This leads us back, then, to the dialogue of the extraction of the advice from the expert by the user of that advice as a source of evidence to back up his side of the argument.

With respect to the third critical question, DeMorgan drew attention to a distinctive type of fallacy that can occur when two or more expert sources are involved.

> It is not uncommon, in disputation, to fall into the fallacy of making out conclusions for others by supplying premises. One says that A is B; another will take for granted that he must believe B is C, and will therefore consider him as maintaining that A is C. But it may be that the other party, maintaining that A is B, may, by denying that A is C, really intend to deny that B is C. In religious controversy, nothing is more common than to represent sects and individuals as *avowing* all that is esteemed by those who make the representation to be what,

upon their premises, they ought to avow. All parties seem more
or less afraid of allowing their opponents to speak for themselves. Again, as to subjects in which men go in parties, it is not
very uncommon to take one premise from some individuals of a
party, another from others, and to fix the logical conclusion of
the two upon the whole party: when perhaps the conclusion is
denied by all, some of whom deny the first premise by affirming
the second, while the rest deny the second by affirming the first.
(1847, 281)

The type of *ad verecundiam* fallacy analyzed by DeMorgan here does
have a logical structure as a distinctive type of argument. It is not, however, a form of the type studied in Chapter 4. Instead, it involves a context of dialogue where several participants are involved. Two experts
testify or give their separate opinions, and then a third party draws an
inference from their collective testimony, presenting it to a fourth party
as a proposition to be accepted, on the basis of appeal to authority.
 DeMorgan relates a series of various distinctive types of errors common in the use of quotations from sources of authority to support argumentation (1847, 281–86). Some of these are quite subtle, but it does
not take much imagination to see that they are also quite common. A
nice example is the following fault:

> Perhaps the greatest and most dangerous vice of the day, in the
> matter of reference, is the practice of citing citations, and quot-
> ing quotations, as if they came from the original sources, instead
> of being only copies. It is in truth the reader's own fault if he be
> taken in by this, or by the false appearance of authority just
> alluded to; for it is in his own power to certify himself of the
> truth: though there may be difficulty when the citations are
> many, or when some of them are from very rare books. Honesty
> and policy both demand the express statement of every citation
> and quotation which is made through another source. If a per-
> son quotes what he finds of Cicero in Bacon, it should be "Cicero
> (cited by Bacon) says, &c." It has happened often enough that a
> quoter has been convicted of altering his author, and has had no
> answer to make except that he took the passage from some pre-
> vious quoter. (283)

The problem here is one of documentation of a source cited. But surely
it is an important aspect of *ad verecundiam* as a fallacy. For many
appeals to authority are problematic and deficient, from a point of view

of using them as evidence in argumentation, precisely because of this type of failure to represent what the source said accurately and document the quotation properly, so that the appeal can be verified.

Thus DeMorgan draws our attention to a whole new dimension of the *ad verecundiam* as a fallacy. The evaluation of an *ad verecundiam* argument surely depends on the question of how accurately and correctly what the source said was reported by the user. Errors, faults, and omissions in such practices, of the kind DeMorgan described, are important parts of the evaluation of *ad verecundiam* arguments. Matters of the dialogue between the user and the expert are therefore very important.

8. Critical Questions and Logical Form

Arthur Hastings conceived of the argument from authority as a species of sign reasoning that has the form: For every statement A, if authority E asserts A then A is probably true (1962, 133–34). Because Hastings thought of this type of argumentation as a species of sign reasoning, he saw it as a kind of argument that goes forward provisionally, subject to certain qualifications. In sign reasoning a known event (e.g., tracks in the snow) are taken as an indication of an unobserved event (an animal passing that way previously) (55). In argument from authority, the source has some contact with some aspect of reality, and for a respondent who consults the source, the opinion given is a sign of that reality (135).

Accordingly, Hastings classified argument from authority as a species of argumentation based on testimony (133). As such, it is seen as a fallible kind of argumentation, best evaluated by subjecting it to several tests that take the form of critical questions. The five critical questions matching the argument from authority, according to Hastings are the following (135–38):

1. Is the authority in a position to know the situation?
2. Is the authority competent in the field?
3. Is the authority motivated to be accurate?
4. What internal evidence (consistency, justification by evidence given, explanation given) supports the conclusion?
5. How accurate is the source?

Hastings's approach is to evaluate a given case of an *ad verecundiam* argument by matching these critical questions to the argument from authority, testing the one against the other, according to the evidence available in the case.

In principle, this approach is quite different from the more usual approach of evaluating arguments used in logical textbooks, where one simply identifies the general pattern of the argument and then examines the given case to see whether the argument, as presented in that case, corresponds to a fallacious pattern or not. In this new approach, if the requirements of the form of the argument are met in a given case of argumentation, then this is sufficient to identify the type of argument as, e.g., an argument from authority. But then, in evaluating the argument, an additional test is needed to see how well the argument, as used in that case, meets the requirements of responding to the appropriate critical questions.

This new type of approach has already been advocated, with respect to the *ad verecundiam,* by Walton (1989a, chap. 7), specifically. But as we shall see in Chapter 7, many of the logic textbooks have, at least implicitly, moved toward adopting this general approach. Many of them— and we have already seen in Chapter 3—have used sets of critical questions as devices to be used by students to evaluate *ad verecundiam* arguments as fallacious or not. One of the implications of this approach is that it fits in nicely with evaluating *argumentum ad verecundiam* as a species of presumptive argumentation that shifts a burden or weight of presumption forward that is defeasible and can be challenged by the asking of appropriate critical questions. If an appropriate critical question is asked in a given case, it shifts the burden of proof back onto the proponent of the original argument to answer the question.

What the Radar Guns and Lorenzo's Oil cases both showed is that the dialectical framework in which the asking of the critical questions are embedded is also very important to an evaluation of an appeal to expert opinion. What needs to be examined as evidence for the evaluation is not only the premises and conclusion of the appeal to expert opinion and the critical questions appropriate for the appeal but also the larger question of how these two things are woven into a longer sequence of exchanges in a dialogue between the proponent and the respondent in a given case.

According to the dialectical method of evaluation, the argument is evaluated according to the performance of the participants in a dialogue (question-reply) exchange. Thus the form of argument outlined in Chapter 4 needs to be supplemented by a dialectical analysis of a case that takes the context of dialogue (or at least certain key factors in it) into account.

9. Drawing Inferences from Expert Opinion

As noted in Chapter 4, appeals to authority are not always only claims that, according to expert E, such and such a proposition A in E's field S is asserted to be true by E. In many cases, an expert is asked for advice on how to solve a practical problem, fix something, or proceed with a course of action. In such a case, the expert may not only be asked to state facts or report on the knowledge in her field but to apply this knowledge to a specific case and give advice on how to deal with that case. Here, the expert may be asked to make inferences or draw conclusions from the knowledge in her field.

Imwinkelried theorizes that the testimony of an expert witness, as used in a legal trial, has a syllogistic structure. The major premise is the "underlying technical principle—often a scientific proposition—that serves as the expert's general explanatory theory" (1991, 3). The minor premise is "the case-specific data to which the expert applies the major premise" (4). The conclusion is an opinion relevant to the issue being judged in the trial. He gives the following example:

Case 5.10: The accused calls a psychiatrist as the next defense witness. Pursuant to court order, the psychiatrist examined the complainant before the trial. Based on that examination, the psychiatrist is prepared to testify that the complainant suffers from a psychosis which produces sexual delusions that the complainant cannot distinguish from real events. In this variation of the hypothetical, the expert is prepared not only to vouch for a general theory, such as the symptomatology for the psychosis, but also to apply the general theory to the specific facts of the complainant's case history to form an opinion about the complainant's credibility. (3)

In this case, the expert supplies both the major and minor premises. However, other possibilities exist. An expert could be called upon only to give facts relevant to a rape case, as illustrated by the following case:

Case 5.11: In some cases, an expert testifies exclusively to facts. Assume, by way of example, that an accused is charged with rape. The alleged victim testifies that, during the rape, she dug her fingernails into the rapist's chest and scratched him badly. The day after the alleged rape, by happenstance, the accused visited his physician. During the visit, the accused removed his shirt and the physician examined the accused's upper torso. The physician could testify that there were no scratches on the accused's chest. Like a layperson, the physician would be permitted to testify to that fact. The physician could qualify as an expert to testify to various opinions, but the physician's expert status does not render her incompetent to relate facts of which she has personal knowledge.

At the other extreme, we can also have a case where the expert is asked to testify only about "general technical principles." An example here would be the use of a psychologist to testify on the general unreliability of eyewitness testimony (2).

One can easily see here how, in some cases, the expert source and the respondent who questions her could reason together, one providing the major premise and the other the minor premise. The argument here might still have the syllogism-like structure identified by Imwinkelried, but since the two parties collaborate in drawing the conclusion, the argument also has a kind of dialogue structure.

This kind of situation occurs commonly when an expert's advice is sought on some practical problem. The expert could supply the general theory, as Imwinkelried indicates, and the layperson could provide the specifics of the case at issue. Or conversely, the questioner could provide his general goals and the expert could provide technical knowledge on the best way to achieve those goals in the questioner's situation. This sort of case frequently occurs when experts are used to provide input into public policy decisions; for example in congressional or parliamentary debates, like those cited in section 4, above.

Here, the dialogue is a kind of deliberation on what is the best general policy or course of action. This type of dialogue has its paradigm in the kind of advocacy that seeks to conclude in a directive to change a policy or commitment to action on a controversial issue of values. Examples cited by Windes and Hastings are: "Motion pictures should be censored by the government," and "The United States should withdraw from the United Nations" (1965, 223). The advocate of change, in these cases, has a burden of proof to show that the proposed changes will have a favorable balance of beneficial consequences over harmful consequences. The opposed party takes the opposite point of view. In this context, practical reasoning is a type of argumentation from projected consequences of an action.

Practical reasoning, as noted in Chapter 4, section 10, is a form of goal-directed, action-guiding presumptive reasoning that takes the form of argumentation in different contexts of question-reply interactive dialogue. The goal of one type of dialogue of this sort—expert consultation dialogue—is to seek advice on a practical problem of action in a particular situation. This important context of dialogue appropriate for the use of practical reasoning involves both advice-seeking and advice-giving dialogue. In this type of interactive dialogue, one party seeks advice on a practical problem and the other party provides advice (often in the form of an expert opinion). This two-person framework of reasoning has the following general format:

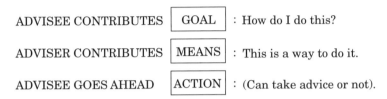

ADVISEE CONTRIBUTES | GOAL | : How do I do this?

ADVISER CONTRIBUTES | MEANS | : This is a way to do it.

ADVISEE GOES AHEAD | ACTION | : (Can take advice or not).

Fig. 5.3. Two-Person Framework of Advice-Seeking Dialogue

In some cases, expert consultation dialogue is a species of information-seeking dialogue only. But in other cases deliberation is involved because the advisee is deliberating upon whether or how to carry out a particular course of action she is considering. Or she may be confronting a practical problem that requires some deliberation on the wisest course of action to take.

Practical reasoning is based on argumentation from consequences, at least in part, because the agent must look to the future and calculate the projected possible consequences of a course of action she contemplates. Practical reasoning is goal-directed but can involve multiple goals because an agent's position may contain numerous different commitments at any point in a dialogue. Practical reasoning is relative to a particular agent and her personal circumstances. An agent will often enrich her plan to include consideration of side effects beyond her goal rather than planning exclusively toward one single goal point that will activate the whole planned sequence of actions.

This process of practical reasoning can be modeled by a state space graph where the linear paths represent the projected sequences of actions (Walton 1990b, 237). But the plan of any action may be revised as it goes along. No general formula could represent the universal search procedure of projective practical reasoning for all commonplace cases of knowledge-based intelligent goal-directed action. But it is possible to indicate certain universal argumentation schemes and critical questions for practical reasoning in a two-person framework of advice-giving dialogue.

There is an agent (planner, reasoner) involved in practical reasoning, and this agent has some knowledge but seeks further knowledge by consulting an expert source. The critical questions of a practical inference are relative to the knowledge bases of the advice-seeker and advice-giver. But the advice-giver has knowledge that the advice-seeker does not have (direct) access to. Practical reasoning involves closure of the agent's commitments relative to the agent's state of knowledge at any point in a dialogue. The initiation of an argumentation sequence of practical reasoning involves five kinds of critical questions posed by the agent: the goal, the alternatives, the side effects, the possibility, and the further steps (Walton 1990b, 109).

Projective practical reasoning may start out as a search tree, but often and characteristically involves trial-and-error searching in middle (gray) areas where the structure is not that of a tree but of a closed state space graph. In the middle areas of a planned sequence of actions exhibiting projective practical reasoning, the agent's commitments to further steps of action must be judged relative to the carrying out of the plan at that point. It follows that projective practical reasoning is irreducibly dynamic and no single search algorithm applied to the initial situation in a sequence will "work" in every case. Projective practical reasoning is an information-seeking type of reasoning that seeks out new input knowledge as it goes along toward a goal. This characteristic is present in expert systems.

In practical reasoning, whether a particular outcome is judged to be a side effect of the agent's actions or part of those actions depends on what the agent could reasonably have anticipated from his knowledge of the situation. Enrichment of an agent's projective practical reasoning may involve taking foreseeable side effects into account. This introduces a new factor into the state space graph of an action. Not only must the agent reason backward from the goal to the middle areas of his plan, he may also have to reason forward beyond the goal to consider possible side effects that may follow upon the successful carrying out of the goal. Side effects characteristically involve multiple goals, but it is possible to have a side effects type of problem in a case where an agent has only a single goal.

One key difference between discursive and practical reasoning is that the former kind of reasoning is often held to start from a fixed "arbitrary" set of premises that does not expand or contract during the sequence of reasoning. Practical reasoning starts from premises relative to an agent's knowledge-base, which may contract and expand during a sequence of dialogue exchanges with a source of knowledge. Practical reasoning is based on dynamic presumptions in a constantly changing situation, i.e., it is a nonmonotonic kind of reasoning.

The argumentation scheme for two-person practical reasoning in advice-giving dialogue is the following, where A and B are actions, X represents the agent who is contemplating carrying out an action, and Y is a source of knowledge (like an expert) consulted by X for advice. There are two variants of this argumentation scheme, the necessary condition schema and the sufficient condition schema, depending on which of the two kinds of conditions is appropriate in the second premise.

> X intends to realize A, and tells Y this.
> As Y sees the situation, B is a necessary (sufficient) condition for carrying out A, and Y tells X this.
> Therefore, X should carry out B, unless he has better reasons not to.

There are five critical questions appropriate for this argumentation scheme:

1. Does X have other goals (of higher priority) that might conflict with the goal of realizing A?
2. Are there alternative means available to X (other than B) for carrying out A?
3. Would carrying out B have known side effects that might conflict with X's other goals?
4. Is it possible for X to bring about B?
5. Are other actions, as well as B, required for X to bring about A?

According to Diggs, the advice-giving context for this type of reasoning results in a conclusion that expresses a technical 'ought': "it represents a course of action as *best,* the *one* to be taken—at least in given circumstances" (1960, 302). Thus practical reasoning is a kind of knowledge-based reasoning that expresses a practical imperative to a course of action that is best, relative to what is known in a particular situation. This kind of conclusion is a kind of presumption that can change (sometimes rapidly and radically) once new knowledge enters the picture.

It was just this kind of collaborative practical reasoning that broke down in the Lorenzo's Oil case, because the experts (the medical researchers) and the advice-users (the Odone family), had somewhat different goals and required different types of argumentation in order to support those goals. Thus the dialogue broke down. There was a kind of mismatch between the scientific goals of the researchers and the practical goal of the Odones, which was to help their son by whatever possible means. Thus the appeal to expert opinion did not function well as a useful argument because the attempts of the Odones to raise questions in the ALD support group meeting were brushed aside as irrelevant to the scientific inquiry required by the experts.

10. Dialectical Structure of Appeal to Expert Opinion

Many of the traditional informal fallacies have been analyzed as correct or incorrect arguments or moves in argument on the model of argument as reasoned two-person question-answer dialogue by Hamblin (1970), Woods and Walton (1982), Walton (1989a), and others. At first sight, however, it appears implausible that the analysis of the argument from appeal to expertise should require such a dialectical model of argument. However, the development of expert systems in AI (outlined in Chapter 4) has very much brought to the forefront the importance of the user interface in relation to the expert knowledge base. Chapter 5 has confirmed this importance. What needs to be taken into account in evaluating appeal to expert opinion arguments is the dialogue exchange, either explicit or presumed, that took place between the expert source and the layperson user, leading to an imperative for a course of action.

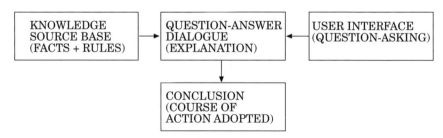

Fig. 5.4. Expert System Argumentation

Thus, contrary to traditional appearances, the use of appeal to expertise in drawing reasoned conclusions does require interactive two-person reasoned dialogue as part of the logical structure of the reasoning process. This is reflected in the inclusion of critical questions as part of the structure of the *ad verecundiam* argument to be used in evaluating a given case.

When asking about the logic of expert reasoning, we need to make the distinction between the internal reasoning of the expert and the use of the expert's conclusion by a second party, usually a layperson in the domain of the request for advice. The two processes of reasoning must have enough of a common basis for there to be communication between the two parties. The user must ask a question or formulate some goal of the inquiry. The expert must then respond to the question by finding one or more solutions to the goal.

But the process of dialogue interaction is not that simple in many cases. The expert may have to ask to have the question reformulated before an answer can be given. The user of the information may have to query the expert on what she means in layperson's terms. And the user may have to engage in a peirastic subdialogue where he critically examines and tests out the expert's advice in relation to his problem to be solved.

In both the Radar Guns case and the Lorenzo's Oil case, the practical problem posed by the situation was life-threatening and demanded some kind of immediate investigation and action be taken on the basis of the investigation. In both cases, the experts could give general advice, but adapting that advice to the particular case also involved anecdotal evidence. These "anecdotal" findings collected personally, although they did not have scientific validity as clinical or medical evidence, supplied a practical kind of practical basis for making a decision that would be unwise for those affected to ignore.

In practical reasoning, a person may have to take such anecdotal evidence into account in order to arrive at a prudent decision on how to proceed in a changeable situation where scientific knowledge, based on expert opinion, may be insufficient (by itself) to solve the problem. In such cases, expert opinions may have to be peirastically questioned and then fitted into a larger framework of practical reasoning used in deliberating on what advice to take and how to proceed with a personal course of action in a particular situation. The framework of dialogue in which the practical reasoning is used may be complex because different ways of using evidence are involved.

The internal reasoning carried out by an expert system involves searching in a systematic manner through a knowledge base in order to satisfy the goals set by the question posed. The search procedures used in an expert system language such as Prolog may involve some elements of deductive logic but will also have requirements that are not familiar from deductive logic. Thus, to use the system effectively, the user must have knowledge of the language used by the expert system to search out solutions to a goal.

A basic characteristic of programming languages for AI is their goal-oriented structure that involves a hierarchical linkage of actions and goals at different levels of abstraction. Philosophers call this "practical reasoning." In advice-giving dialogue, the structure of the *ad verecundiam* argument is not deductive but takes the form of practical reasoning. In such cases, the appropriate critical questions are those characteristic of practical reasoning, as used in a personal deliberation. These questions might not be relevant in a scientific inquiry by experts in a field of knowledge but they might be relevant in applying the knowledge in that field to a particular case where an individual decision to take action is the issue.

Who should ask these questions? In the information-seeking or advice-giving dialogue, presumably, it is the function of the advice- or information-seeker to ask these questions, and the function of the expert is to answer them (or at least to give appropriate and informative replies). In the next chapter, as I examine the role of the expert witness in legal argumentation, we will see that this dialectical approach is generally the most useful in the reasoning needed to intelligently evaluate the testimony of an expert witness in a trial. Just as in the cases studied in Chapter 5, the expert's opinion may need to be questioned in a peirastic subdialogue. And just as in the Chapter 5 cases, the central problem in many legal cases may be the existence of a conflict of opinions between experts, or groups of experts, on two sides of a disputed question.

6

EXPERT TESTIMONY AS LEGAL EVIDENCE

Legal argumentation provides a good source of insights on evaluating *ad verecundiam* arguments, for expert opinion has for a long time been recognized as a legitimate type of evidence in legal trials. The law has developed criteria and guidelines for the use of expert opinion testimony, and it is interesting to see what they are and how they have evolved.

Problems of dealing with scientific testimony have been a source of much concern and debate in law. Critics have argued that the courts have become too permissive in admitting evidence based on appeal to expert opinion. The "battle of the experts" in trials and the problem of "junk science" are two areas that have been especially controversial.

To many lawyers more and more cases turn critically on expert testimony. Imwinkelried goes so far as to say that since the enactment of the new Federal Rules of Evidence in 1975, "litigation has fast become trial by expert" (1991, 1), and "the expert has assumed a virtually ubiquitous role in contemporary litigation" (2). Bailey cites an incident where he asked a court reporter how a case was going and got the answer, with a weary sigh, "The usual war of the experts" (1993, 65).

1. The Adversarial Setting of a Trial

The legal framework for trials in North America is an adversary system. A charge is made and then, in a trial, the attorneys or advocates are supposed to use the strongest arguments they can find for their side. The prosecution has a burden of proof, to prove the charge by whatever legal standard is appropriate—"beyond a reasonable doubt" in a criminal case—and the defense, to win its case, must throw enough doubt on the prosecution's argument to show that it has failed to meet the required burden of proof (Degnan 1973). This process is adversarial in the sense that each side is supposed to try its best to attack and defeat the argumentation of the other side. Unless there is a mistrial, the judge or jury has to declare a winner and loser at the end of the proceedings. One side wins if and only if the other side loses.

In a trial, both sides can, and most often now do, call forward expert witnesses to testify on behalf of their side. These expert witnesses are chosen and paid by the attorney. The experts are paid on an hourly basis for their time spent testifying and for whatever research they have to do to get their testimony ready. More and more, the practice of experts who make a lot of their income from appearing as expert witnesses in court is increasing. Lawyers tend to get in the habit of using experts who have been useful and successful in testifying for them in previous cases (Graham 1977; Younger 1982).

The process of the trial, as noted above, is basically adversarial, and the attorneys, when they cross-examine the other side's expert witness, tend to be aggressively hostile. Their aim is to make the expert witness look as bad and as unconvincing as possible, even if it means attacking their competence and character (Weber 1981). The witness is under an oath to tell the truth and, therefore, attacks on an expert witness's character for veracity are regarded as relevant in the law (Graham 1977; Weber 1981). Although the system is adversarial, and the attorney is not under an oath to tell the truth, the judge is obliged to hold the lawyer's arguments to a codified set of rules of evidence. These rules impose some limits on the kinds of arguments lawyers can use in court. Most of the evidence presented in a trial comes from witnesses, who are supposed to be competent, and who take an oath to tell the truth. Their testimony is produced in response to questioning by the lawyers for both sides, who take turns examining and then cross-examining the witness.

Expert witnesses are employed for two purposes: "to observe first-hand knowledge that only specialists can perceive," and "to express opinions on matters so technical that the judge or jury would have

difficulty understanding them without the aid of expert knowledge"
(Degnan 1973, 908). Physicians and ballistics experts are two kinds of
experts that are frequently called in to testify in trials. When an attorney cross-examines an expert witness in court, the attorney can demand
a direct answer to his question (even a yes-no question), and request
that the reply be struck from the record if it is not a direct answer. In
the case below from Hoffman, an expert quarryman was testifying to
the value of industrial valuable limestone on a tract of land, after the
removal of the "overburden" covering the limestone on the land (1979,
331). His estimate was based on core borings of stone taken from the
land.

Case 6.1: Q: Can we agree that without core borings you could only
guess as to the depth of the overburden?

A: It is my best guess that it runs at an average of eight to
ten feet in this part of the county.

Atty.: Your Honor, I object to the witness's answer as not
responsive to the question. I ask that his answer be
stricken; that the jury be instructed that it is improper
and to be disregarded. I also ask the Court to instruct
the witness to answer the question yes or no because it
called for no explanation.
[After the court struck the answer and instructed the
jury to disregard it as not responsive to the question,
the question was read by the reporter and the following
ensued.]

A: Yes sir.

The legal rules of courtroom dialogue allow the attorney to request that
the expert's reply be struck from the record on the grounds that it did
not directly answer the question. These rules give the cross-examiner
a way of forcing the line of answers in a particular direction, which is
very important in understanding the strategy behind this type of
expert-interview dialogue in court. Note, however, that even if the
expert's reply is struck off the record by the judge after it has been spo-
ken, it may still have significant effects because the jury will have
heard it anyway.

One way of attacking the expert testimony of the other side in cross-
examination is called *impeachment,* defined clearly by Degnan.

Impeachment is the process of discrediting testimony by showing facts which tend to reflect upon the veracity of the witness

and thus to authorize rejection in whole or in part of the testimony he has given. This can be done in many ways. The elicitation of testimony of contrary facts from other witnesses forces judges or jurors to choose which to believe. Again, doubting a witness' perceptive capacities—hearing, sight or his opportunity to perceive—may discredit his testimony. In addition, a body of formalized rules govern certain established forms of impeachment. There are four universally recognized forms: (1) showing that the witness has previously made statements inconsistent with those made on the stand (i.e., in the box) under oath; (2) showing that the witness is biased either for or against one of the litigants; (3) showing general bad moral character of the witness; and (4) showing that his character for truth and veracity is bad. Two others are sometimes added. One is the introduction of evidence contradicting the witness on facts in the case. This is not subject to the specialized rules here treated. The other is virtually extinct; it consisted of questioning the witness about his belief in God, upon whom he had called in oath to vouch for his testimony. (1973, 908)

The purpose of cross-examination of an expert witness is to "neutralize or destroy that expert's theory," or to "get him to acknowledge the validity of your theory of the case" (Weber 1981, 299). Hence impeachment, or discrediting the expert's credibility in any way, are common forms of attack.

A recent book by Harold Klawans (1991), a distinguished neurologist, describes the experiences of a seasoned expert witness, depicting the "order of cross-examination, which often endures for hours, by aggressive even insulting attorneys whose purpose is to humiliate, denigrate and confuse physicians brought in as expert witnesses" (Posner 1991, 1142). Reviewing Klawans book, Posner's description of this process gives a good idea of the adversarial nature of cross-examination of experts in court (see also Graham 1977). But one can see why lawyers are so hostile to expert witnesses when, as shown in section 2 below, typically the experts are carefully selected by the opposing lawyers to support their side of the case. And these experts do so enthusiastically, even being paid to testify. It seems, then, that the dialogue in court is not simply a situation where the attorney asks questions in order to get information or explanations of technical matters and the expert answers these questions, supplying the required information in order to give information to the jury. This ideal represents the normative model of the information-seeking dialogue. In many cases, however, there has been a shift to an eristic or quarrel type of dialogue.

Ideally, what should happen in a trial is that the expert in a domain of scientific knowledge should present the results of the research in her field as established by the cumulative process of verifying the scientific facts established in that field. The attorney should examine the testimony of the scientific expert in a peirastic kind of subdialogue that clarifies what the expert has said, for the jury's information and understanding, and also critically question and challenge the expert's arguments in an enlightening examination that helps the deliberations of the jury to be more informed and intelligent. But does this model represent what is really happening in the courts? Not in the North American adversarial justice system of the present.

Even while not on the witness stand, the expert can also play a decisive role in a trial, according to Holmström-Hintikka. She cites a case where a forensic scientist failed to tell the jury certain facts about the victim's blood that were very important to the case (1995, 490). He omitted telling these facts to the jury because nobody asked him. Moreover, he undoubtedly knew these facts. A case like this shows that the expert can also have a role in explaining to the attorneys, before the trial, what facts are important and what questions they should ask.

2. The Battle of the Experts

The way the adversarial framework of a trial works, in cases where the outcome depends on expert testimony, the prosecution and defense sides will tend to find their own experts who will support their own side of the case. In this framework, then, it is natural, and even typical, for a case to turn into what generally is called the "battle of the experts" (Imwinkelried 1986; Simon 1992; Brooks 1993). Younger outlines a typical kind of case (1982, 2).

Case 6.2:   Take, for example, a "spleen-out" case where the main issue is the amount of damages. The plaintiff's attorney will call an expert who will testify that the spleen plays a vital, though as yet unidentified, role in the body's immunological system. The expert will testify that without a spleen this little boy has a life expectancy of a great big question mark, and the case is worth at least half a million dollars. The defendant's attorney will call an expert with equal credentials to testify that the spleen is left over from the days when we were fishes; it is a vestigial organ like the appendix. It is of no significance whatsoever. The little boy is just as good now as he was before he was run over; he is probably *better* now as a matter of fact—maybe he ought to pay *us*.

The outcome of this kind of case will tend to depend on which of the two opposed appeals to expert opinion is the more credible, on the apparent authoritativeness of the expert in the eyes of the jury, which in turn is likely to depend on how the experts react to questioning under cross-examination by the opposing attorney.

It is surprising to see the extent to which even criminal cases are dominated by the battle of the experts (Imwinkelried 1991). This has come about because the law allows for excuses, conditions that defeat or reduce responsibility for an action that would otherwise be a criminal offense. The basic idea, as stated in *Regina v. Oxford* (1840), a case where a man with a history of insanity took a shot at Queen Victoria, is that if a "controlling disease" was the "acting power within the defendant, which he could not resist" then he is not responsible for his action (Walton 1975, 546). There are different rulings in different jurisdictions, but what it comes down to is that a defendant can be found not guilty by reason of insanity if what he did was caused by a mental disease, so that he did not really know what he was doing, at the time.[1]

The jury is supposed to make the decision of whether or not the defendant knew what he was doing at the time, and to determine whether he is not guilty because he did not know.[2] But in order to decide this, they need to determine whether he was suffering from a mental illness, at the time, of a kind that would block his knowing what he was doing. Different jurisdictions phrase this in different ways, but the gist of it is that an expert on mental illness—a psychiatrist or psychologist, normally—is brought in by the defense as an expert witness to testify that the defendant was insane.[3] To counter this argument, typically an expert witness will be brought in by the prosecution who will testify to the opposite of this opinion, claiming that the defendant was not insane. Psychiatrists and psychologists often differ when it comes to

1. For these different rulings and the historical background of the insanity defense, see Goldstein (1967).

2. According to the McNaghten Rule, the defendant is supposed to understand the "nature and quality of the action" at the time it was committed. See Goldstein (1967). Walton (1975) also contains a summary of the various rules used to test conduct in the insanity defense.

3. For the history of this defense, see Walton (1975).

offering explanations of individual human conduct, so it is not too surprising that, usually, genuinely authoritative experts are found who testify convincingly on both sides of a case. Direct conflicts of opinion in such cases are extremely common in trials.

A famous case in point was the trial of John Hinckley Jr. in 1982 for the attempted assassination of then president Ronald Reagan. Waller cites the following expert opinions on the state of Hinckley's mind at the time he shot Reagan (1988, 129–30).

Case 6.3:   "[Hinckley suffers from] process schizophrenia." (Dr. William T. Carpenter [psychiatrist who interviewed Hinckley at length after the assassination attempt], June 7, 1982.)

"Hinckley does not suffer from schizophrenia." (Dr. Park E. Dietz [specialist in forensic psychiatry], June 7, 1982.)

"[Hinckley was suffering from] a very severe depressive disorder." (Dr. Ernst Prelinger [psychologist at Yale University], May 20, 1982.)

"There is little to suggest he was seriously depressed [the day of the shootings]." (Dr. Park E. Dietz [specialist in forensic psychiatry], June 4, 1982.)

"[CAT scans] were absolutely essential [to my diagnosis of schizophrenia]." (Dr. David M. Bear [Assistant Professor of Psychiatry at Harvard Medical School], May 19, 1982.)

"[CAT scans revealed] no evidence of any significant abnormality whatever." (Dr. Marjorie LeMay [Associate Professor of Radiology at Harvard Medical School], May 21, 1982.)

"There's no possible way that you can predict people's behavior, or whether they're schizophrenic or not schizophrenic, from a CAT scan, period." (Dr. David Davis [Head of Radiology Department at George Washington University Medical Center], June 3, 1982.)

"It is a psychiatric fact that Mr. Hinckley was psychotic." (Dr. David M. Bear [Assistant Professor of Psychiatry at Harvard Medical School], May 18, 1982.)

"Mr. Hinckley has not been psychotic at any time." (Dr. Park E. Dietz [specialist in forensic psychiatry], June 7, 1982.)

Cases like this really make one wonder. Certainly, it shows that such appeals to expert opinion cannot be taken as completely authoritative or as the final word. If there is value in this kind of evidence, it is to be found in questioning the experts and judging how they respond.

Other cases that really make one wonder are those where expert testimony from psychiatrists or psychologists is stretched so far in the insanity defense that the argument borders on absurdity. According to Vatz and Weinberg (1992), the public is losing patience with psychiatric excuses for criminal behavior and is increasingly skeptical about this form of escape from criminal responsibility. The following case, summarized from the detailed account of it given in Klawans (1991, chap. 12), is a famous case where an attorney used expert testimony to argue that his client, who killed two people, had suffered diminished mental capacity at the time of the killings because of eating junk food. It is sometimes called the Twinkie Defense.

Case 6.4: Dan White, a city supervisor in San Francisco had resigned his job, but when he wanted it back, he attributed his failure to get it to George Moscone, the mayor of San Francisco, and Harvey Milk, a politically influential city employee. On November 28, 1978, Dan White shot both these men, in the body, and then later twice in the head.

Charged with two counts of first-degree murder, White pleaded "not guilty by reason of diminished responsibility" under California law, on grounds of reduced mental capacity. This claim was supported by expert testimony from four psychiatrists and one psychologist, who all came to the conclusion that White was suffering from a psychiatric disease, recurrent attacks of depression, caused by eating junk food.

Dr. Martin Blinder, one of the psychiatrists, testified that White had a manic-depressive syndrome: "White's frequent episodes of depression were escalated by an exclusive diet of junk food—Twinkies, cupcakes and Cokes." (Klawans 1991, 164). The testimony was that when White was depressed, he would go on high-sugar junk-food binges, and that just before the killings, he had stayed awake all night, gorging on chocolate Twinkies, chocolate bars and Cokes. As a result, Blinder claimed, White had suffered a biochemical disorder of the brain causing intoxication and diminished capacity similar to that shown in recent scientific evidence where cerebral allergic reactions were caused by eating highly processed foods.

The jury brought in a verdict of voluntary manslaughter. As a result White was eligible for parole in less than five years (his sentence was seven years and eight months).

Cases like this, where not very credible arguments seem to persuade juries, are testimony to the power of the *ad verecundiam* argument. Science and its qualified, representative experts seem to have the power and institutional aura to make a not very credible argument appear to a jury to be acceptable.

In a Canadian case, wealthy socialite Dorothy Joudrie shot her former husband, Earl Joudrie, a prominent corporate executive, six times with a .25 caliber Beretta pistol. She admitted shooting her former husband but her attorneys claimed that she was not guilty of murder on grounds of "automatism," a defense seldom used in Canadian law (Mitchell 1996, A7):

Case 6.5:   Psychiatrists have examined Mrs. Joudrie and said she was in a brief dissociative, or robotic state during the critical moments of the shooting, and so, in legal terms, was unable to form the intent to harm her husband. Because criminal acts depend on intent, the jury would have a hard time accepting the psychiatric evidence and still convicting her.

Three psychiatrists, including the Crown's own witness, told the jury that Mrs. Joudrie was in that robotic state, based both on the fact that she can't remember the shooting and the fact that Mr. Joudrie testified that his wife acted coldly, without emotion.

He said she was unlike the person he had known for more than 40 years since they were childhood sweethearts. Later, he testified, she seemed to become her old self again, seeming frightened and plaintive, and agreeing to call the ambulance, a move that saved his life.

However, Crown prosecutor Jerry Selinger, in closing arguments that he read to the jury yesterday, questioned whether they could accept this psychiatric evidence. He noted that the field of automatism still is developing, quoting the testimony of Mrs. Joudrie's regular psychiatrist, Dr. Alan Weston, who said not a great deal of research has been done on it.

"You may want to question the value of their opinions in this area."

Selinger added that psychiatrists had testified that Mrs. Joudrie was in a state of "massive denial" about her problems, "including her alcoholism, beatings by her husband, and the fact that he had left her for good" (A7). He argued that clues showed that Mrs. Joudrie had planned for months to shoot her husband, and that while shooting him, she mused aloud about inheriting his money and dumping him in a ditch.

A jury of eleven women and one man found Mrs. Joudrie not criminally responsible for shooting her husband by reason of mental disorder, based on the defense that she was "in a trancelike state when the shooting took place," described as a "robotic condition" by the defense experts, and "was not aware of her actions" (Laghi 1996, A4). Here we have reached the outer limits of junk science used by expert witnesses in the courts.

3. Junk Science in the Courts

Peter Huber warns of the severe problems in the courts caused by the testimony of pseudo-scientists, or genuine scientists who appeared impressive in court, but who advocated scientifically eccentric opinions that were convincing to juries but turned out not to be based on real scientific evidence. Huber recounts cases where courts awarded huge settlements to claimants who, backed by testimony from scientific experts, advocated the theory that physical trauma (e.g., tripping while alighting from a streetcar), causes cancer (1991a, chap. 3).

In other cases scientific experts found all sorts of causes for the sudden acceleration of the Audi 5000 (chap. 4). After a prolonged series of lawsuits that depressed Audi sales and cost the company a fortune, scientific experts eventually came to the conclusion that these accidents were caused by the driver accidentally putting his or her foot on the accelerator instead of the brake pedal.

One fringe area of science that comes in for lengthy criticism by Huber is that of clinical ecology (chap. 6), a field populated by scientists who have excellent credentials as experts but take the extreme and eccentric view that chemicals and environmental pollutants cause almost every human affliction. Court experiences with these experts is summarized by Huber (1991a, 69).

Case 6.6:   Consider the courtroom antics of a fringe group of quasi-experts broadly known as "clinical ecologists." Clinical ecologists believe that trace chemicals in the environment are the cause of all manner of maladies, from depression to charley-horses. More specifically, they believe in "chemically induced AIDS," a subversion of the immune system by minuscule exposures to environmental pollutants. A pair of clinical ecologists arrive in court in Missouri in late 1985, testifying on behalf of 32 residents of the town of Sedalia. At a nearby plant, Alcolac, Inc. manufactures specialty chemicals for soaps and cosmetics.

The clinical ecologists will blame pollution from that plant for dozens of different afflictions, spanning nerve damage and heart disease, brain damage and vomiting, kidney infections and headaches. Using a battery of laboratory tests, the clinical ecologists claim to find "pervasive abnormalities" in the immune systems of every person tested. Utterly convinced, a jury awards $6.2 million in compensatory damages plus $43 million to punish Alcolac. The trial judge concurs. So does the court of appeals, though it sends the case back for a recalculation of damages.

Huber urges that the source of these problems with the abuse of expert testimony in the courts is the "let-it-all-in" approach sanctioned by the Federal Rules of Evidence (1991, 17). He argues that the best way to stop these abuses is to return to the *Frye* ruling and restrict expert testimony to opinions generally accepted by the scientific community in a field.

As an absolute rule, however, Huber's approach seems too rigid because, in some cases, real uncertainty may exist in science. Against the risk of admitting junk science, there is the other risk of barring new techniques, like DNA fingerprinting, from consideration before they have become accepted by the majority of the scientific community (Herrera and Tracey 1992). The problem is well stated by *Harvard Law Review* (1992, 105: 937–38).

[Huber] trivializes the genuine possibility that the very rigor of the scientific process may bar expert testimony that should be heard. For example, often the only way to determine a chemical's carcinogenic properties is to wait for a statistically significant number of cancers to appear above the appropriate baseline. For diseases with long gestation periods, data collection may take decades. Meanwhile, because of the lack of scientific consensus, *Frye* would exclude any evidence indicating the carcinogenic link. Furthermore, notwithstanding Huber's historical observation that mainstream science, when erroneous, corrects itself before litigation begins, nothing in the nature of science *requires* that result. Therefore, Huber should acknowledge more explicitly that he is balancing the cost of excluding relevant evidence against the admittedly high cost of including irrelevant junk.

Huber has amassed ample evidence of the enormous costs and appalling consequences of the current "let-it-all-in" approach. But going back to the *Frye* ruling, without allowing for any exceptions to even be considered, does not seem to be the best solution to the problem.

One problem is that scientific knowledge continually advances, so that what is generally accepted is always in a process of change. This, in itself, will cause scientists to disagree. And it will generally make it difficult for the courts to decide what is "generally accepted" and what is not, and what is worth considering as evidence, even if it is not yet generally accepted by the majority of the scientific community in a field. Another problem is that the number of fields that lay claim to expertise is increasing. One factor in this increase is that the supply of potential experts has also increased.

> Americans have record numbers of degrees. In 1940, all colleges and universities awarded only 217,000 degrees, and most of those (187,000) were bachelors' degrees; there were only 27,000 masters and 3,000 doctorates. By 1991, the total had passed 2 million, with 337,000 masters and 39,000 doctorates, including 430 Ph.D.s in "public affairs." (Samuelson 1995, 49)

Another factor is that demand for expert opinion has increased dramatically. Use of expert testimony has become a more significant part of the legal evidence used in trials than ever before. The number of radio talk shows and television news programs that feature guest experts has expanded considerably. All these factors make it difficult to judge borderline claims to expertise based on skill or experience or academic qualifications, where the scope and exact nature of the techniques used in the field may not be well defined.

Another problem is that of fads in science, such as "clinical ecology," that may be on to something but, for all we know, may be "kooks" or extremists who hold a fashionable but not very well-supported theory.

4. The Go-It-Alone Expert

An even more subtle and difficult problem is the genuine scientific expert who uses the accepted methodology (at least, to all appearances) but gets novel, and even spectacular, results that the other scientists in the field are suspicious of but do not yet have enough evidence to categorically condemn.

The following case is a story reported by the CBS News program *48 Hours* in 1992, summarized below from the account given in Hansen (1993, 65–66).

Case 6.7:   Louise Robbins was a professor of anthropology at the University of North Carolina at Greensboro who appeared as an expert identifier of footprints in more than twenty criminal cases, before she died in 1987 at the age of fifty-eight. Her testimony helped to send at least twelve people to prison.

Professor Robbins claimed to see things in a footprint that no one else could see. She once astounded her colleagues by identifying a 3.5 million-year-old fossilized footprint found in Tanzania as that of a woman who was five and a half months pregnant. Using her unique skills of identifying footprints and boot marks, she was instrumental as an expert witness in securing convictions in several murder cases. This expertise was unique to Robbins.

Other experts can match feet with footprints or shoes with shoeprints, provided that the two samples being compared share enough of the same ridge details or random characteristics. But Robbins was alone in claiming that she could tell whether a person made a particular print by examining any other shoes belonging to that individual.

Robbins built her reputation on the theory that footprints, like fingerprints, are unique. It was her contention that, because of individual variations in the way people stand and walk, everyone's foot will leave a distinct impression on any surface, including the inside sole of his or her shoe. Those impressions, she contended, show up as "wear patterns" on the bottom of every shoe.

"Footprints are better indicators for identifying people than fingerprints," Robbins told the *ABA Journal* in July 1985. "With a footprint, you use the entire bottom surface of the foot. With the fingerprint, you only use the tip of the finger."

The problem is that the rest of the scientific community has disagreed with Robbins's claims. Her colleagues claimed that her observations were unreliable, and that she was overly suggestible in interpreting evidence. A panel of more than one hundred scientific experts, shortly before her death, "concluded that her footprint identification techniques didn't work." Other colleagues were quoted as saying "the scientific basis for her conclusions was completely fraudulent."

This case led to much controversy. The defendants in some of the cases in which she testified as an expert witness have appealed their convictions. Thomas Knight, a former Illinois prosecutor who used Robbins as an expert in court, ranks "her credibility as a witness and her integrity as a scientist right at the top," who has been "terribly maligned by some of the things that have been said about her" (66). In this case, the expert testifier had the right academic credentials to justify being classed as a genuine expert in the appropriate field. Her methodology was based on scientific techniques in that field and she was a credible witness who appeared to be conscientious, and who honestly believed the opinions she put forward. The problem is that her opinions, and her theory, were eventually, generally rejected by the other experts in the scientific community in her field. But this consensus took quite a long time to establish and, by that time, the scientist had already appeared in cases where, as a highly credible expert witness, she had given expert testimony that was the basis for legal decisions.

A comparable case described by Yang concerned a statistician who has testified against some of the leading drug companies in court (1993, 61).

Case 6.8:   A Berkeley Ph.D. in statistics with impressive credentials testified in many cases that statistical evidence proves a causal link between drugs and birth defects. During a Benedictin case, however, the defense lawyers charged that the methods this expert used (which have never been published) are skewed to fit the testimony.

This was another case where the jury struggled to understand enough of the science to reach some decision on how credible the expert testimony should be. The problem once again in this case was that this scientist's conclusion contradicted the conclusions of studies in the prevailing scientific literature.

Should such go-it-alone scientific testimony be rejected simply because it goes against the prevailing opinion in the field? Or does a case of this sort need to be fought out on its merits as science?

Case 6.9:   According to a report released by the West Virginia Supreme Court in 1993, Fred Zain, a police serologist whose job it was to match blood and semen samples found at crime sites, had lied and systematically manufactured evidence in at least 133 rape and murder cases ([60 Minutes, 1994, p. 8]). According to Stanley Schneider, a Houston attorney, in one of the many cases in which innocent persons were convicted on Zain's testimony, Jack Davis, a maintenance man in an apartment building was convicted of murder of a woman after Zain testified that his blood matched blood found at the murder scene ([9]). A year after Davis's conviction for murder, Zain changed his story. After four years of imprisonment, Davis was finally released—he had come within one vote of being sentenced to death by the jury ([10]).

Zain had a B.Sc. in biology, but it turned out that he had lied in his job application and had never taken any courses in chemistry. His grades in college had been poor but he had been hired in the 1970s when it was difficult to get qualified staff (11–12). Apparently, he was able to get away with evidence tampering for so long because he gave police and prosecutors the kind of evidence they needed to get convictions.

What is particularly scary in this case is how long this giving of expert forensic evidence—by someone who was not even seriously investigating the facts of a case—went on, and how many rape and murder cases were affected. The court ruled that all evidence examined by Zain over a ten-year period needed to be retested (8). But after ten years, much of that evidence had deteriorated or disappeared.

5. Legal Criteria for Scientific Testimony

Who qualifies as an expert witness in court? Federal Evidence Rule 702 states that a witness may qualify as an expert by reason of "knowledge, skill, experience, training, or education" (Saltzburg and Martin 1990,

170). However, as Giannelli and Imwinkelried point out, determining whether a witness is qualified is a matter of the court's discretion (reviewable for an "abuse of discretion") (1986, 154). They cite a court ruling that an expert "need not have certificates of training, nor memberships in professional organizations," and in the end, the only question for a judge to consider is "whether his [the supposed expert's] knowledge of the subject matter is such that his opinion will most likely assist the trier of fact in arriving at the truth" (155). Thus, it seems that courts have quite a bit of latitude to admit as an expert witness anyone whose testimony is relevant (that being an additional requirement) and helpful.[4] However, in the case of scientific experts, degrees and qualifications, experience, and publications, are the kinds of evidence needed to qualify a scientist as an expert witness (Spellman 1968, 165–71).

The criterion used until recently to evaluate expert scientific testimony in U.S. courts was the so-called Frye Rule. In *Frye v. United States* (1923), the Court of Appeals for the District of Columbia rejected the systolic blood-pressure deception test (an early form of the polygraph or lie-detector test). The Frye Rule requires that the major premise (the scientific technique or theory used) must have "gained general acceptance," and not be merely "experimental" in nature (as noted in Chapter 1). The key passage is quoted by Giannelli.

> Just when a scientific principle or discovery crosses the line between the experimental and demonstrable stages is difficult to define. Somewhere in this twilight zone the evidential force of the principle must be recognized, and while the courts will go a long way in admitting expert testimony deduced from a well-recognized scientific principle or discovery, the thing from which the deduction is made must be sufficiently established to have gained general acceptance in the particular field in which it belongs. (1981, 13)

The majority of the courts enforced the Frye Rule for more than fifty years, but during the late 1970s and early 1980s, courts began to repudiate or seriously question it and loosen the requirements for expert opinion testimony (Imwinkelried 1986, 22).

In 1975, new Federal Rules of Evidence were introduced that gave guidance on how expert testimony was to be used in the courts. Rule

---

4. Saltzburg and Martin cite a case where a person trained in tractor-trailer skid control, but did not have a scientific or engineering background, was allowed to testify as an expert in a personal injury truck accident case (1990, 170).

702 states: "If scientific, technical, or other specialized knowledge will assist the trier of fact to understand the evidence or to determine a fact in issue, a witness qualified as an expert by knowledge, skill, experience, training, or education, may testify thereto in the form of an opinion or otherwise" (Saltzburg and Martin 1990, 170). Rule 704 says that admissible expert testimony should not be rejected just because it "embraces an ultimate issue," except in a criminal case, where the expert must not "embrace" the ultimate issue by determining an element of the crime charged (183). This means that experts are generally free to give opinions that bear on an issue to be decided. But the restriction is that in a criminal case—for example, in an insanity defense case—the ultimate issue of whether the defendant is insane is for the jury (not the expert) to decide. 'Insane' is meant here in the legal sense appropriate for a jurisdiction, e.g., meaning that the defendant did not know what he was doing at the time. Rule 705 says that the expert may give an opinion without giving reasons ("underlying facts or data") for it, but if questioned on cross-examination, she may be required to disclose these reasons (187).

It is generally believed that the Federal Rules are much more liberal than the Frye Rule, but not everybody accepts that interpretation.

> Under the Rules, qualified experts are allowed to testify about "scientific, technical or other specialized knowledge" if their testimony "will assist [in understanding] the evidence or to determine a fact in issue." Many courts have interpreted this language to mean that scientific evidence must be "helpful and reliable" to be admissible, a test no more illuminating and just as much a shorthand rule as "general acceptance." Some lawyers have argued that the Rules are more liberal than *Frye*, and that evidence that was inadmissible before their adoption can now be introduced. Published decisions, however, indicate that in practice there is no great difference between the two approaches. (Ayala and Black 1993, 232)

These rules did not include the general acceptance test, and that was taken by some critics as an implicit rejection of the Frye Rule.

Rule 704 has sanctioned an increasing relaxation of the courts on standards of admitting expert evidence, as indicated by the stated recent demise of the *ultimate-fact prohibition,* which barred expert witnesses from answering a question (like determination of guilt) that is supposed to be resolved by the trial.

> The ultimate-fact prohibition is today largely a dead letter in most jurisdictions; physicians are now routinely allowed to testify about the cause as well as the effect of an injury, pathologists to characterize a wound as homicidal, and psychiatrists to testify directly on questions of the defendant's sanity. Experts must still stop short of expressing opinions on questions of law (a physician may not, for example, testify as to the liability of a plaintiff's employer for a work-related ailment), but that, for all practical purposes, is the only vestige of the old prohibition. (Imwinkelried 1986, 23)

The outcome of these developments is that courts now accept as evidence expert opinions that would previously have been inadmissible. Many now feel that the courts have gone too far, and the subject has been debated in recent years.

In the case of *Daubert v. Merrill Dow Pharmaceuticals Inc.* (1993), the U.S. Supreme Court rejected the Frye Rule, instead advocating as the criterion for admissibility of scientific testimony that it be "not only relevant but reliable." According to the majority opinion, "reliable" means "derived by the scientific method" and "supported by appropriate validation." The term "relevant" comes from Federal Rule 702, meaning that expert evidence should "assist the trier of fact to understand the evidence or to determine a fact in issue" (Dyk and Castanias 1993, 18). The Court made it clear that the intent of this ruling was to make the judge the "gatekeeper" to determine the admissibility of scientific testimony in a case. Among the criteria given were (1) "testability" of the theory or scientific technique, (2) peer review and publication, (3) known or potential rate of error, and (4) general acceptance, not as the exclusive criterion (as in the Frye Rule), but as part of the court's assessment of reliability.

In *Daubert,* the issue was whether an antinausea prescription drug, called Benedictin and used in pregnancy, had caused children to be born with limb deformities. The plaintiff's expert testimony was based on test-tube and live-animal studies, chemical studies showing similarity of structure between Benedictin and other substances known to cause limb deformities, and reanalyses of previously published epidemiological studies (17). Their argument prevailed against the contention of Merrill Dow that this expert testimony did not meet the requirements of the Frye Rule. The implication is that new or controversial scientific theories or techniques will no longer be disqualified as expert evidence (Mervis 1993, 22).

Benedictin had been used since 1956 to treat "morning sickness" in pregnant women, an unpleasant affliction that is only fatal to mother or child in a few cases. In 1986, William McBride, an Australian gynecologist, known for being among the first to suggest a link between thalidomide and birth defects in 1961, claimed that Benedictin is a teratogen (causes birth defects). McBride published a paper describing animal tests on rabbits, showing "two out of eight rabbits receiving higher doses of a Benedictin-like chemical produced deformed fetuses" (Huber 1991a, 113). Although there was very little other scientific evidence supporting this claim and a large body of published data that showed no significant correlation between Benedictin and birth defects, McBride's claim was enough to form the expert evidence to sustain many lawsuits against the manufacturer of the drug, Merrill Dow. In the end, the scientific evidence against Benedictin was discredited by the scientific community. Even though Merrill Dow was vindicated in the end, the company, over a series of lawsuits, lost a huge amount of money in court costs and was ultimately forced to take Benedictin off the market.

6. Hearsay Evidence in Expert Testimony

If an expert is asked for the basis of her opinion, should part of the evidence she cites in reply be allowed to consist of the quoted opinion of another expert? This question is one that lies in the background of the study of one important critical question for an appeal to expert opinion, for it calls into question the specification of what should count as "evidence" when an expert cites the evidential basis of her judgment.

There are two points of view on this issue: a *pro* and a *contrary* line of reasoning. The *pro* point of view argues that an expert would customarily, properly, and even perhaps necessarily reply on the judgments of other experts in the normal course of his reasoning in his field of expertise, at least on some points. For example, an expert in chemistry, in the course of running an experiment or other form of scientific inquiry in his field, might take the conclusions given in textbooks or other authoritative works in the field as acceptable premises of the inquiry. Therefore, according to the *pro* point of view, since the expert relies (at some points) on the conclusions of other experts in the course of his normal reasoning in the field, he should also be allowed to cite these expert conclusions in defending his own line of reasoning. The *contrary* point of view argues that the expert should not be allowed to use the opinion of another expert in defending his own opinion because it leaves no way for a critical questioner to challenge or further question this part of the opinion. For example, suppose expert E1 cites the opinion of expert E2 as part of his basis of his (E1's) line of reasoning, and a critical questioner, Q, wants to challenge E1's reasoning behind his conclusion. When it comes to the part vouched for by E2, Q has no further recourse in his line of questioning. He cannot ask E1: "Why do you accept this?" For the only reply E1 can give is: "I accept it because it is the opinion of E2." The problem is that E2 (we presume) is not a participant in the dialogue between Q and E1. In fact, E2 may not be available for questioning at all. Hence the line of critical questioning comes to a dead end at this point. Therefore, according to the *contrary* point of view, the expert should not be allowed to rely on the pronouncement of other experts in defending his opinion (even at some points in this explanation), because it defeats the basic purpose of critical questioning a dialogue exchange of arguments.

Thus there is something to be said for both points of view on this issue, and the problem is not an easy one to resolve. In practical terms, this problem arises in legal argumentation in connection with expert testimony in the courts. Younger (1982) cites two cases that illustrate the legal problem.

Case 6.10:   In the first case [p. 24], a physician is called to testify as an expert witness on the ailment of an elderly lady. Upon questioning, he reveals that his diagnosis was arrived at on the basis of five pieces of data: (1) he looked down her throat and saw red patches, (2) he felt her neck and noted a spasm in the muscles, (3) he sent her to a neurologist, who made a report on her nerves, (4) he sent her to a hematologist, who made a report on her blood chemistry, and (5) he sent her to a roentgenologist, who sent x-rays. But items (3), (4), and (5) are legally "hearsay," because the experts who made these reports have not testified. So should these three items be counted as evidence? According to Younger [1982, 25], Federal Rule of Evidence 704 counts them provided that it is customary in the expert's field to rely on this type of information, and provided the judge finds this custom a reasonable one. However, Younger disagrees with this general ruling, citing a second type of case.

Case 6.11:   In the second type of case cited by Younger [1982, 26], a psychiatrist is called upon to testify that a defendant was sane, and he gives four items of evidence. The fourth item

of evidence is a statement made by the defendant's girlfriend, even though the girlfriend has not herself testified
in the case. Should this count or not? It is customary for
psychiatrists to rely on statements about a patient's personal affairs in treating that patient. For this reason, it
could be argued that the statement should be allowed. And
according to Younger [26], the New York Court of Appeals
did in fact allow this opinion, in a case of this sort.

As Younger notes, the problem in this case is how the jury is supposed
to assess such an opinion (27). How do you attack it? Since the girlfriend herself is not being questioned, there seems to be no real avenue
to evaluate the opinion by any further line of questioning.

These types of cases have posed a dilemma for legal theorists. According
to Imwinkelried, the early common law view in the United States would
have supported the kind of evidence presented in the first case above,
but would not admit the statement in the second case as evidence
(1991, 17). But the drafters of the Federal Rules of Evidence opposed
this common law view, instead taking the view that the expert may
take such a statement "as part of the basis for his opinion so long as the
information is of a type reasonably relied on by experts within the witness' discipline" (18). In fact then, the tendency is to relax the nonad-
missibility of hearsay evidence in expert testimony by making
exceptions to the normal barring of this kind of evidence.

However the courts deal with this, it is also a problem for logic as
applied to the evaluation of appeals to expert opinion in everyday argumentation. One of the primary critical questions for any such argument
is whether the expert can justify her opinion if questioned, by showing
that it is based on the scientific evidence in her field of expertise (see
Chapter 7, section 9). But can she do this without appealing to what
other scientists in the field say? Or should such (hearsay) opinions be
allowed in as part of the body of evidence in the field used to justify her
claim?

This is not an easy question to give a simple answer to. It seems that
the expert should be allowed to use as premises in her argumentation
propositions that are taken as true because they are found in professional handbooks or encyclopedias, or in other accepted sources generally accepted as authoritative in the field. But, if appropriate, she should
be able to be questioned about the scientific evidence supporting these
propositions, over and above their being generally accepted by authorities in the field. The best solution, from a logical point of view, to this
problem, is to allow for subquestions under a critical question, so that

an expert can be questioned more and specifically, about the basis of her opinions, in a continuing sequence of dialogue. However, in court, clearly there will have to be practical limits set on how far such a dialogue can go. At a certain point, presumptions will have to be made.

We saw an instance of this in the Radar Guns case in Chapter 5. In this case, Adair cited a number of scientifically authoritative regulating agencies to back up her claim that the safety standards would certify the hand-held radar unit as safe for use by police officers. This is quite a reasonable argument on her part even though, by citing other scientific authorities, it is a kind of appeal to expert opinion argument within another appeal to expert opinion argument. What should be kept in mind is that her citing of these expert sources should only give a small extra weight of evidence to support her argument. It should not be regarded as final or beyond challenge.

It should be regarded as acceptable for a respondent to ask critical questions about the scientific evidence presumably used by these authorities to back up their rulings. In effect, the argumentation in the case did this when it was claimed that these safety standards were not meant to apply to the special circumstances of the way these handheld radar units were actually being used by the police.

7. Science As a Body of Knowledge

The foundation of the rules of expert evidence in the Anglo-American system of law were laid by Lord Mansfield in *Folkes v. Chadd* (1782) in the following terms: "The opinions of scientific men upon proven facts may be given by men of science within their own science."[5] However, the expert does not need to have formal qualifications in a science in order to testify as an expert nor is it necessary for her discipline to be an academic branch of study or a professional area with qualifications. For example, handwriting experts have been allowed to give expert testimony in the courts, and experts in stylometry, the statistical study of literary style, have given expert testimony on authorship of letters and other documents in court. Neither of these disciplines could be called an established science, indicating that Lord Mansfield's dictum has come to be interpreted very liberally in law. Moreover, since the courts have recognized expert testimony from authorities on "obscenity" and

5. Quoted by L. J. Lawton in *R. v. Turner,* 1975, Q.B. 834, 841, and in Kenny (1983, 199).

"literary merit" in obscenity cases, it has become clear that expert opinion is not always required to be based on "proven facts" of "science."

Another case in point is psychiatry. Although psychiatry, as a branch of medicine, is a science, psychiatric testimony in the courts is often allowed to include opinions that go beyond "proven facts" or scientific evidence, as indicated by their challenge by opposing psychiatric experts. It follows then that an expert opinion in legal testimony is not necessarily an opinion based on proven facts of science.

The paradigm case of an expert opinion in court, however, is that of a conclusion pronounced by an expert in a scientific discipline or field of inquiry where the conclusion comes within the field in question. However, it is by no means always true that a reasoned appeal to expert opinion has to be the scientific conclusion of a scientific expert. And, indeed, it may be hard to know, in some cases, whether an opinion in a field advanced by a scientific expert in that field is in fact a scientific conclusion derived from facts established within that scientific field. For, as noted in Chapter 3, an expert opinion may be based on skilled judgment that is intuitively based on skilled practice and practical experience rather than scientific knowledge. These observations lead to many interesting questions about how one knows, or could know, whether an expert opinion is truly based on an inference from "facts" in a scientific discipline.

A basic philosophical question is then posed: What is a science? Kenny (1983, 205–6) ventures four required criteria for a discipline to be scientific: (1) it must be *consistent,* meaning that the opinions of two different experts must not conflict on a question that is central to their discipline, (2) it must be *methodical,* meaning that the practitioners basically agree on the basic methods of their field, so that procedures of collecting data by one expert can be duplicated by those of another expert in the field, (3) it must be *cumulative,* meaning that findings are built on previously laid foundations, previous basic findings that do not need to be re-researched or called into question by the next generation of researchers, and (4) it must be *predictive,* meaning that it must predict the not-yet-known from the already-known in a "falsifiable" manner, that is, the hypotheses must be subject to Popper's criterion of falsifiability—evidence that would falsify the hypothesis must be available, at least in principle.

In practical terms, however, this kind of question, whether something is really a science or not, would be very difficult to settle or even try to debate in court. In fact, certain disciplines are designated or have been generally accepted as sciences, and others are not. Science is an institution of a well-organized sort, with its hierarchies, titles, rituals, and established doctrines. As such, it exerts a kind of institutional authority, as well as the kind of authority based on expertise (see Chapter 8).

But what really gives scientific testimony its strongest claim to evidence as an appeal to authority is precisely the aspect of it cited by Kenny (1983). Science, in a given discipline or field, is supposed to be an organized body of knowledge that exists and has weight as evidence independent of any of its individual practitioners or of what they might say. It is this supposedly cumulative and consistent body of knowledge that gives an appeal to scientific expertise its authority as an opinion in argument. When something is officially pronounced in a scientific discipline, this functions as evidence of a special kind—evidence that this theory or technique is generally accepted. But science is a changing, growing body of knowledge. The new syndromes are a case in point.

According to Block, the term *rape trauma syndrome* was introduced by Burgess and Holmstrom (1974).

> From their interviews, Burgess and Holmstrom identified an acute stress reaction to a life-threatening situation which they named "rape trauma syndrome." The syndrome consists of behavioral, somatic, and psychological reactions to the attack. The symptoms usually occur in a two-phase reaction, i.e., the acute phase and the long-term phase. During the acute phase, which starts at the time of the rape and continues for the next 2 to 3 weeks, the rape victims undergo a number of acute somatic manifestations such as physical trauma, skeletal muscle tension, gastrointestinal irritability, and genito-urinary disturbance and a number of emotional reactions ranging from feelings of fear, humiliation, and embarrassment to anger, revenge, and self-blame.
>
> During the long-term phase, which starts after the acute phase and can last for 6 months to a year or longer, the victim begins to reorganize her life-style. The victims reported motor activity changes such as the acquisition of a new residence and/or a new phone number and a turn to support from family members not normally seen daily. (1990, 310)

The American Psychiatric Association recognized rape trauma syndrome as a psychiatric diagnosis in 1980, including it as a post traumatic stress disorder. Block states that, because of this recognition, rape trauma syndrome meets the *Frye* test for scientific testimony (313). Based on case precedents, Block states that rape trauma syndrome does not give evidence that a victim was actually raped (309), but can be used "to (i) prove lack of consent, (ii) show the amount of damages in a civil suit, (iii) form a defense to culpable behavior, or (iv) explain behavior of the victim inconsistent with a claim of rape" (313). Now that rape trauma syndrome has been accepted by the science of psychiatry, its general acceptance as a scientific explanation of conduct in a court case is no longer subject to critical questioning in the same way it once was, before it was accepted.

Battered Woman Syndrome (BWS) is a kind of testimony used to support a self-defense claim by a woman who kills her abusive spouse or lover.

> The theory of Battered Woman Syndrome was developed primarily by Dr. Lenore Walker, who has testified in over 150 murder trials. Dr. Walker describes the dynamic of battering relationships as a "Cycle of Violence," involving three phases: the tension-building phase, the acute battering incident, and the tranquil period of "loving contrition." The cycle begins with the tension-building phase, where minor battering incidents occur. The woman attempts to placate the batterer in an effort to prevent the escalation of violence, but these efforts become less effective as the cycle progresses and the tension grows. Eventually the violence spirals out of control into an acute battering incident, in which the violence reaches the level of "rampage, injury, brutality, and sometimes death." The acute incident is followed by a period of loving contrition, in which the batterer exhibits loving behavior and tries to atone. A woman is most likely to kill the batterer during the tension-building phase. She is aware that at any point the violence may erupt into an acute incident in which she will lack the strength to protect herself. (Murphy 1992, 295)

When BWS was first introduced in the 1970s, it was often ruled as not admissible scientific testimony by courts, but in the 1980s it has come to be widely accepted.

These newer syndromes either gain general acceptance in a field and are announced as such in the scientific literature or they are not. This internal, official recognition by the appropriate scientific authorities sets something in place as generally accepted. And this, in turn, has important consequences when appeals to scientific, expert opinions are used by nonscientists to support argumentation—for example, in a trial.

To call something a "syndrome" gives it an air of scientific validity, as an objective entity that has been established in a scientific domain of technical knowledge. Once the syndrome has been accepted as such by the experts in a field, as part of the established knowledge in a field, it appears to have an objective existence that cannot be disputed by a nonexpert in that field. But are scientific syndromes as objective as they appear to be? Remember the study by the Norwegian researchers cited in Chapter 1 that failed to find cases of whiplash in Lithuania, a country where there was nothing to be gained from a diagnosis of whiplash. What is suggested by such a finding is that although chronic whiplash is accepted in most western countries as an objective syndrome that can be diagnosed by physicians on the basis of empirical data, it might really only be a legal artifact useful for suing people and collecting insurance claims. Raising such questions about the scientific objectivity of syndromes suggests that many expert scientific opinions may really be based on socially constructed definitions and concepts as much as on purely objective models of empirical data. Such a postmodernist view of syndromes challenges the modern view of science as a cumulative body of knowledge that cannot be questioned by someone who is not an expert in the technical discipline of scientific research that is being used to decide an issue.

8. Solutions to the Junk Science Problem

Occasionally attempts have been made to deal with the problem of scientific testimony in the courts by modifying the existing adversarial process. One judge in Colorado has assembled panels of scientists to provide consensus information to juries, and a Carnegie Commission advocated placing the expert witnesses for both sides together in court and allowing the jury to ask questions of both (Schrof 1992, 68–69). Others have proposed the appointment of "neutral" experts to aid the court.

> The most widely touted antidote to extremist testimony is the court-appointed witness, chosen by a judge to act as a neutral voice of reason in the midst of scientific disputes. The American Association for the Advancement of Science has promised to aid judges in their quest for court experts by screening scientists and providing lists of suitable candidates. A related group, the National Conference of Lawyers and Scientists, is preparing a demonstration to test the referral system and to overcome judges' general reluctance to appoint experts. A Federal Judicial Center study reveals that although 80 percent of judges think

appointing neutral experts can be useful, only 20 percent have ever done so, and half of those used the measure just once. Most judges express concerns about affecting the outcome of a trial and worry that they lack the scientific expertise to choose an expert. (69)

The basic worry about this proposed solution to the problem is that the court-appointed expert may turn out to have unanticipated bias for one side, especially in those kinds of cases where there is a real division of opinions in the scientific community, e.g., on a new theory or technique.[6] Although having court-appointed experts to help in some cases, it would seem that the adversarial nature of the trial, especially in criminal cases, precludes any proposed solution of this sort from entirely solving the problem in a satisfactory way.[7]

Huber's proposed solution (1991a), of going back to the *Frye* criterion, would undoubtedly eliminate much of the junk science. But by tilting the balance the other way, it would leave the courts ill-equipped to deal with new technology, or generally with the kinds of cases where the community of scientists disagree. And one can see from just looking at recent trends in legal trials, such disagreements are both common and significant as contentious matters for the courts to deal with.

Thus we have strong arguments on both sides. Huber's argument that junk science is a huge problem is widely recognized as a serious challenge to the legal system. But many influential scientists have also argued that going back to the *Frye* type of ruling would be too restrictive. The argument on the other side contends that the ruling that science is "good" if and only if it is "generally accepted" and peer reviewed is too conservative an approach, which would overlook innovative research in some cases. In a brief supporting the Benedictin parents, Harvard University science historians Everett Mendelsohn, Stephen Jay Gould, Gerald Holton, and nine other scholars, cited cases where scientific theories at first deemed eccentric later became accepted generally (Begley 1993, 63).

Case 6.12: In a letter last month in the journal *Nature,* physicist Juan Miguel Campanario of the University of Alcalá in Madrid

---

6. Although the system of court-appointed neutral experts is widely used in Continental Europe, Howard (1991) argues, from an English law perspective, that such a system would have great disadvantages. One of the central problems noted by Howard (101) is that of bias.

7. For some other proposals for methods dispute resolution to aid in problems of appeal to expert opinion in court, see Hensler (1991).

listed four papers that *Nature* had rejected. One, on how cells synthesize an energy-making molecule, and another, on the biochemistry of hormones, went on to win their authors Nobel Prizes. The others, on biochemistry, have been cited in other scientists' papers almost 2,000 times each (citations measure how valuable a paper is).

Case 6.13: In 1950, geneticist Barbara McClintock discovered that genes jump around on chromosomes. This find was so at odds with prevailing dogma that it was dismissed for years. McClintock won a 1983 Nobel Prize.

Another factor is that unpublished work has often been rightly judged, in the past, as a sufficient basis for banning pesticides, and establishing standards for exposure to hazardous chemicals in the workplace (Begley 1993, 63). These cases suggest that if the courts hold to a standard of what is generally accepted in science as the guideline for allowing scientific testimony as good evidence, it would shut off many valuable results of scientific research from being considered as evidence.

This is certainly a serious legal problem, and it seems that none of the solutions advocated so far will solve it adequately. Neutral experts are not the answer, and neither cleaving strictly to the Frye Rule nor having a "let-it-all-in" approach is the answer. This is really a problem for lawyers to resolve, by modifying the rules of evidence. But logic can throw some light on the problem that can point the way toward arriving at legal solutions based on a coherent way of evaluating appeals to expert opinion.

The logical problem underlying the current issue of junk science relates to expert opinions that appear to be in conflict with what is generally accepted in a field. This problem relates to the consistency critical subquestion of Chapter 6.

9. The Framework of Dialogue in a Trial

A trial is regulated not only by rules of evidence but by other legal rules that apply to particular cases and particular jurisdictions. It is a special speech event, and therefore we cannot draw conclusions about argumentation in the law from premises about argumentation on the model of a critical discussion or vice versa. However, a legal trial does share some important characteristics with the critical discussion (Feteris 1989), a subtype of persuasion dialogue where the goal is to resolve a conflict of opinions by reasoned argumentation. Both the critical discussion and the legal trial are essentially types of dialogue where the goal is to resolve a conflict of opinions by having both sides put forward their strongest arguments in an adversarial way. However, a critical discussion is regulated only by implicit rules of politeness, while a legal trial is presided over by a judge, who is supposed to see to it that the legal rules of argumentation are enforced on both parties (Feteris 1987).

In their analysis of the critical discussion as a type of dialogue, van Eemeren and Grootendorst use the *intersubjective testing procedure* (ITP), a source of knowledge or set of propositions that the participants agree on at the outset of the discussion, as authoritative information (1984, 167). This is a way of testing propositions that the participants do not know as true or cannot agree on as true or false. Van Eemeren and Grootendorst write that such a source might consist of written works, such as encyclopedias or dictionaries, or of observations or experiments jointly conducted by the participants.

What the legal problems of junk science and the battle of the experts indicate, however, is that while such a source of knowledge testing is vital to the intelligent resolution of a conflict of opinions on controversial issues, it should not be regarded as a fixed set of propositions—a final or ultimate authority that is agreed to, one that cannot be challenged by the opposing parties in the dispute.

The battle of the experts in courtroom dialogues can exhibit intricate and subtle dialectical shifts. The trial itself is a kind of persuasion dialogue, where a conflict of opinions is supposed to be resolved. Within this outer framework of dialogue, the expert is brought in to provide the court with "facts," information, or knowledge, thus introducing an information or knowledge elicitation type of dialogue into the persuasion dialogue. However, a real danger is that, since the expert witness is brought in especially to testify for the one side, she may, in reality, be engaging in a kind of persuasion, or even negotiation, dialogue to make a good case for the side she has been brought in to support. Indeed, the use of the expert witness has become so prevalent in the courts that, as noted in section 1, above, there are "professional expert witnesses" around who derive a good portion of their income from appearing in court. Naturally, these experts want to please the lawyers who hire them, so there could be a real danger of bias in how they present their testimony. The trial process itself is an adversarial procedure that does not exclude the use of arguments designed to support one's own side of a case. So dealing with persuasive expert testimony is an important skill for the trial lawyer.

The legal use of expert testimony in the court shows many new dimensions of the dialectical framework of the *argumentum ad verecundiam*. For, in court, the attorneys on both sides of the persuasion dialogue may cross-examine the expert witness. This process of cross-examination is ostensibly a kind of information elicitation dialogue. But, in practice, it may frequently turn into a highly adversarial species of exchange. The dialectical structure that is revealed is the embedding of one type of dialogue within another, as described in the dialectical contexts of argument analyzed in Chapter 5. If the structure of argumentation in a legal trial can be described as a type of persuasion dialogue, then within that dialogue there needs to be an information-seeking (expert consultation) type of dialogue where the scientific or technical expert gives testimony that will help the judge or jury to understand the facts relevant to a case that can only be supplied by an expert.

But because the trial is an adversarial process, and because scientific opinions can be questioned or disputed by the experts, in some cases, and because it can be hard for a layperson to grasp expert opinions, clearly it is necessary for the attorney to examine what the expert says in a peirastic subdialogue of questions and replies. Basically, the problem is that a scientific theory or concept, like a syndrome, has to be applied in a legal trial to a particular case. And it is a case that is subject to dispute. So the scientific opinion is used for a purpose, in the context of a persuasion dialogue, or for purposes of deliberation. But the users are not themselves scientific experts.

What is revealed is that the secondary dialogue between the expert and the user-participant in the original persuasion dialogue can itself be subject to logical problems and abuses that could be identified with species of *argumentum ad verecundiam*. This calls for a careful approach to devising the appropriate structure of critical questions to be used in evaluating this type of argumentation.

What the legal experience in dealing with expert testimony in argumentation shows is that expert sources need to be critically questioned, in a dialogue, by the primary participants in the argument. And it is this interactive process of critical questioning that provides the normative framework for evaluating appeals to authority as arguments.

Logic alone cannot solve these legal problems. It is up to the lawyers, legal scholars and judges who formulate and work with the rules of evidence to construct rules that serve the interests of justice by permitting fair trials. However, the argument from appeal to expert opinion is an important part of courtroom argumentation, and at bottom, it is only through a critical and logically structured use of this type of argumentation that the courts' rules of evidence will serve these purposes, without being aggravated by, or even overwhelmed by the kinds of problems we have cited in this chapter.

10. The Consistency Critical Question

One very important, primary critical question appropriate for dealing with an appeal to expert opinion is whether the expert's opinion is consistent with what is said by other experts in the same field. Any field of expertise, especially if it is a scientific discipline, represents a cumulative body of knowledge (see section 7). The expert is an expert because she is a repository of, or at least has access to, this knowledge base. However, the expert is also an individual person, who is (normally, in these cases) a human being, who has personal opinions, and also human failings. Hence the expert's opinion may, in some cases, not be the same as the generally accepted opinion in the field.

One important step in evaluating an appeal to expert opinion is to first ask whether the opinion agrees with what is generally accepted in the field. If the answer is 'yes,' then that critical question is satisfied, but if the answer is 'no,' logic requires that further subquestions be asked before the appeal can be evaluated. Basically, what needs to be known is why this expert opinion differs from what is generally accepted by the other experts in the field. There can be various reasonable explanations for this divergency: (1) the kind of question asked to the expert in the first place—some questions are controversial or unsettled in a field, so that you would expect different opinions by different experts; (2) new technology or theories—some findings are new, and have not yet received wide general acceptance in a field, but may be accepted by some leading experts; (3) if the opinion is about a particular case, experts may differ on what they know about this case, or how they interpret its special circumstances; (4) experts from different schools of thought, or fields of subspecialty, may have differing points of view that explain a difference of opinion.

In general then, if the expert's opinion is different from what is generally accepted in the field, questions need to be asked to determine why it is different. Any of the above four explanations may suffice. But if none does, a burden of presumption should be cast back upon the original argument from expert opinion. Reasons need to be given to show why there is good evidence for what the expert said, in order to meet this burden. These reasons then should be scrutinized on their merits.

The danger here is the reason the expert diverges from what is generally accepted in the field is that she is going it alone, venturing her own personal opinion instead of an opinion based on the knowledge in the field of expertise. This can be dangerously deceptive if the expert really is qualified as a scientist in the right field for the opinion in question, has clearly and authoritatively asserted this opinion, and is willing and able to defend it. For, in such a case, all the requirements of the form of the argument from appeal to expert opinion are met. And such an expert may have the right appearance and scientific demeanor to appear highly persuasive to laypersons who lay no claim to being experts in the field.

To sum up, then, what we need is essentially a two-tiered approach when it comes to devising critical questions for the *ad verecundiam* argument. If the opinion in question agrees with what is generally accepted in the field, then that strengthens the appeal to expert opinion, and the evaluation can go on to ask other basic critical questions. If the opinion disagrees with what is generally accepted, however, then the evaluation should go into a set of critical subquestions.

Hence the dialectical method of evaluating appeals to expert opinion involves three tasks: (1) identifying the form of argument of appeal to expert opinion; (2) identifying the critical questions appropriate for that form; and (3) constructing sequences of nested sets of pairs of the two moves of kinds (1) and (2) so that deeper critical questioning of a contested argument is possible, when useful.

7

CRITICAL QUESTIONS

The next task in the development of a structure that can be used to evaluate appeals to authority in argumentation is the construction of sets of appropriate critical questions matching the various forms of argument from authority. This task is carried out here as the required prerequisite for carrying out the third task of seeing how the matched pairs of arguments and sets of critical questions are properly (and improperly) used in a context of dialogue. This third task is the subject of Chapter 8.

Many of the more recent textbooks, and even some of the older ones, have now (at least judging by the practical methods they use for evaluating cases of appeal to expert opinion in argumentation) begun to adopt the technique of using sets of critical questions. In this chapter, I shall begin with a survey of the various proposed sets in the textbook accounts. Finding significant disagreements and differences of emphasis among these accounts, I shall turn then to a discussion of the various points of agreement and disagreement. While many accounts appear to agree on a few fundamental points, there is in fact not a great deal of uniformity or consistency in their treatments of the subject.[1] There are also

---

1. As will become clear, as well, some of the textbook accounts are improving, but even among these better accounts, there are definite conflicts, differences, and problems.

several key points on which some of the textbook criteria for evaluation of the *ad verecundiam* are misleading, unfavorable, and in need
of revision.

Arising from the ensuing analysis, a new, unified set of critical questions is formulated below. The technique of evaluation proposed uses a
set of six general critical questions along with a set of subquestions
attached to each general question.

1. Premises and Critical Questions

We have certainly begun to see now that the argument from expert
opinion admits several important kinds of qualifications and complications. This was evident in Chapter 3, section 4, to some degree, when
we set out form (G4), which had five premises to be taken into account.
One way to take these various complicating factors into account is to
add new premises that pose additional requirements.

One textbook that has adopted this approach is *A Practical Study of
Argument* by Trudy Govier, where appeal to authority is said to have
the following form as an argument (1992, 127).

(G5) 1. Expert *X* has asserted claim *P*.
      2. *P* falls within area of specialization *K*.
      3. *K* is a genuine area of knowledge.
      4. The experts in *K* agree about *P*.
      5. *X* is an expert, or authority, in *K*.
      6. *X* is honest and reliable.
      Therefore,
      7. *P* is acceptable.

However, for practical purposes, not all of factors 1 through 6 may need
to be considered as relevant or necessary in a given case.

Another approach would be to streamline or strip down the form of
the argument into something simpler that represents the main basis
or initial thrust of the argument, and then add in these other factors as
considerations that can be raised as appropriate in a given case. Taking
this approach, we might simplify the form of the argument from expert
opinion to something like the following:

(G6) *E* is a reliable authority in domain *S*.
      A is a proposition contained in *S*.

E asserts that A.
Therefore, A.

Then, accompanying this form of the argument or argumentation scheme, we might have a set of appropriate critical questions such as "Is S a genuine area of knowledge?" or "Is A consistent with what other experts say?"

According to this proposal, an argument having the form (G6) that is advanced by a proponent in a dialogue would have a certain weight of presumption in its favor (provided it really is of that form). But then the asking of one of the appropriate critical questions by a respondent would shift the weight against the argument. However, if the proponent were to answer the question adequately, it would once again shift the weight of presumption to her side. And the strength or weight of presumption attached to the appeal to expert opinion argument, generally, would depend on how strongly the premises are supported by the evidence in the given case.

If (G6) is taken as the form (argumentation scheme) for the argument from authority (see also [G7], below), one might expect that the first three critical questions to be naturally raised would concern the truth or justifiability of the three premises. This approach would suggest the following three critical questions:

1. Is E a genuine authority (as opposed to someone who only has glamour, prestige, etc.)?
2. Did E really assert A? That is, was E quoted exactly as saying A, or if not what did E say, and how was A inferred from it?
3. Is E an authority in the right field, i.e. is the domain of A some field other than S?

These three critical questions are appropriate in evaluating many common cases of *ad verecundiam* arguments. And, in fact, many of the examples of the *ad verecundiam* fallacy so often cited in the logic textbooks can be evaluated helpfully with the use of these three questions (Walton 1989a, chap. 7). However, as we will see, these three questions do not exhaust all the considerations cited by the textbooks. Some textbooks cite other critical questions that are clearly important to consider.

As we look over the textbook accounts in the survey given below, we see that some only give a few (often three) critical questions, while others give substantially more. And while they generally agree on the kinds of critical questions thought to be relevant, some omit ones that others think important. These differences are partly due to differences

in length of treatment of the *ad verecundiam* fallacy. Many of the textbooks devote only a half page to it. But a few of them have gone into the
treatment in quite a bit more detail (W. Salmon 1963; Fearnside and
Holther 1959; Johnson and Blair 1983; Capaldi 1971; and Little, Groarke,
and Tindale 1989).

The differences are more than merely trivial, however, or only matters of emphasis and depth. In general, the texts fail to refer to any central theory or scholarly work on appeal to authority in logic, nor do they
refer to (or appear to be unaware of) each other.

2. Early Accounts

A. E. Mander gives four conditions that must be complied with to justify acceptance of a judgment of the recognized expert authority who is
quoted: (1) the expert cited must be identified; (2) she must be "recognized as an authority on that particular subject," and recognized by her
"peers and co-workers in that field"; (3) we may only accept the judgment of a dead (i.e., historically influential) authority if it is up to date
with current authorities; and (4) the authority must be unbiased (1936,
41–43). According to Mander, if any one of these four conditions is not
met, the statement in question cannot be accepted as resting on "recognized expert authority" (43).

All four of these conditions are important. Number 2 seems to come
under the heading of critical question 1 in section 1, above. Identification
of a cited expert is important, as we saw in Chapter 4. The textbook
accounts of the *ad verecundiam* fallacy indicate that being up to date
is important for an expert authority. And bias was found to be significant in Chapter 5.

According to Beardsley, an argument from authority is not one of the
illegitimate kinds if it meets three conditions.

> A speaker is not relying on illegitimate authority when he gives
> *reasons* for believing that the opinion he quotes was reached by
> someone (a) who had access to the relevant information, (b) who
> was capable, by training and ability, of thinking about it, and (c)
> who was fair and unbiased in his thinking. For these are the
> marks of a *legitimate* authority. (1950, 134)

Once again, bias is cited in condition (c). And condition (b) seems to
relate to our critical question 1. Condition (a) sounds similar to Hastings's

requirement of being in a position to know.

Here we might recall the five critical questions posed by Hastings (1962), cited in Chapter 5, section 8, which required the authority to be in a position to know, be competent, and be motivated to be accurate. The fourth and fifth critical questions concerned the justification by the authority of her conclusion and her accuracy as a source. Putting these three sets of requirements together gives us quite a list of factors to consider already, but an even more elaborate account, given by Fearnside and Holther, adds several more.

Fearnside and Holther (1959) distinguish several conditions for giving weight in argument to an appeal to authority under two headings—personal reliability and qualification as an expert. An authority is said to be *personally reliable* only if three conditions are met.

1. There is reason to believe that the witness is telling the truth as he sees it, or at least no reason to suppose he is lying. The witness, for example, is not an habitual liar. If he were, it would be foolish to trust his words even though he might know a great deal about the matters he is reporting on.
2. There is reason to believe that the witness is disinterested, or at least no reason to suppose him swayed by bias. A highly biased or partisan report would convince no one who recognized it as such. Such reports, even from acknowledged experts, usually result in learned confusion at the best.
3. There is reason to believe that the witness is conscientious, or at least no reason to suppose that he has not been attentive to the problem and diligent in gathering data. Casual statements from a witness, however competent, who has been too busy or too lazy to investigate properly, ought not to be regarded as authoritative.

An authority is qualified as an expert only if the following conditions are met.

1. The authority is clearly identified. The assertion "A leading expert says . . ." is a device of slovenly journalism. How can it be a proper appeal to authority? Since the expert is not named, his qualifications cannot be examined.
2. The authority has professional standing. The qualifications of experts are properly judged, not by laymen, but by fellow experts. The standing of a surgeon should be established by his colleagues, not by the size of his practice or by his popularity among his patients.

204 APPEAL TO EXPERT OPINION

3. The authority is current. Darwin is a great name in biology, but
   before relying on Darwin as an authority, one would want to check
   present opinion in the science. In some fields today the growth of
   knowledge is so rapid that a few years or even months may suffice
   to render an opinion obsolete.
4. The authority is expressing an opinion within the field of his special
   competence. Einstein may have held very worthy opinions on world
   peace, but he was not to be regarded as an expert on international
   relations just because of his reputation in physics. It is of course possible—and this may have been the case with Einstein—for a man to
   be expert in several fields, even as far apart as physics and politics.
5. The authority in the opinion cited must hold representative views in
   his field. Where there is controversy, it is not proper to cite one side
   without acknowledgment of the other. (85–86)

A similar account is given in Fearnside (1980), where four of the above
conditions of an authority's being "professionally qualified" are cited
(328), and the matter of personal reliability is also addressed (330).

Some of these requirements are questionable. Condition 5 of the second list bars the opinion of any expert whose opinion is not generally
accepted in the field, reminding us of the Frye Rule (Chapter 6, section
5). And condition 2, which requires "professional standing," would out-
law expert opinions from sources in trades or with practical experience
and skills but not in a profession. The first list rightly emphasizes bias
as a factor to be considered but it is unclear whether the factors of
truthfulness (condition 1) and conscientiousness (condition 3) are distinctive of *ad verecundiam* arguments or apply to all kinds of testimony-
based evidence generally. Some of the textbooks cite bias as a factor,
while others concentrate on other factors.

Moore states that three questions should be asked before accepting
the opinion of an authority (1967, 41): (1) How much does the authority know about the specific question at issue? (2) Is the authority objective about the matter in question? (3) What do other authorities conclude
about the matter? Here question 2 raises the possibility of bias.

As mentioned in Chapter 2, Wesley Salmon states that appeal to
authority is misused if the authority is (1) misquoted or misinterpreted, (2) has only glamour, prestige or popularity, and not special
competence, (3) makes a judgment outside the field of special competence, (4) expresses an opinion on which there is no possible evidence,
or (5) disagrees with other competent authorities (1963, 64–66). Salmon's
account is addressed to an assessment of the "reliability" of an authority in a statistical sense, referring to the likelihood that what the

authority said is true. Perhaps because of this orientation, he does not include "personal" reliability in the sense of Fearnside and Holther (1959).

3. Accounts in the 1970s

Byerly offers three considerations for judging the qualifications of an authority (1973, 47).

1. An authority should be clearly identified rather than vaguely alluded to, as in phrases such as "leading physicians say . . . ."
2. An expert should have current status in the field in question.
3. The authority should represent the predominant view of experts in the field, or, if not, the controversial nature of the opinion should be openly acknowledged.

This account is fairly typical of the textbooks that devote only a short space to the *ad verecundiam*. Byerly's third consideration is nicely put, however, modifying the requirement of general acceptance to suit circumstances.

Crossley and Wilson cite three questions that should be asked about an authority cited in an argument (1979, 42).

1. Is the person cited really an authority?
2. Is the authority talking about something within his or her special field of competence?
3. Are there *rival* authorities? It is not uncommon for authorities to differ in their opinions. Consider the controversy among doctors and scientists, all authoritative in their fields, about the effects of Vitamin C in preventing and curing the common cold.

This, too, is a typically short account, but notice that it does differ from Byerly's significantly.

In other textbooks of this period, one also finds some longer and much more elaborate accounts.

Capaldi lists eight qualifications to be used when citing the opinion of an authority:

1. You "should be sure that the authority you cite is not considered a liar."

2. The authority should "not have a vested interest in the case you are
   discussing."
3. "The authority should be considered conscientious . . ." and "careful
   about details."
4. The authority should be "well known."
5. The authority "must be an expert in the relevant field."
6. The authority should be "if possible" . . . "both current and historical."
7. The authority's opinion should be "representative of the general
   expertise in his field."
8. The authorities, if more than one is cited, "should be as numerous,
   as diverse, and otherwise as different as possible." (1971, 23–27)

Capaldi's intent in using these eight criteria is to help make an appeal
to authority as convincing as possible to an audience. But one can easily see that the same criteria are relevant to critically questioning an
appeal to authority.

Capaldi, like Fearnside and Holther, cites a conscientiousness factor
(condition 3, above). Also, like Fearnside and Holther (their condition
5), Capaldi requires that the authority's opinion should be representative of those generally accepted in the field (his condition 7). No mention of this requirement is made in the fairly extensive set of conditions
given by Purtill (1972). Purtill does, however, mention bias and being
up-to-date in his list.

Purtill offers a list of five questions said to be useful in deciding how
much weight to give to the authority of experts.

1. *Who?* If an appeal is made to the authority of an expert, we must
   first know who the expert is. A device often used in advertising is the
   faceless expert.
2. *What?* We must also know what the expert is an expert *on,* what
   qualifications he has. The opinion of "Dr. Smith" on the safety of the
   birth control pill may be of little value if he is a rural GP with little
   knowledge of the latest research.
3. *Where?* The geographical location of the expert, as well as the region
   to which his statement is intended to apply, can be important. An
   expert who has lived all his life in a tropical country may be unfa-
   miliar with conditions outside the tropics, and his expertise may not
   apply to conditions that he is not familiar with.
4. *When?* Again we can apply this question in two ways. How long ago
   the expert made his statement can be important, especially in fields
   where knowledge increases very rapidly.
5. *Why?* The motive for an expert's testimony may be important in

judging the worth of that testimony. If an expert stands to gain financially or in other ways from making a certain statement, we must take this fact into account (1972, 67–69).

Another factor mentioned by Purtill is that "the testimony of an expert cannot and should not convince us if we have personal experience to the contrary" (69). The novelty in Purtill's list is question 3, a factor that does not always apply to *ad verecundiam* arguments, but one that is possible to subsume under the "position to know" condition already encountered in Beardsley's account (1950).

Woods and Walton give five conditions that must be met for an appeal to authority to be adequate.

1. "The authority must be interpreted correctly." Under this heading, the various problems in the citing of sources warned of by DeMorgan are noted (1847; see also Chapter 4).
2. "The authority must actually have special competence in an area and not simply glamour, prestige or popularity." Three indicators of special competence are given: (1) previous record of predictions, (2) tests or hypothetical predictions the expert has successfully performed, (3) access to qualifications, like degrees or testimony of other experts.
3. "The judgment of the authority must actually be within the special field of competence."
4. "Direct evidence must be available in principle."
5. "A consensus technique is required for adjudicating disagreements among equally qualified authorities" (1972, 88–90).

This account, although fairly elaborate in some respects, fails to mention bias as a factor (like Wesley Salmon's account does, and several others above).

A set of five rules specifying the conditions for proper appeals to authority are given by Johnson and Blair quoted below from the second edition (1983):

> Rule I: If an authority is appealed to in support of a statement, Q, then Q must belong to some specifiable set of statements, S, which constitutes a domain of knowledge.

> Rule II: If M is appealed to as an authority on Q, then Q must belong to a class of statements, S, on which M is an authority.

Rule III: If there is no consensus among authorities in S, to which Q belongs, then this lack of consensus must be noted in any appeal to authority about Q, and the conclusion qualified accordingly.

Rule IV: The authority, M, whose judgment is appealed to, must not be in a situation of bias, or conflict of interest, about Q.

Rule V: If M is appealed to as an authority on S, then M must be identified (147–53).

According to Johnson and Blair, the violation of any one of these rules "undermines the argumentative force of the appeal" to authority (155).

Rule I, requiring a "domain of knowledge," like some other accounts noted above, appears to exclude appeals based on skill and practical expertise, as opposed to appeals based on theoretical, academic, or professional knowledge. But Rule III, like Byerly's version is commendably flexible (1973). Other than that, these rules are fairly consistent with many of the previous accounts. Bias is included (or excluded) as well, as a factor, in Rule IV.

4. Recent Accounts

One might expect the recent accounts in the new textbooks to have benefited from the buildup of considerations cited by earlier texts in some of the more detailed accounts cited so far. But that has not generally been the case. A few recent accounts are now fairly elaborate, but many of the textbooks still continue to give only brief and selective accounts, without referring to any of the more complete analyses that can be found in prior texts.

Kelley gives three conditions for the credibility of an appeal to authority: (1) "that the alleged authority be competent—an expert on the subject matter in question," (2) "that the alleged authority be objective," and that the issue "requires special knowledge or skill that the ordinary person does not possess" (1988, 118–19). This account adds nothing to comparable earlier accounts like that of Beardsley (1950).

The problem with these textbooks that give three conditions is that they give different conditions, although there is usually an overlap of at least one condition. This sends out a bad message to students or to anyone consulting these texts, that there is no real basis for unanimity or consistency in the field of logic on how *ad verecundiam* arguments are supposed to be judged.

Soccio and Barry cite three questions to be asked when a claim relies on an authority as a source of knowledge.

> How do we know when to lend faith to the statements of a particular authority? We must ask ourselves: Is the authority a recognized expert in the field? Do the authorities in the field agree? Can we check the claims of authority for ourselves? (1992, 54)

We seem to be getting random combinations of three conditions chosen by the different textbooks, among the various conditions that could be selected.

Another account also gives three conditions, but does elaborate on one of them, suggesting a number of critical subquestions. According to Russow and Curd, there are three factors that are the main criteria to be used when evaluating appeals to authority.

1. The first thing to check is the legitimacy of the authority. Is it true that the person or source providing the testimony has special knowledge or training in the appropriate field? In the case of testimony from individuals, we assess their legitimacy by asking the following sorts of questions: (a) Is the person in the relevant field? What is he trained in? (b) Does the person have the kind of background, education, and experience that would make him an expert? (c) What is the person's status in his field? Is he eminent or respected by other experts in the same area? If the testimony derives from a group or organization, we look for similar factors, with special emphasis on the last questions. When testimony relies on printed matter such as a book, we must try to assess its author. In the case of words which, like encyclopedias and reports, have no single author and may contain unattributed material, we must rely on the reputation of the work as a whole and the credentials of the organization that produced it.
2. The second major factor to consider when trying to use testimony is the presence or absence of consensus among authorities. Do the experts in the field agree with each other on the issue in question?
3. The third factor to keep in mind when looking for good testimony is the trustworthiness of the authority. Having a vested interest in presenting testimony of a certain sort, or in a certain way, will undermine an authority's trustworthiness (1989, 192, 194–95).

The subquestions listed under factor 1 are very useful in judging *ad verecundiam* arguments, in many cases, and relate to the comparable ones in Walton (1989a, 195). They would come under critical question 1 in our list of the three initial critical questions given in section 1 of this chapter.

In general, the approach of having more specific critical subquestions under a general or primary critical question looks promising. This allows for the possibility of a more detailed evaluation in a given case, subsequent to a general evaluation.

Little, Groarke, and Tindale cite five factors that must be incorporated in a good argument from authority.

(i) You must *state the credentials* of the person or group to whose opinion you appeal. If you fail to state them, a person who hears your argument has no reason to accept the views of the person or group you endorse.

(ii) You must make it clear that the stated credentials are *relevant* to the issue under discussion. This is an essential aspect of arguments from authority that is often overlooked.

(iii) You must ensure that the authorities to whom you appeal are *not biased*. The most obvious kind of bias arises when individuals have a vested interest, when they stand to gain from expressing some view or making some claim.

(iv) You must ensure that the claim is one for which there is *wide agreement* among the relevant experts.

(v) You must ensure that the claim belongs to an area of knowledge where *consensus* is in principle possible because there are universally accepted criteria for making judgments. (1989, 263–64)

Little, Groarke, and Tindale state that a good argument from authority requires that each of these criteria be established in a given case, but that in some cases they can be taken for granted "because they can be assumed as part of the general knowledge of your audience" (265). This is a good combination of the most important of the requirements already considered by the other textbooks, but (iv) and (v) are perhaps stated in too narrow a way as to be universally applicable.

The account of the *ad verecundiam* argument given by Walton identifies the following form of argument (1989a, 193):

(G7)   *E* is an expert in domain *D*.
       E asserts that *A* is known to be true.
       A is within *D*.
       Therefore, *A* may (plausibly) be taken to be true.

(G7) is similar to (G6) in section 1 above except that the third premise in (G7) is explicitly epistemic (knowledge-based), in contrast to the comparable premise in (G6). This makes (G7) preferable, in light of the analysis of expert systems given in Chapter 3. The form (G7) is called an argumentation scheme in Walton (1989a), and in the sense of Hastings (1962), and is evaluated by balancing it off against six critical questions.

1. The first question is whether the judgment put forward by the authority actually falls within the field of competence in which that individual is an expert.
2. The second main question with regard to any appeal to authority is whether the cited expert is actually an expert, and not merely someone quoted because of his prestige, popularity, or celebrity status.
3. The third critical question is that of how authoritative a particular expert is. Even if the individual cited is a legitimate expert in the field in which the question lies, there still remains the question of how strongly the appeal should be taken as a plausible argument.
4. The fourth question is whether there is disagreement among several qualified authorities who have been consulted. Here there are several methods that may be used to resolve the disagreement.
5. The fifth question is whether objective evidence on the cited opinion is presently available, and whether the expert's opinion is consistent with it.
6. The sixth question is whether the expert's say-so has been correctly interpreted. It must be in a form that is clear and intelligible. Yet it must not be only a simplistic rewording of what the expert said that may overlook necessary qualifications or exceptions. Preferably, the expert should be quoted directly. If not, it could be reasonable to question whether his view has been presented fairly and accurately. (194–96)

In addition to these six critical questions matching the argument from authority, sets of critical subquestions (that is, more specific questions) are given under two of the questions.

Under the first critical question, the following five critical subquestions are given (Walton 1989a, 195):

1. What degrees, professional qualifications, or certifications by licensing agencies does this person hold?
2. Can testimony and evaluations of colleagues or other experts be given to support his status?

3. Does the expert cited have a record of experience in the field or particular technique being discussed?
4. What is this individual's previous record of predictions or successful accomplishments in this field of expertise?
5. Can evidence be given of publications or other projects that have been evaluated, refereed, or reviewed by other authorities?

Under the fourth critical question, it should be noted that while a track record is a helpful indicator, care should be taken because this factor needs to be weighed in with other factors and judged in perspective. In 1991, New York became the first state to release surgeon-specific death rates for coronary bypass surgery (Bumiller 1995, D8). This "cardiac report card" had the effect of lowering risks of undergoing a bypass operation but it also led to controversy due to the belief among physicians that some surgeons are turning away severely ill patients because they are afraid a death will hurt their rankings. Questions were also raised about how risk-factors are defined in the ratings. Hence there are questions about whether the ratings may be biased or misleading in certain respects. Track record should not be the only basis for deciding to choose a particular surgeon.

Even so, making the surgeons' track records available to the public gives someone who is thinking of having this type of operation a much better base of information for making a decision. It is unfortunate that, in many other kinds of cases of medical decision making, information on track records of this type is not available to patients.

Under the sixth critical question, the following four critical subquestions are given (190):

1. Is the expert's pronouncement directly quoted? If not, is a reference to the original source given? Can it be checked?
2. If the expert advice is not quoted, does it look like important information or qualifications may have been left out?
3. If more than one expert source has been cited, is each authority quoted separately? Could there be disagreements among the cited authorities?
4. Is what the authority said clear? Are there technical terms used that are not explained clearly? If the advice is in layman's terms, could this be an indication that it has been translated from some other form of expression given by the expert?

These four subquestions reflect the kinds of concerns raised by DeMorgan (1847) about the problems inherent in the quotation, and citation generally, of expert opinions used as authoritative sources (Chapter 5).

5. Personal Reliability and Bias

One factor that is conspicuously missing in the list of six critical questions for the *ad verecundiam* given by Walton (1989a) is bias (see also Blair 1988, and Walton 1991; 1992a; 1992b). This seems an unexpected omission in view of the citing of bias as a factor in other accounts, and because it is recognized in Walton that querying financial interest in a case is a permitted form of cross-examination question for lawyers in court (183). At any rate, questioning bias in an expert's testimony is cited by so many of the textbooks as an appropriate category of critical question for *ad verecundiam* arguments, and also in the courts, as we saw in Chapter 5, that it is clear that it should be an important consideration in evaluating this type of argumentation. But bias and trustworthiness of the expert as a source of testimony generally seems like a separate kind of factor from the kinds of critical questions cited in Walton (1989a), which stress matters of the expert's competence and interpreting what the expert asserted.

In general, the approach taken by Fearnside and Holther (1959) of dividing the conditions for giving weight in argument from authority into two broad categories—one on expertise and one on trustworthiness, or "personal reliability" as they call it—makes a good deal of sense. There seem to be two quite clearly distinct types of considerations in evaluating *ad verecundiam* arguments. One is a more factual question of the source as a competent expert, a source of knowledge. The other is an ethical question of the sincerity and trustworthiness of the source as a reliable testifier to the truth of what was asserted.

Waller agrees, stating even more generally that testimony of any sort needs to be evaluated by two distinct kinds of standards, which raise separate types of questions of evaluation.

> Testimony must be evaluated by two standards: Is this source of testimony trustworthy, honest? (The testimony of a lying expert is no more helpful than the testimony of a sincere incompetent.) If a witness identifies the defendant as the person who ran from the scene of the crime, we want to know: Is this witness *trustworthy* (does the witness have a special bias, such as a deep hatred for the defendant; does the witness have

> a reputation for honesty) *and* is the witness a careful observer
> with good eyesight (an honest witness whose eyesight is so bad
> that he or she could not have made an accurate identification
> will not provide strong testimony). (1988, 126)

In the case of expert testimony, the one category of evaluation is that of
trustworthiness, and the other concerns the justification for thinking
that the expert's opinion is based on her knowledge of the subject. Thus
the second category has to do with factors like whether the expert is a
competent authority in that subject, and whether her expressed opinion really flows from that authority and being in a position to know, i.e.,
from the knowledge base in that subject.

This distinction seems fundamental to evaluation of *ad verecundiam*
arguments, and its centrality suggests breaking down the list of critical questions into two main subsets: reliability questions and knowledge questions.

But Fearnside and Holther (1959) listed three factors under personal reliability: telling the truth, bias, and conscientiousness (see section 2, above). What about these two other factors? Should they be
included as critical questions along with the question of bias?

The question "Is the expert witness lying?" could be relevant, apart
from cases where there is reason to think that the witness is lying
because of a bias. But it seems like lying might be more appropriately
dealt with under the third critical question in our initial list (section 1):
"Did the witness assert *A*?" For if the source is lying, then the problem
is that she is asserting a false proposition *A*, or a proposition she knows
or thinks to be false.

However, the question of whether the witness asserted *A* and the
question of whether the witness knows or thinks *A* is true or whether
she is lying to us are really separate types of questions. The first is
about what the source asserted—whether it is *A*, for example, or probably *A*, or possibly *A* that was asserted, or even some other proposition
altogether. This is a question of interpreting what was said or of judging
what can be inferred from what was actually asserted and of documenting what in fact was actually asserted. The second is about whether
the source is being truthful: Is what she said really her honest opinion
on the matter? And this seems to be an inherently different type of
question, from a logical point of view. One is a question of honesty (sincerity) of the source in saying what was said, while the other is a question of documenting and interpreting the meaning of what was said
(apart from whether the source really believes it to be true or not).

Conscientiousness was also cited as a question apart from bias by

Capaldi (1971), as well as by Fearnside and Holther (1959, 85; see also section 2). But should conscientiousness, in Fearnside and Holther's sense of being "attentive to the problem and diligent in gathering data," be treated under the heading of the expert's competence or her ability to justify her opinion by showing the evidence on which it was based? If so, this question should come under the other broad category of the expert's competence and qualifications rather than under the category of honesty or personal reliability. Conscientiousness, it seems, is somewhat of a borderline consideration, falling between the two broad categories perhaps, or perhaps more in the competence category. It seems to have more to do with being in a position to know.

Whatever the outcome is here, we certainly ought to have a broad category of critical questions under personal reliability, including both bias and dishonesty (lying) as critical questions. This broad category I will call the *trustworthiness* question.

6. The Trustworthiness Question

It is important to note that, in formulating the critical question relating to bias, a finding of bias in itself should not be regarded as sufficient to refute the argument from expert opinion. It is true, as stated by Russow and Curd (1989, 195) that if the expert is found to have a "vested interest" in presenting testimony "of a certain sort," this will undermine her trustworthiness, as an authority, to give testimony. But we should recall, from Chapter 6, that experts are often paid to testify, which does not, in itself, make their testimony suspect or undermine it as credible evidence. This is not how bias works as a critical question.

A finding of vested interest, especially if it was concealed initially by the testifier, is an indicator of bias but not a conclusive refutation of her opinion as being credible. It is only certain sorts of indicators of bias that raise doubts about the personal reliability of a source.[2] Just being paid to testify or having some sort of financial interest in a case is not enough, in itself, to rule out an appeal to authority as illegitimate.

It is for these reasons that Johnson and Blair's Rule IV, which requires that the authority "must not be in a situation of bias, or conflict

---

2. Blair cites misrepresentation of an opponent's position in a dispute as evidence of a kind of bias that is a violation of a norm of fairness that should be expected in a rational discussion (1988, 96).

of interest," is too strong (1983, 195). It is acceptable for an expert to have a bias, but what raises a critical question of personal reliability is the kind of situation where this bias is a critically bad bias, an obstacle to honest and credible testimony for one side over another. This could occur in the kinds of legal cases noted in Chapter 6, for example, where an expert witness works full time for a law firm and gets all her income from supporting a particular point of view in appearing as an expert in court cases.

Normally, expert witnesses used in courts do have some sort of bias. Giannelli cites not only the fees paid to expert scientific witnesses, but also the inherent institutional bias posed by the control of crime laboratories by the police. Giannelli describes cases where police officers admitted they were under strong pressure to go ahead with evidence known to be scientifically false or inadequate (1993, 117).

Guy Morin was wrongly convicted of rape and murder in 1992 (as shown by later DNA evidence), partly on the basis of a study of tiny clothing fibers conducted by a forensic expert. The defense argued that the fibers did not match, and that even if they did, there had been numerous opportunities for them to be accidentally deposited (Makin 1994, A6). However, what really pushed the prosecution forward was the police determination to get a conviction, expressed in their strong effort to collect any kind of potential evidence that might indicate that Morin was guilty.

So the expert does not have to be free of bias to give credible testimony, but she has to be free of the kind of strong or "bad" bias that would throw her personal reliability into question (Blair 1988). In other words, if challenged on the question of bias, by being shown to have some sort of vested interest or something to gain by offering the opinion she has advanced, the expert must be able to respond to this challenge by maintaining that her opinion was based on her knowledge in the field and not on a motive for gain. The question shifts a weight of presumption against the expert testifier (if appropriate), and requires an explanation or appropriate response, if the weight of presumption in favor of her opinion is to be restored. However, while bias is the most important factor in the area of trustworthiness of an expert source, as Fearnside and Holther noted, there are other factors to be considered here as well.

I recommend that the general critical question for trustworthiness of an expert source should be formulated as follows: Is E personally reliable as a source? Then under this general critical question there should be three critical subquestions.

1. Is E biased?
2. Is E honest?
3. Is E conscientious?

The second critical subquestion is one of E's character for veracity. If E has a criminal record, if there is evidence that E has lied in the past, or if there is any reason to think that E is lying or is not being honest or sincere in advancing the opinion in question, then it should be appropriate to have doubts or reservations about the credibility of E's testimony.

The third critical subquestion needs to be carefully separated off from the question of whether in fact E has done her homework and taken the time to search out the relevant evidence and base her opinion on this knowledge. This comes under a different heading I will call *position to know* (section 7, below). Question 3 above pertains to E's scholarly habits or carefulness and professionalism as a skilled technician.

7. Position to Know

Another consideration not explicitly covered by the list of six critical questions in Walton (1989a) is whether the expert was in a position to know the special circumstances concerning the proposition A she asserts. This might not be so relevant if the expert is only pronouncing on general knowledge of what is accepted in the field. But it might be more important if the expert is commenting on a particular situation. This factor could come under Beardsley's heading of "access to the relevant information" (1950), or Purtill's "where" question (1972), concerning the region to which the expert's statement is intended to apply, for example. The question is whether the expert has access to or has studied the localized data or special circumstances of the case.

In the case of a physician testifying as an expert witness in court, for example, the question might be whether the physician has actually examined the patient in question or she is relying on reports from another physician. Or the question might involve whether or not the physician examined the patient at various crucial times during the development of a disease or the history of an injury and recovery.

Another critical question in this area concerns the kind of case where no possible evidence could verify or falsify an opinion—where a hypothesis or speculation is not scientifically testable (W. Salmon's factor 4). Here, again, it is a question of access to data.

These kinds of questions, as we have seen, have arisen in the courts' use of expert testimony on questions of psychiatric testimony, the various syndromes that have been the subject of debate, and other areas where junk science has become a problem. But in court cases generally, the experts do disagree, no doubt because the attorneys on both sides have selected their respective experts because their opinion supports their own side of the disputed question.

Especially in cases where experts disagree, there ought to be a critical question to ask the expert to give us the evidence (the knowledge in the field) on which her opinion was supposedly based. Thus we ought to have as a general critical question: Can the expert explain or justify her opinion by citing the evidence on which it was based? Using this question depends, of course, on the expert being available to engage in a dialogue defending her viewpoint. In evaluating cases in a logic course, this is generally not possible unless the given case already includes an account or transcript of such a dialogue. In court, as we have seen, use of hearsay expert testimony is frowned upon precisely because it cannot be challenged or questioned by the triers of fact.

There should be three subquestions under this general critical question.

1. What is the internal evidence the expert used herself to arrive at this opinion as her conclusion?
2. If there is external evidence, e.g., physical evidence reported independently of the expert, can the expert deal with this adequately?
3. Can it be shown that the opinion given is not one that is scientifically unverifiable?

The third critical question relates to Wesley Salmon's factor 4 that the opinion should not be one on which no possible evidence could be brought to bear.

8. General Acceptance in a Field

As we have seen in the legal controversies surrounding the Frye Rule, it is a moot point whether an opinion given in expert testimony ought to be representative of the views in the field or to have gained general acceptance in the field in question. Fearnside and Holther required (condition 5 in their second list), that the authority "must hold representative views in his field" (1959, 86). Capaldi also held (his condition 7) that the authority's opinion should be "representative of the general expertise in his field" (1971, 26). This conservatism, in effect, imposes the Frye Rule as a requirement for expert testimony to be acceptable. But as we saw in Chapter 6, this conservative approach has its problems, and there are strong arguments against it.

One much-discussed case arose from two books written by biochemistry Nobel laureate Linus Pauling, advocating the taking of large doses of Vitamin C to cure or prevent the common cold. Pauling also advocated the taking of large doses of other kinds of vitamins for longevity and better health, even claiming that if you follow his regimen, you can "increase the lifespan by 25, 35 years" (Knight-Ridder 1986, 39). Understandably, physicians and nutritionists expressed strong disagreement.

Case 7.1:   In a program last week at Thomas Jefferson University's medical school, another researcher on vitamins told his audience that "vitamin supplements are misused."

"There's a feeling that people have if a little is good . . . more is better," said Dr. Richard Rivlin, a professor of medicine at Cornell University Medical College and chief of the nutrition service at Memorial Sloan-Kettering Cancer Center in New York.

"Vitamins taken in excess can cause significant damage," he warned.

Rivlin, who spoke at Jefferson under the sponsorship of the National Dairy Council, said vitamins can be beneficial to patients who are taking certain drugs, but "healthy people do not gain much health advantage by taking vitamin supplements." Large doses of vitamins such as A and C—far in excess of the Recommended Daily Allowances, or RDAs—can be dangerous and in the case of Vitamin D, for instance, even deadly, he said.

"Vitamins are drugs and in large amounts they can cause toxicity," he said.

"I think most of the studies have suggested Vitamin C is not particularly helpful in the treatment of the common cold," Rivlin said in an interview. He also disagreed with Pauling's finding that large doses of Vitamin C, along with conventional therapy, are helpful in the treatment of cancer and may help patients survive longer.

In this case, the newspaper report is citing the two expert opinions in such a way that a conflict of opinions is posed. So there are two contexts of dialogue: (1) an expert consultation type of dialogue where the books or speeches of the two experts are quoted and interpreted, and (2) a critical discussion turning on the conflict of opinions—are large doses of Vitamin C good for you (in particular, for treating the common cold) or not?

The issue turns on argumentation from consequences. Dr. Rivlin claims that "Vitamins taken in excess can cause significant damage." Dr. Pauling claims that following his megavitamin regimen "you can increase the lifespan by 25, 35 years." One cites the allegedly good consequences of the course of action at issue as supporting his side, the other supports the claim that the bad consequences that would ensue from this course of action as a decisive reason for not doing it. Thus the conflict of opinions is a practical issue that concerns the prudential advisability of certain possible (opposed) courses of action.

The problem with appealing to Pauling as an expert authority is posed by the fact that he is an expert in biochemistry (even a Nobel Prize winner) but is not a physician. Rivlin is a well-qualified expert in medicine, but the problem with his opinion, as cited from the interview quoted, is that it is nonspecific and therefore weak or open to further critical questioning. He is quoted as saying, "I think most of the studies have suggested Vitamin C is not particularly helpful." This claim, carefully qualified by only citing "most of the studies" without giving details, is subject to further questioning. It is not a fallacious *ad verecundiam* argument but rather a weak kind of appeal, a point of departure that is open to challenge and requests for further justification.

The conflict in this case is a "battle of the experts," a case where qualified experts disagree; however, as such the conflict is not purely symmetrical. Pauling is an acknowledged maverick on this particular issue (and not an expert in medicine), and Rivlin represents the "official" or "established" point of view of the medical profession. Both sides clearly recognize this aspect of the dispute, however. So it would not do to simply say that Pauling's argument is a straightforward case of the *ad verecundiam* fallacy because he is not a medical doctor. As a biochemist, he has expert standing in a related field, so it would be simplistic to reject his opinion too strongly as having no claim to expert status at all.

In a case like this, it would not be a good evaluation to simply reject Pauling's viewpoint out of hand because he is the "maverick" and accept Rivlin's viewpoint because it represents the established, representative views in the field of medicine. This conservative approach does not do justice to the balance of factors in the case, which need to be seen in a dialectical perspective. It is better to say that while there is a strong presumption in favor of Rivlin's side of the case, there are critical questions to be posed on both sides in relation to the particulars given in the media report in Case 7.1.

Both Byerly (1973) and Johnston and Blair (1983) present more flexible conditions that take representativeness in the field into account but do not absolutely require it in order for an expert's opinion to carry weight in an argument. Byerly's condition 3 requires that the authority's opinion should *either* "represent the predominant view of experts in the field" *or* "if not, the controversial nature of the opinion should be openly acknowledged" (47). Johnson and Blair's Rule III states that any lack of consensus in the field must be noted (and the conclusion "qualified accordingly"), if there is not a consensus (150). Both these rules are flexible in that they do not absolutely exclude giving an expert's opinion weight even in some cases where it is not representative of what is generally accepted. What is required is that this factor of non-representativeness should be noted and the case dealt with specially.

These accounts suggest an approach that could be very useful in dealing with the cases that are proving so troublesome in this area. We could have a general critical question: Is the expert's opinion representative of what is generally accepted in the field? If the answer is yes, then this avenue of questioning ends and we go on to another type of critical question. But if the answer is no, then a series of critical subquestions that go into the question of why the expert's opinion is non-representative must be asked. Is it because the question is one on which you would normally expect experts in this field to disagree? Or is it a question where the preponderance of other highly qualified experts agree on an opinion other than the opinion of the expert source cited? If the latter, then some explanation is required. Does it mean that this expert simply has not done her homework (lacks knowledge in the field), is a maverick of some sort, or has unusual but nevertheless defensible views? Or does it mean that this supposed expert is some sort of crank or crackpot or is perhaps out of date? Unless some explanation that is defensible can be given, failure of a view to represent what is generally accepted in the field is a strike against the expert's opinion as being based on the knowledge in the field. However, the strike against it is only presumptive and not absolute. It can be recovered by an appropriate explanation or justification, e.g., in the case of a new technique or technology that has been tested and verified as reliable but is so new that it has not yet reached the stage of widespread or general acceptance by the majority of practitioners in the field. One thinks here of DNA fingerprinting and other techniques that took time to become generally accepted as routine forms of expert evidence.

The question of general acceptance of an opinion in a field is one aspect of a broader critical question that pertains to disagreements between equally well qualified authorities. Such disagreements frequently exist, as the controversies surrounding the battle of the experts, outlined in Chapter 6, clearly show. But they are not a problem in all cases. In some cases, a proposition may be uncontroversial, in the sense that nearly all the qualified experts in the field will agree on it. In other cases, for various reasons, a proposition can be very controversial, and experts can easily be found to vouch both for the proposition and also its direct opposite (or negation).

Under the broad critical question of consistency with what other experts say, there should be two related critical subquestions.

1. Does A have general acceptance in S?
2. If not, can E explain why not, and give reasons why there is good evidence for A?

The linking of these two critical subquestions is based on the requirement expressed by both Byerly (1973) and Johnson and Blair (1983), to the effect that a lack of consensus among authorities should be noted and the conclusion drawn should be qualified accordingly. To reflect this flexible way of dealing with the issue of general acceptance, we link the subquestions as follows: The first subquestion does not have a yes answer as a general requirement. But if the answer is no, then it is obligatory to go on to ask the second subquestion.

9. General Recommendations

The argumentation scheme (G7) expresses the basic thrust of the appeal to expert opinion, as a type of argumentation that carries presumptive weight, very simply and appropriately. The most useful approach is not to complicate it with further premises because these further premises do not always need to apply or be considered in a given case. Better we think to match it with the three critical questions posed in section 1 above, along with three additional critical questions.

Granted, the considerations of this chapter have shown that there are a large and complicated variety of factors that should properly be taken into account. But it is not a useful approach to simply generate a long list of critical questions to be tested against the argumentation scheme in every case. Instead, I have recommended the use of general critical questions. If the general question is replied to appropriately then the argument from expert opinion can be further tested by posing more specific subquestions.

It is my recommendation that the following six general critical questions, matching the argumentation scheme for the argument from expert opinion, be called:

1. *Expertise* question: How credible is E as an expert source?
2. *Field* question: Is E an expert in the field that A is in?
3. *Opinion* question: What did E assert that implies A?
4. *Trustworthiness* question: Is E personally reliable as a source?
5. *Consistency* question: Is A consistent with what other experts assert?
6. *Backup evidence* question: Is A's assertion based on evidence?

Critical question 1, the expertise question, has the function of determining whether E, the individual cited, really is an expert or not. If so, then the second function of E is to get some indication of the degree of expertise of E so that the user can get an idea of how credible he should take E to be as a source of opinion founded on evidence of an expert who has a high degree of credibility who will give a high degree of plausibility (other things being equal) to her stated opinion. If E has less credibility as an expert, then the proposition stated in E's opinion will have less plausibility for the rational user. Under the expertise question, the following critical subquestions are appropriate.

1. What is E's name, job or official capacity, location, and employer?
2. What degrees, professional qualifications or certification by licensing agencies does E hold?
3. Can testimony of peer experts in the same field be given to support E's competence?
4. What is E's record of experience, or other indications of practiced skill in S?
5. What is E's record of peer-reviewed publications or contributions to knowledge in S?

This list is a modification of the five critical subquestions given in Walton (1989a). The first one above is new, however. It expresses the requirement that the expert source needs to be specifically cited as an individual who can be traced, as opposed to a vague or generic attribution like "according to leading experts" (195).

In some cases, a group of experts who allegedly have a particular opinion are referred to in generic terms, by a general description; then an example of one expert's opinion may be cited. Even so, that particular expert may not be named but again labeled in a generic way by referring to his or her field or position. In the following case, the issue was whether hunting should be allowed on Sundays or not. Various expert opinions on whether Sunday hunts should be legalized or not were quoted including the following citation (Sawyers 1985, 4):

Case 7.2: The men and women with their fingers on the pulse of wildlife agree that Sunday hunting would not harm animal populations. One Maryland game biologist said that Sunday hunting would have no effect on the present four-month squirrel season. "Only when considering a short hunt for a closely-watched species, such as the wild turkey, would Sunday hunting make any difference," he remarked. "Even then, we could shorten the season at the tail-end to compensate for opening the hunt on Sunday."

In this case, the general claim made is that the "men and women with their fingers on the pulse of wildlife" agree that Sunday hunting would not be harmful. But who exactly are these men and women? We are not told. But there is a strong claim made by appeal to expert opinion here, because these people, who are said to be those who are in a practical position to know what is really going on, are in agreement on one side of the issue.

However, in partial substantiation of this generic claim, one expert is cited. However, she or he is not named, only identified as "one Maryland game biologist."

The critical subquestions for the second critical question, the field question, include the four following questions:

1. Is the field of expertise cited in the appeal a genuine area of knowledge, or area of technical skill that supports a claim to knowledge?
2. If E is an expert in a field closely related to the field cited in the appeal, how close is the relationship between the expertise in the two fields?
3. Is the issue one where expert knowledge in *any* field is directly relevant to deciding the issue?
4. Is the field of expertise cited an area where there are changes in techniques or rapid developments in new knowledge, and if so, is the expert up-to-date in these developments?

The critical subquestions for the third critical question, the opinion question, are similar to those given in Walton (1989a, 190), but with some changes.

1. Was E quoted in asserting A? Was a reference to the source of the quote given, and can it be verified that E actually said A?
2. If E did not say A exactly, then what did E assert, and how was A inferred?
3. If the inference to A was based on more than one premise, could one premise have come from E and the other from a different expert? If so, is there evidence of disagreement between what the two experts (separately) asserted?
4. Is what E asserted clear? If not, was the process of interpretation of what A said by the respondent who used E's opinion justified? Are other interpretations plausible? Could important qualifications be left out?

The opinion question—which could also be called the assertion question—relates to the opinion asserted by the expert and to how what is presumed to be this opinion (a proposition) was extracted or inferred from the text of discourse the expert actually put forward in dialogue with the respondent. As noted in Chapter 4, this set of questions both presupposes and provides a normative model for the dialogue exchange between the expert source and the respondent.

10. Using Critical Questions for Evaluation

In principle, it is reasonable in argument to appeal to the opinion of an expert source to support one's side of the argument. Such an appeal to authority is, therefore, not in itself fallacious in argumentation. However, correct extraction and use of expert opinion in this way is complicated by problems of accessibility. Expert opinion is best seen as inherently fallible, especially deployed in dialogue on controversial issues, and experts are imperfect when it comes to explaining (to a layperson, especially) how they themselves arrived at a certain conclusion on the basis of their skill and competence in their domain of expertise. Moreover, two distinct levels of dialogue are involved. First, the extraction of the conclusion from the expert, and second, its later deployment in support of an argument on an issue that may be controversial. First, there is the expert-user dialogue, which is a type of knowledge elicitation (or information-seeking) dialogue. Then second, there is the deployment of the extracted opinion by a proponent in a critical discussion, in order to support his side of an argument against a respondent.

When an expert opinion is used in a critical discussion, it is proper for the respondent to ask critical questions concerning the documentation of the appeal to authority. Our case studies have shown that if such documentation is not explicitly included in an appeal to expert authority in dialogue, the argument may be judged weak or questionable. But it does not necessarily follow that the argument is fallacious. The argument should only be judged fallacious if the fault is more serious—for example, if the proponent refuses to answer any of these critical questions if challenged by the respondent or if his manner of presentation of the argument, as indicated by the context of dialogue, forecloses such questioning in advance, as suggested by Locke's account.

When the proponent of an argument, in a persuasion dialogue, backs up her argument with an appeal to what she alleges to be an expert opinion that supports his argument, the respondent of the argument is entitled (and, unless she accepts it, obliged) to ask one or more of the appropriate critical questions. The expertise question asks, with its subquestions, the following range of questions. Has a particular expert been cited, and if so, is he a genuine expert, and can it be shown that he is a genuine expert in the relevant field? Showing that the authority cited is a genuine expert in the relevant field means giving evidence that the individual cited has attained a level of skill in this field.

The opinion question centers on what the expert actually said. Did the expert cited actually assert some definite proposition that supports the proponent's argument? The problem exposed by this query is that, notoriously, what an expert actually says can be distorted, misquoted, misinterpreted, and generally misunderstood. For example, there are many shortcomings in the use of opinions from expert sources by quoting out of context, changes of wording and emphasis, and neglect of important qualifications. The problem is that experts are often guarded and careful in their advice or predictions and it may be extremely difficult for a layperson to "translate" technical terms in a special field of expertise (jargon) in a nonmisleading fashion that is true to the content of the expert's assertion.

The field question raises the following concerns: Is the cited opinion of the expert actually within the expert's domain of expertise, and does this domain coincide with the area or topic of the proponent's argument that the opinion is supposed to support? The problem here is a common one cited in the textbooks—for example, in Copi (1953; 1986, 98), where a legitimate expert's opinion may be cited, but he is not an expert in the area of the argument that his opinion is used to back up.

The fourth critical question I suggest is the question of trustworthiness, which centers on the personal reliability of the expert as a source or witness who vouches for an opinion. If there are good reasons to think that the expert may be too strongly biased to one side or to a particular view, or if there is any reason to doubt the expert's honesty and character for veracity, this throws doubts on the expert's support of a particular opinion as a credible argument to support the truth of that opinion. This factor is closely related to the *ad hominem* argument, which often (and characteristically) takes the form of an attack on an arguer's character for veracity. There are important connections here between *ad verecundiam* and *ad hominem* argumentation.

The consistency question, critical question 5, compares the expert's opinion to that of other experts in the same field. What do other experts say and, if known, how does what this expert says square with what the other experts say? Much depends on the issue here. On some issues, we expect a solid consensus among experts in a field of knowledge, whereas on other issues, controversy and a wide range of opinions would be normal. Here, too, the legal problems with the use of expert testimony cited in Chapter 5 would suggest asking whether the technique or theory used in the expert's judgment is one that has gained general acceptance in the field of knowledge it falls under. Is it accepted by most experts in the field, or only a few?

The backup evidence question, the sixth critical question, queries the expert's basis of support for her opinion. Can the expert defend and explain his line of reasoning so that we can understand the evidence that his conclusion is based on? In principle, for an appeal to expertise to be acceptable the expert must base her judgment on real, objective evidence in her field of competence. However, as we have seen, the problem is that this evidence will not usually be directly available to the user. Therefore, where there is any doubt about the basis of the expert's claim, a questioning of the basis of the claim by a call for evidence is a reasonable and appropriate response in dialogue.

In many cases, however, our expectations of how well an expert should be able to perform in answering the backup evidence critical question must be tempered by the inherent limitations of experts outlined in Chapter 3. In principle, an expert should be able to cite evidence that explains the basis of her reasoning. But for a layperson to be successful in extracting such an explanation may require skilled questioning in a lengthy sequence of dialogue interactions between the layperson and the expert. The peirastic interval may require a kind of critical examination that Socrates is portrayed as using in the early Platonic dialogues.

A subtlety inherent in the evaluation of any text of discourse where *ad verecundiam* argumentation is said to occur is the dual nature of the context of dialogue. The proponent who has advanced the appeal to expert opinion has done so in order to advance an argument in a critical discussion where her goal is to persuade his respondent that she (the proponent) has a conclusion (point of view) that is right. But in order to make her appeal to expert opinion have weight, or to be based on good reasons in the critical discussion, the proponent presupposes a secondary dialogue where she has correctly interpreted the opinion of a genuine expert in a field relevant to the topic of the persuasion dialogue in such a way that it supports her argument. This secondary dialogue involves the correct dialogue management of the process of extraction of knowledge from an expert source.

The above six critical questions are at the core of any evaluation of a given text of discourse where it has been alleged that a fallacious *argumentum ad verecundiam* occurred, or where an appeal to authority has been challenged as weak, unsupported, or questionable. The use of appeal to authority in argument is, therefore, from a point of view of its logic—inherently dialectical. The argumentation scheme (G7) provides a core argumentation form around which a context of dialogue can be reconstructed, revealing the weight of backing for the *ad verecundiam* argument as used in a given case. How the use of the argumentation scheme in a context of dialogue can be evaluated to see if it was used in a dogmatic way, closing off critical questioning, is indicated in Chapter 8, section 8.

An appeal to authority commits a fallacy in reasoned dialogue when the argumentation technique of appealing to expert opinion to support one side of a dialogue is misused by its proponent as a tactical device for preventing the respondent from raising the appropriate critical questions about the proponent's side of the argument. Generally speaking, an argument that uses expert opinion to support its conclusion is a kind of defeasible, presumptive reasoning that shifts burden of proof in reasoned dialogue. It can be abused if pressed too hard by the proponent as a tactic for making his case against an opponent. Detection of abuse in a particular case is determined by an analysis of the context of dialogue, which includes factors in the style of presentation of the proponent's profile of argument.

Specifically, a fallacy is indicated, according to Locke's analysis, if the opponent refuses to answer or presses ahead in the dialogue in too powerful or aggressive a manner, so that the effect is to try to wave aside or even block the legitimate critical questions posed by the respondent. Thus the fallacy is the use of the argument to unduly prevail on or to silence the opposition by techniques of forcing closure of the dialogue without allowing the respondent room to continue with proper critical questioning of the appeal to authority. Thus, determining the fallacy involves studying the sequence of question-reply dialogue both prior to and subsequent to the particular move in the dialogue where the proponent appeals to authority to support his argument.

But what exactly is the borderline between a presumptively weak or unjustified *ad verecundiam* argument, where one or more of the six critical questions has not been adequately answered, and a fallacious *ad verecundiam* argument? In Chapter 8, we turn to a detailed consideration of this question.

8

EXPLAINING
THE FALLACY

We now have explored a good basis for evaluating arguments from authority as strong or weak: the argumentation scheme and the matching set of critical questions. But is there more to it than this? I have argued that solving the problem of what makes an *ad verecundiam* argument fallacious needs to go beyond this point and involves a forced or premature closure of the interactive dialogue between the two primary participants in an argument.

But going beyond this point raises a very controversial, yet general question that we cannot entirely resolve here, namely, What is a fallacy? (Walton 1987). The textbook treatments of the *ad verecundiam* fallacy often treat cases where there has been an overlooking of or failure to address critical questions as instances of the *ad verecundiam* fallacy. But in this chapter, I argue that such cases are not necessarily fallacious arguments, and that the fallaciousness of such an argument resides in how it is presented in a given case—a matter of the interactive factors in the context of dialogue, as outlined in Chapter 5.

According to the explanation of the *ad verecundiam* fallacy given in this chapter, fallacious cases occur where what is basically a presumptive and defeasible type of argument is presented in an absolutistic and final manner in a dialogue.

1. Suspect and Fallacious Appeals

Already surveyed in Chapter 3 were a number of textbooks, especially among the earlier ones, that simply dismissed appeal to authority as fallacious without explaining why, or defined this type of argument as inherently fallacious. However, the emerging trend in the more modern textbooks is to portray appeal to authority as a type of argument that is reasonable in some cases, and questionable (suspect, weak) in others. Among this latter type of text, there are many that do not offer explanations of what they think makes such an argument fallacious, over and above being weak or questionable.

The problem here is that the use of the term 'fallacious' is a strong condemnation of an argument, which seems to mean more than saying the argument is weak or open to questioning. The word 'fallacy' implies a systematic, underlying, logical pattern of misuse or error in the structure of the argument whose presence shows that the argument is not only structurally incorrect, as used in a given case, but is also the kind of argument that can be used to unfairly get the best of a speech partner because it has a plausible appearance of being correct or persuasive (Walton 1995; Hamblin 1970). If an argument is open to critical questioning, does it follow that it is fallacious? Not necessarily. For, perhaps the question can be easily answered without any pattern of deceptive misuse being involved. What, then, is the difference?

Although Fearnside and Holther label the appeal to authority as a fallacy, under the heading of 'psychological fallacies,' their actual treatment of it is more as a weak argument, open to critical questions. They use a set of criteria (which works like critical questions) to evaluate this type of argumentation (see Chapter 7, section 1), indicating that the appeal can be proper in cases where the criteria are met. Where the criteria are not met, they judge the appeal "suspect."

> In summary, an appeal to authority is proper where the problem is technical and the expert cited is qualified and personally reliable. Otherwise, the appeal is suspect: at best the speaker may not realize what is required for a proper appeal to authority; at worst he may be trying to give some opinion of his own a weight it would not have without the aid of great names or unidentified "expert opinion." (1959, 87)

But what is the difference between an appeal to authority that is merely "suspect" or open to critical questioning, and one that is fallacious? Fearnside and Holther do not seem to answer this question. In the "at best" situation, the improper appeal seems to be just a blunder, or self-inflicted error. In the "at worst" situation, it seems more like a deliberate attempt in argument to mislead the other party. But what is the difference?

Kelley takes the positions that it is "perfectly appropriate to rely on the testimony of authorities if the conditions of credibility are satisfied," but that if they are not satisfied, "appealing to authority is fallacious" (1988, 118). This implies that if a critical question is not answered (if one of the requirements for an appeal to authority is not satisfied in a given case), then that case is an instance of the *ad verecundiam* fallacy. Yanal identifies fallacious and weak appeals to authority. He defines a *weak* argument from authority as one where the person cited is "either an inappropriate or unreliable authority on the subject." Then he adds that "such weak appeals to authority are *fallacious appeals to authority*" (1988, 383). These accounts make a logical leap that is not justified. Just because an appeal to authority is weak in a given case, it does not follow that it can automatically be categorized as fallacious.

Gensler treats appeal to authority under the heading of "Informal Fallacies," but does not specifically claim it is a fallacy or try to show why. Instead, he writes that it is good reasoning in some cases, but "wrong" reasoning in other cases.

> If [the cited expert] is a *great* authority and the consensus of authorities is *large,* then the argument becomes stronger. But it's never 100 percent conclusive. All the authorities in the world might agree on something that they later discover to be wrong! So we shouldn't think that something *must* be so because the authorities say it is. It's also wrong to appeal to a person who isn't an authority in the field (a sports hero endorsing coffee makers, for example). And finally, it's wrong to appeal to one authority (regarding the safety of an atomic power plant, for example) when the authorities disagree widely. The appeal to authority can go wrong in many ways. (1989, 338)

Since nothing is said about fallaciousness here at all, we are left hanging. Is an appeal to authority fallacious when the argument is taken as "100 percent conclusive"? (This seems an interesting hypothesis). Or is it the nature of appeals to authority that they "go wrong in many ways," and so are bad and defective arguments, but not so bad that they should be called fallacious? This leaves an avenue open that many of the texts appear to take. This is to forego any discussion of fallaciousness of appeals to authority and remain content with the task of distinguishing between the weak and the strong ones.

Purtill stays away from calling appeals to authority fallacious. Instead, he concludes that some of them should be taken seriously, but many more are "weak arguments" that should receive a critical examination (by asking critical questions) (1972, 69).

This approach could be based on the following philosophy. Perhaps the whole idea of fallaciousness is just too difficult to address, too problematic, or is an old idea that is no longer appropriate to appeal to, in modern logic. Now that we have various critical questions or requirements for the goodness (correctness) of appeal to authority as a type of argument, we should simply evaluate such an appeal as adequate (credible, justified), in a given case, if all the requirements are met. And then we should evaluate it as weak (incomplete, inadequate) if some of the requirements are not met. That is all we need to do, to evaluate cases, and we can give up the old, traditional idea of condemning such arguments as fallacious.

Many recent textbooks do, in fact, de-emphasize the fallacy aspect of appeals to authority. Soccio and Barry, in their section on appeal to authority do not even mention the word 'fallacy.' They state that we often have to rely on authority as a "secondary source of knowledge," but that there are "dangers in relying on authority as a source of knowledge" (1992, 53–54). To deal with these dangers, they use three critical questions as criteria to test an appeal to authority. But nowhere do they describe appeal to authority as a fallacy.

Little, Groarke and Tindale use the same style of approach, using critical questions, and not the concept of fallacy, in their evaluation of arguments from authority (1989, 260–65). They take a positive approach, setting out five critical criteria (see Chapter 7, section 3). Then they conclude their evaluation by saying that a "good argument from authority" must meet all five criteria (265).

This kind of approach could be justifiable. Once we have identified the form of the argument and the appropriate critical questions, then we can carry out the task of evaluating appeals to expert opinion as presumptively strong or weak (suspect), using these tools, as applied to a given case. We do not need to address, or even discuss, the additional task of evaluating such arguments as "fallacious" or not, in accord with the traditional concept of a fallacy, as outlined in Hamblin (1970). Perhaps we should be content, in the textbooks, to accomplish the former task and not worry about the concept of fallaciousness, implying a stronger form of condemnation. This approach could be a good one for the textbooks to take, at least provisionally. The main problem is that many of them continue to use the word 'fallacy,' identifying the committing of the *ad verecundiam* fallacy with the failure to answer one or more critical questions.

2. Specific Defaults Cited

Some textbooks appear to construe the fallacy quite narrowly. Copi equates the *ad verecundiam* fallacy with the kind of case where the opinion cited falls outside the authority's field.

> *Argumentum ad Verecundiam (appeal to authority)*. The *argumentum ad verecundiam* is the appeal to authority—that is, to the feeling of respect people have for the famous—to win assent to a conclusion. This method of argument is not always strictly fallacious, for the reference to an admitted authority in the special field of his competence may carry great weight and constitute relevant evidence. . . . But when an authority is appealed to for testimony in matters outside the province of his special field, the appeal commits the fallacy of *argumentum ad verecundiam*. (1953; 1972, 80)

Little, Wilson, and Moore also equate the fallacy with this same type of failure.

> *Misuse of Authority*. To quote a respected authority on an issue in his own field is a legitimate kind of argument, for in many situations we are forced to rely on the opinions of authorities. This kind of argument becomes a fallacy, however, when we cite an authority on an issue unrelated to his field of competence. (1955, 28)

Little, Wilson, and Moore recognize other critical questions that need to be answered in order to evaluate evidence from authority (178). But when it comes to the question of what makes this type of argument fallacious, the only explanation they give is the one above.

According to Hurley the appeal to authority (*ad verecundiam*) fallacy "occurs when the cited authority or witness is not trustworthy" (1991, 126). This approach, like those of Copi (1953) and Little, Wilson, and Moore (1955) cites one specific default, the failure to meet one particular requirement, as the basis of the fallacy. This is simply too narrow, however. For, as we have seen in Chapter 7, section 9, there are five other requirements, or critical questions, that ought to be considered in evaluating a case of the *ad verecundiam*. There is another factor to be considered, as well.

Suppose that a proponent of an argument supports it by an appeal to expert opinion, and a respondent then brings forward evidence to show either that this authority is not trustworthy, or that she is not an expert in the right field for that opinion. Does this mean that the proponent has committed an *ad verecundiam* fallacy? Not necessarily, it seems, especially if he acknowledges the weakness in his argument, as shown by the new evidence, and concedes that his presumptive argument from authority has defaulted.

Many of the textbooks focus on only two of the critical questions, and equate the *ad verecundiam* fallacy with failure to meet these two requirements. Blyth states that because the words 'expert' and 'authority' are "honorific" terms, the *ad verecundiam* fallacy results.

> As a result, the opinion of some authority is frequently quoted in support of a conclusion which lies wholly outside the field of competence of the authority quoted. In advertising it has become a common practice to buy an endorsement of a well-known figure without even presuming that the endorser really knows anything about the merits of the advertised product. This irrelevant appeal to authority has traditionally been called the *argumentum ad vericundiam*. (1957, 39)

Rescher notes only two standards, cited as the most common forms of "misappeal to experts."

> Utilization of expert opinion is, of course, a perfectly legitimate mode of reasoning, but it must always be safeguarded by two prerequisite standards: the opinion in question must actually be that of a genuine expert, and not simply a person whose notoriety excites interest, and it must be that of an expert in the field of the particular topic at issue. (1964, 81)

Barker, like Blyth, sees the fallacy as one of irrelevance, citing the failure of the same two conditions.

> If we appeal to some admired or famous person as if he were an authority on a certain question when really he is not, we are making this fallacious appeal to authority [the *argument ad*

verecundiam]. It is not always illogical to appeal to authorities; but we should not trust an authority outside his special proven field of competence. (1965, 192)

Carney and Scheer narrow the fallacy down to two factors, whether or not the person appealed to is an authority, and whether or not the field is right. "In order for an argument which is an appeal to authority to be a fallacy, it must be the case that the person whose opinion is being appealed to is not an authority in the area under consideration" (1964, 26). The accounts have broadened the basis of the fallacy somewhat, but still do not seem to be adequate to explain it properly.

Some textbooks go further than citing the failure of three conditions as the explanation of the fallacy. Facione and Scherer cite three factors:

> The fallacy of the misuse of authority occurs when people cite authorities whose competence is outside of the subject matter at hand, make up fictitious authorities or facts, or confuse genuine authority with popularity, fancy titles, and ceremonial behavior. (1978, 315)

Damer also defines the fallacy of "irrelevant" or questionable appeal to authority by citing three factors.

> *Definition*: This fallacy consists in attempting to support a claim by quoting the judgment of one who is not an authority in the field, the judgment of an unidentified authority, or the judgment of an authority who is likely to be significantly biased in some way. (1980, 93)

But these accounts still omit to mention the three other factors that, as we saw in Chapter 7, are equally important in evaluating *ad verecundiam* arguments.

The lack of agreement in the accounts of the fallacy surveyed above is confusing. But perhaps it suggests that some faults in appeals to authority are more serious than others. If the "authority" cited is definitely not an expert at all or is an expert only in a field that is not related to the issue at all (even remotely), then these seem to be serious violations. Could we say that these two faults should be singled out, among the list of critical questions, as especially devastating to the logic of an appeal to expert opinion? This kind of error seems to make the appeal totally worthless as an argument.

A hypothesis then would be that some of the types of failures to meet the six requirements are especially destructive and that, therefore, the *ad verecundiam* fallacy should be identified with these faults.

Johnson and Blair evaluate the fallacy of improper appeal to authority as a violation of one or more of five conditions (1983, 155; see also Fig. 8.1). These five conditions correspond to their five rules (see Chapter 7, section 3).

According to Johnson and Blair, any violation of any one of the five conditions "undermines the argumentative force of the appeal," but "some violations are more grievous than others" (1983, 155). This is an interesting and unusually subtle approach to evaluating appeals to authority as arguments because it distinguishes between certain violations that are weaker faults or errors that can be corrected or overcome by appropriate replies, and more serious types of violations that have a greater impact on the worth of the argument. Is it possible that these more serious types of violations could correspond to the fallacious uses of the argument from authority?

---

1. M appeals—tacitly or explicitly—to the authority of N in supporting claim Q (which belongs to domain of assertions, S).

2. (a) S is not a domain in which authoritative knowledge can, or does, exist; or
   (b) N is not an authority about matters in domain S; or
   (c) Although S is in general a domain of knowledge, there is among authorities in S a lack of consensus that such claims as Q are true; or
   (d) N has a special interest in Q's being accepted; or
   (e) N is not identified sufficiently to enable one to check N's credentials.

Fig. 8.1. Improper Appeal to Authority (Johnson and Blair 1983)

Johnson and Blair write that if 2(a) or 2(b) is violated, "there is no way to patch up that part of the argument." But the force of violating 2(c) can vary widely, depending on whether there is an established theory in the field, on the proposition Q. The effect of a violation of 2(d) is to "put a question mark beside Q" but is not "fatal" to the argument. The effect of a violation of 2(e) is only to postpone acceptance of Q until N's credentials can be checked out (155–56).

In fact, however, this attempt to single out certain requirements as more grievous than others does not work very well. For all six of our conditions (given in Chapter 7) can fail to a greater or lesser degree. The worst failure generally seems to be the first one (not being an expert), but even that can be partial, if the authority cited is not a fully qualified expert, but still has some skills or experience in a field greater than that of a layperson.

And the other five requirements can fail so drastically to obtain, in some cases, that it would justify calling the *ad verecundiam* fallacious. But it does seem that Johnson and Blair are onto something here. What is important, it seems, is not so much which particular requirement has failed, in a given case, to make us call it "fallacious" as opposed to "weak." What is important is how it failed, or how strongly it failed. If a requirement fails so badly it seems to somehow block the whole argument exchange, that is when it appears to be appropriate to call it an *ad verecundiam* fallacy.

The problem with the kinds of cases of worrisome appeals to expert opinion that are identified with the fallacious *ad verecundiam* is that the appeal poses as an expert scientific conclusion, while at the same time, it shows evidence of a mind-set that is closed to scientific information or testing. Gardner comments on Case 1.2 (1993, 374), the kind of court case where recovered memory is put forward as evidence, that the therapists are motivated not by money, but by a sincere feeling that they are helping their patients. But this feeling appears to be ideological in nature, even perhaps religious. Gardner compares it to the church officials that "cured" witches by torture, burning, and hanging.

The problem of appeal to expert opinion in these kinds of cases is that the whole framework of the dialogue is one-sided. In their zeal to push ahead with their cause, the advocates of one side leave no room for the other side to even raise critical questions about how they got their evidence. According to Gardner, although the therapists usually deny asking leading questions in their interviews, tapes of their sessions yield questions like, "You sound to me like the sort of person who must have been sexually abused. Tell me what that bastard did to you" (374). This kind of approach is problematic, because it shows a consistent pattern of blocking out any consideration of any argument or evidence for the opposing (or questioning) point of view.

The comparison between use of expert "scientific" testimony of abuse therapists—so-called traumatists—and the persecutions in the European witch craze of the sixteenth and seventeenth centuries in Europe was noted in connection with the discussion of Case 1.2. Theological experts using demonological manuals supplied evidence, including so-called spectral evidence, of a kind that was impossible to critically examine or to test by counterevidence. This "evidence" was not possible for a nonexpert to observe, and anyone who questioned it was said to be in league with the devil—a "heretic" or nonbeliever. This kind of use of appeal to expert opinion is closed to questioning by a nonexpert.

3. Dogmatic Appeals to Authority

A different hypothesis now put forward for consideration is that the *ad verecundiam* fallacy is not to be identified with the failure to meet any one or any combination of the six critical requirements but instead should be identified with how the appeal to authority was put forward in the dialogue in the text of discourse in a given case. This test for the fallaciousness of an *ad verecundiam* argument is a pragmatic one because it relates to how the form of argument for appeal to expert opinion was used in dialogue, in a given case, in relation to the potential use of the appropriate critical questions.

Some textbooks have already advocated such an approach by linking the committing of the *ad verecundiam* fallacy with a particular way of putting such an argument forward, to appear to make it unchallengeable (not open to critical questioning).

Creighton stated that appeal to authority becomes fallacious when put forward uncritically, i.e., when "we suppose that [the authority's] opinion amounts to proof, or forbids us to consider the matter for ourselves." The explanation of fallaciousness given here is that the fallacious appeal is one that is put forward so dogmatically or absolutistically that it blocks out "consideration of the arguments which are advanced for or against the position" (1904, 170). This seems to suggest the Lockean distinction between *ad judicium* and *ad verecundiam* arguments, the problem indicated being that the former is taken in an inappropriately absolutistic way, so that it blocks out the former (which should really have priority, or at any rate, not be excluded). This account also suggests that the blocking of critical questions is what makes such an appeal fallacious.

Black outlined a number of critical questions or tests to be used to judge whether an appeal to authority is a good argument or not. But then he went beyond this to suggest a factor (dogmatism) that can make such an argument fallacious.

> To call an authority good is to say that he satisfies the tests outlined in the preceding paragraphs. When a person regularly submits the authority upon which he relies to the tests described, the appeal to authority may be said to be critical or undogmatic. When the authority is held to have the last, unchallengeable word upon a subject, we have dogmatic appeal to authority. (1946, 234)

According to Black, "the need to discriminate between dogmatic from undogmatic appeals to authority calls for constant vigilance." But what defines a dogmatic appeal to authority? Black writes that when it is "set out baldly," it is the argument, "I believe X because A says that X is true; and I believe in A because I believe that A ought to be believed" (235). In other words, in a dogmatic appeal to authority, the arguer tries to shield off the need to produce any evidence that the authority is credible.

Schipper and Schuh (1959, 39–40) see dogmatic authority as only one of five distinct fallacies of illicit appeal to authority. But it is interesting to see how they define the concept of a dogmatic appeal to authority.

> An appeal can be made to a specifically named authority, and still be fallacious, if the authority is dogmatic rather than expert. Of course, the words "dogmatic" and "expert" are used in a number of different ways. In the present context, however, the term *dogmatic* characterizes an authority beyond which there is no appeal—a final, ultimate, infallible authority, neither requiring nor offering any reasons or evidence for his specific pronouncements. An *expert* authority, on the other hand, is one whose prestige in some field is based, not so much on title or rank or number of academic degrees, as on special training and the ability, if questioned, to support his pronouncements with reasons or evidence that is open to public scrutiny.

They go on to add that the dogmatic assertion of authority is not the fallacy we are seeking to analyze here. It is only when one party in an argument tries to prove his opinion by appealing to an authority in a dogmatic manner that is not open to critical examination.

> We must be careful, however, not to confuse the *appeal* to dogmatic authority with the *assertion* of such authority. It is not a fallacy to assert or claim to be a final, irrefutable authority in any or even all fields. For this assertion is not an argument and thus, while it might be false, cannot be fallacious. Only when the attempt is made to *prove* a statement by calling upon some incontestable authority may we speak of the *fallacy* of dogmatic authority. (40)

The point here, harking back to our dialectical analysis of Chapter 4, is that three participants are involved. It is a matter of how one party presents or uses the opinion of an expert he cites, in an argument with a third party.

What is important here in evaluating whether or not an *ad vere-cundiam* fallacy can justifiably be said to have been committed in a particular case is not just whether the form of argument for appeal to expert opinion was used, but how it was used. But how do we identify dogmatic usage in a particular case? What sort of evidence is to be used in evaluating a claim that such an argument is fallacious or not?

The answer is that we should look at the discourse in a given case, looking for evidence of closure or finality in how the argument has been put forward.[1] We need to remember, above all, as Chapters 3 through 7 indicated, that the appeal to expert opinion is a presumptive type of argument characteristically that should be regarded as open to default and critical questioning. If it is put forward, in a given case, as an unchallengeable argument, the "last word" on the subject, this use of it is an especially serious kind of failure that can have the effect of blocking a critical discussion.

Toulmin, Rieke, and Janik think that appeal to authority can be reasonable, and questionable in other cases, but that it only becomes "fallacious at the point where authority is invoked as the *last word* on a given topic" (1979, 171). Or, as they put it, "appeals to authority become fallacious only when expert opinion is invoked in an argument precisely to stifle further inquiry rather than to illuminate the issue in question" (172). What is to be looked for here, to identify an argument from authority as fallacious, is evidence of the proponent treating the appeal in a certain way, in his exchange of views with the other party in the dialogue. The argument is fallacious, as opposed to being merely suspect, if the proponent treats the authority as infallible, or the final word, implying that the dialogue is closed and the argument settled.

In the fallacious kind of case of the appeal to expert opinion, the proponent who uses the appeal carries on the dialogue in such a way as to shield off the critical questioning of the respondent, implying (or even stating) that a peirastic interval for asking critical questions is inappropriate in the dialogue the participants are supposed to be engaged in. The Lorenzo's Oil case is not a particularly good illustration of the *ad verecundiam* fallacy, because those opposing the attempts of the Odones to ask critical questions were not supporting a particular appeal to expert opinion argument (that is easy to specify). But the Lorenzo's Oil case is an excellent illustration of the kind of case where

---

1. A study of verbal indicators of this preemptive attitude to critical questioning in argumentation has been undertaken by Snoeck Henkemans (1992).

critical questioning in a peirastic interlude in a dialogue is treated as inappropriate.

How a dialogue can shield off critical questioning that is deemed inappropriate in a scientific inquiry is well illustrated in the family conference in the Lorenzo's Oil case. When the Odones asked questions about treatments for ALD, or asked for a show of hands that would indicate how well the current experimental treatment was working, the chairpersons of the meeting deflected off this questioning by arguing that it is the "solemn responsibility of the doctors" to conduct experimental research with "strict protocol" and use of clinical trials and control groups. The questions raised by the Odones were portrayed as inappropriate for the discussion at the meeting, and even "meaningless." Each time the Odones raised questions, the reply was that the questions were not appropriate for medical science.

The family conference dialogue serves as an excellent case study to typify the attitude of an arguer in a dialogue, as revealed by his repeated attempts to close off critical questioning by asserting or implying that any critical examination or testing of what the experts said is inappropriate in the type of dialogue the participants are supposed to be taking part in. Thus the *ad verecundiam* fallacy, when it is indicated by dialectical evidence of this sort, is not just an error of missing a premise in the form of the appeal to expert opinion, or failing to respond to a particular critical question. It is a more global failure to allow for any sort of peirastic argumentation at all. It has to do with an attitude of not being open to critical questioning at all.

Evidence for this "final word" characteristic of the use of *ad verecundiam* arguments is to be found in how the argument is put forward, and in how attempts to raise critical questions, in subsequent dialogue, are dealt with. The attitude of the proponent who commits this type of fallacy is one of not being open to critical questioning, by suggesting to the other party that the other party has no right to such critical questioning, that raising questions is inappropriate. As Locke put it, "it is looked upon as insolence" to set one's own opinion up against that of some "learned doctor" or "approved writer" (see Chapter 2, section 7). Thus an arguer displays this dogmatic attitude by putting forward his argument from authority in such a way that it is implied that it would be inappropriate for the other party to question it.[2] The fallacy is aimed to exploit the submissiveness or obedience to authority of the other party.

2. A dogmatic attitude as characteristic of the committing of fallacies has been studied in Walton (1992a, 284).

4. The Halo Effect and Milgram's Experiments

The Lockean concept of "respect" or "submission" was often incorporated into the logic textbooks, who tried to explain the *ad verecundiam* fallacy by appeal to the concept of "relevance," as we saw in Chapter 3.

Beardsley explained the *argument from illegitimate authority* (the word 'illegitimate' defining it as a fallacy or bad argument) in Lockean terms of respect and reverence.

> *The argument from illegitimate authority.* "As the atomic scientists say . . . as great men of the past agree . . . as I was taught at my mother's knee. . . ." By such appeals to authority, by invoking our willingness to be guided by those who really know more than we do, the speaker seeks to bolster up his claims. (1950, 134)

Ruby explained the *ad verecundiam* as a fallacy using a Lockean analysis that invokes the concept of reverence.

> The appeal to authority is often called the "Argumentum ad Verecundiam," a learned-sounding Latin phrase which means the "appeal to reverence." A revered authority or tradition is often regarded as infallible, so that anyone who disagrees is in some sense disloyal to that which ought to be revered. (1950, 129)

But what does "respect" or "reverence" really mean? Is it a concept that could be defined in a more specific way?

One way to do this is to link this older concept of submissive respect or "reverence" with recent experimental findings in social psychology. Social psychologists have observed that responding to social and institutional expectations in certain kinds of structured situations is powerfully influenced by something called the "halo effect." This means that someone such as a physician, who appears in a clinical setting, appears as a powerful figure, so that whatever he says appears to have authority. One textbook has even cited this "halo effect" as a factor in the fallaciousness of *ad verecundiam* arguments. Cederblom and Paulsen describe appeal to authority as a type of argument that is often legitimate, but can also be a type of argument that uses "sleight of hand" and is fallacious. They attribute this to a "halo effect."

> It is certainly not a fallacy to say you should take a particular medicine because a doctor prescribed it. Since we don't have time to become experts in every field, it often makes sense to

trust someone (without limits) who has proof of expertise in a certain field. Unfortunately, a "halo" effect seems to apply to statements that lie outside an expert's area of knowledge. (1991, 156)

What then is this "halo effect" and how does it work?

Amabile and Hasdorf define the *halo effect* as arising from the "logical error" of seeing different traits as "belonging together when they logically do not": "When the halo effect occurs, the error consists of assuming the presence of many positive traits from the existence of one favorable characteristic" (1976, 247). Thorndike (1920, 29) found, when army officers were asked to rate their subordinates on traits like intelligence, leadership, physique, and so forth, he found that if a special ability was found as a trait in one soldier, the officer tended to exaggerate the other positive traits of that soldier, extending a "halo of general merit." Cialdini (1988, 161–63) found that physical attractiveness produces a halo that favorably influences ratings of other perceived traits like kindness, honesty or intelligence. Fairweather (1988, 345) found an "institutional halo" that leads respondents to judge departments or programs of prestigious universities more highly than they merit. It is this institutional halo in particular that is such a powerful factor in explaining obedience to authority.

The classic experiments on obedience to authority were carried out by Milgram (1974; 1977). The point of the experiment was to find out how strong an electric shock a subject is willing to administer to a victim, following instructions given (authoritatively) by an experimenter. The machine used was a "shock generator," marked with a series of switches going from "slight shock" to "moderate shock," and so forth, all the way up to "severe shock": "The subject was told to administer a shock to the learner each time he gave a wrong response to a test question." If the subject asked whether the victim would suffer injury from these shocks, the experimenter replied, "Although the shocks may be painful, there is no permanent tissue damage, so please go on" (1974, 20). These experiments were conducted in a modern scientific laboratory which would convey an atmosphere of scientific authority to the situation, as the subject saw it.

Actually, the victims did not receive any shocks but they could be seen by the subject, to make painful groans and protests when the more severe shocks were given. But if the subject indicated he did not wish to continue giving more stronger shocks, the experimenter would reply firmly, but in a neutral voice, something like, "It is absolutely essential that you continue" (21). Or if the victim cries out that he can no longer stand the pain, the experimenter says to the subject, "You have no other choice, you must go on!" (Milgram 1979, 104).

The results of the experiments showed that ordinary, decent people were persuaded to perform what they thought were harsh and punitive acts to a remarkable degree that surprised the psychologists.

> With numbing regularity good people were seen to knuckle under the demands of authority and perform actions that were callous and severe. Men who are in everyday life responsible and decent were seduced by the trappings of authority, by the control of their perceptions, and by the uncritical acceptance of the experimenter's definition of the situation, into performing harsh acts. (Milgram 1977, 120)

Milgram added that even when the victim claimed heart trouble, cried out, or pleaded to be set free, subjects continued to shock him. A quarter of the subjects went to the highest shock level.

What could explain this curious and unanticipated result? Milgram attributes a lot to the "situational etiquette" that governs behavior appropriate for a given social occasion (149). If the subject discontinues the shocking, he will appear "arrogant, untoward and rude," by "turning against the experimental authority" as the experimental situation has been designed to appear to him (150). Although the subject could, in reality, quit at any time (and some did), a surprising number seemed to be cowed by a respectful attitude to someone whom they perceived as a scientific authority, as the experimenters had defined the situation. The institutional setting of the situation seemed to be a powerful factor in this.

5. Institutional Setting of Authority

When an appeal to expert opinion is used to support an argument, it should normally be presumed that the appeal is open to critical questioning and scrutiny and evaluation by logical reasoning (Van Eemeren and Grootendorst 1984 and 1992). However, science and professional fields of expertise (like medicine) also have a definite institutional character. They are, in fact, institutions that are closed to nonmembers, and like other institutions they have their customs, codes of conduct, hierarchies, and rulings affecting how one is permitted to behave. Thus they have an institutional authority that makes their claims appear generally not to be subject to critical questioning or logical challenge by an outsider, which may, in fact, make it difficult for an outsider to even dare to ask such questions.

So it is not only the halo effect that tends to discourage people from asking questions of respected doctors or scientists. There are very real deterrents. One can easily be made to look foolish or even "crazy" by questioning the opinion of a physician or scientist. There are also punitive sanctions for such behavior that might be brought into play.

The questioning of the expert opinion of a physician by a patient is a special type of case in point. As Inlander, Levin, and Weiner point out, there is a special aura about medicine, and American medicine in particular, that confers a high level of respect and privilege on anyone who has the special designation *doctor of medicine* (1988, 14). Even though the doctor-patient relationship has changed over the years, from a passive one-sided relationship to more of an economic relationship of consumer-provider, one where more active questioning and criticism by users of the system should be invited, the tradition of the passive, one-sided doctor-patient dialogue persists.

> Doctors over recent generations have established the ground rules for patient behavior, especially regarding the patient's relationship to (and critique of) the doctor. Many of us are taught (or intuit) that it is not good form to play too active a role, never mind a contentious one. Questions to doctors should be polite and deferential, acknowledging their superior knowledge and the wisdom of experience. If we are irritated with the doctor's demeanor in any way or left with any uneasy feeling that something is not right in the care being given, we might save our gripes for relatives or friends. Challenging the doctor is simply too difficult, too embarrassing, too fraught (we believe) with the potential for retribution. (15)

Patients who want access to their medical records or who try to become informed about their problem by studying medical literature may be treated by their physician as meddlesome or "difficult." They may even be diagnosed as showing symptoms of psychological instability. In fact, there has been a tendency to categorize patients who take notes to try to keep track of what a doctor is telling them as "emotionally disturbed." A tag given by doctors to describe this condition is *la maladie du petit papier,* stigmatizing the notetaker as psychoneurotic (197). What is particularly intimidating about these tendencies is that the doctor has the power to shield off or close down the patient's questioning of his opinions by disqualifying the patient from taking part in any kind of rational argument at all on purely medical grounds. The institutional framework of modern medicine and the aura of the doctor as a professional with superior knowledge not only create a halo effect that inevitably leaves the patient in a vulnerable and epistemically weak position to argue, even when arguments that would normally be considered highly persuasive are used. It also puts sanctions in place that can be and are used to penalize patients who appear to the doctor to be too inquisitive.

On the other hand, as more and more medical information has become available to consumers—for example, in the form of computerized data bases—more people are increasingly willing to critically assess medical information themselves, get a second opinion, try alternative therapies, and generally take what physicians say less uncritically, on a trust basis alone, than they used to. In general, respect for opinions purporting to represent the findings of science tends to be more qualified than it used to be.

In Chapter 1, I noted that in postacademic science the increased funding and control of scientific research by corporate and government bodies has meant a decline in public respect for scientific objectivity. In Chapter 6, the intrusion of junk science into the justice system has been documented in cases where expert opinions have been used successfully to support jury decisions that appear to be absurd to the casual observer who is not involved. Indeed the adversarial American justice system, in particular, seems to feature cases where expert opinions on one side conflict with opinions claimed by experts with equally impressive credentials on the other side. The circus atmosphere of these trials, some of which have been widely televised, must have had some effect on lowering public respect for scientific objectivity.

The institutional aura and the halo effect for physicians, scientists, and other qualified experts still exist and are strong factors in explaining how people react to appeals to expert opinion. But a certain erosion of respect has been the trend of recent years, restoring the balance somewhat to an acceptance of the need to evaluate the uses of expert opinion in a more dialectical and open-minded way. The key to evaluating appeals to expert opinion used in arguments is to balance qualified respect with an openness to critical questioning.

6. Fallible Arguments Absolutized

Cederblom and Paulsen were right to stress that there is nothing logically wrong or fallacious about taking the advice of your physician, or at least giving her opinion special weight in deciding what form of action to take in relation to some concern about your health (1982). Such an appeal to authority is fallacious only when the argument is put forward in such a way that it is made to appear stronger than is justified, or even absolutely conclusive to determine your actions.

The nature of appeal to authority as a type of argument that needs to be seen as open to criticism was well expressed by Fowler.

> We have to learn not only that men are to be trusted exclusively within the limits of their own experience, in their own profession or pursuit, but that even within those limits their authority is apt to become tyrannical and irrational unless it is constantly confronted with facts and subject to the criticism of others. (1870, 269–70)

The problem is that it is easy to become overconfident or absolutistic in using appeal to authority and "leap" to the conclusion that an authority can be relied upon unquestionably.

Collier argues that the claims based on an appeal to expert opinion are justified as *rules of thumb*—time- and labor-saving devices that help us to act rationally, for practical purposes, in situations where we lack access to complete information (1992, 156). Rules of thumb correspond to rules warranting what I called "presumptive inferences" in Chapter 3. They are rules based on generalizations that do not hold for *all* cases, but only for normal or typical cases (subject to exceptions, and to default, as new information comes in, in a case) (Rescher 1976). On such a basis, following the advice of an institutional authority can have provisional justification.

> Following the advice of better informed and more experienced 'authorities' (who cannot or will not share their information and experience with us) spares us the time and trouble of re-examining every decision on the merits *au fond;* and coordinating the actions of many people may be possible only if they delegate some authority of decision and surrender some rights to assess the soundness of various courses of action and to determine for themselves what to do. Under these relatively normal conditions, the fact that a superior has issued a command or order is *a* reason, though not necessarily an overriding reason, for obeying it; and it is a reason that does not go to the merits of the decision in the sense of rationally justifying it 'on the balance of reasons.' (Collier 1992, 156)

But the problem Collier sees is that scientific authority can also have a "dark side" that is a special case of institutional authority—the "biasing halo" of the trappings of institutional science can "secure a form of compliance that cannot be justified on intellectual grounds" (157). Although its being attested to by an expert opinion may be one reason for accepting an argument, what needs to be recognized is that there can be other relevant reasons that should count against accepting the argument.

The older textbooks often saw the *ad verecundiam* fallacy as purely a failure of logical form—a kind of error or failure of correctness of an argument that could be determined by examining the premises and conclusion of the argument. For example, Wesley Salmon saw the fallaciousness of an argument from authority as something that is determined by its logical form. Arguments of the form (F1) are according to Salmon "clearly fallacious," while arguments of the form (F3) are "inductively correct" (1963, 63; see also Chapter 4, section 3). On how this fallacy works to deceive people, Salmon does not have much to say, except that it "appeals to emotion": "To sum up, arguments of form [F3] are inductively correct, while those of form [F1] are fallacious. Fallacious appeals to authority are usually appeals to emotion rather than appeals to evidence" (67). But what is really the basis of fallacious appeals to authority is a dialectical failure—the argument has been put forward as though it were unquestionably correct, as though the premises, once accepted as true, make it absolutely necessary to accept the conclusion as true as well, without any possibility of raising doubts. Thus the basic *ad verecundiam* fallacy in its most general form is the presenting of an argument from authority in such a way that the asking of appropriate critical questions is blocked by making it seem improper.

One insightful early textbook account hit on something very important in stating that the *ad verecundiam* fallacy is committed "when an 'authority' is accepted uncritically" (Werkmeister 1948, 61). The observation made here is that the fallacy resides in the matter of how the opinion of the alleged authority was brought forward by the arguer who used it. The fallaciousness is to be sought in the manner of presentation (Chapter 5, section 6). The word "uncritically" is key. If the manner of presentation does not allow for the asking of appropriate critical questions, that is the mark of fallacy.

I have argued that the appeal to authority is, by its nature, a fallible and defeasible type of argument that is open to critical questioning. But the problem is that we sometimes tend to forget this, or even to ignore or suppress it, treating the appeal to authority as much more final than it should be taken.

The view of 'fallacy' presented in Walton (1995) is the dialectical view that a fallacy is not just a weak or questionable argument, but an argument used to block or interfere with the legitimate goal of the type of dialogue the arguer is supposed to be engaging in. The dialectical framework of Walton 1995, when used as a normative structure for evaluating appeals to expert opinion that are used to support arguments, does have a certain postmodern quality. For this framework recognizes several types of dialogue—in effect, what is advocated is the use of several standards of rational argument, depending on the context of conversation being used. In particular, the framework for evaluating appeals to expert opinion involves an embedding of one type of dialogue into another. It begins with an expert consultation type of dialogue and then embeds a persuasion dialogue into it as the dialogue framework for a peirastic interlude where the layperson critically questions, probes, and tests out the opinions the expert has put forward in the expert consultation dialogue. But this analysis is not the whole story of the *ad verecundiam* fallacy.

7. Confusing Two Types of Authority

Another explanation of the basis of some cases of the *ad verecundiam* fallacy is that the appeal rests on a confusion between cognitive authority, which is always subject to critical questioning, and institutional or administrative authority, which often tends to be more coercive and absolutistic in nature. The fallacy, according to this explanation, is to treat or portray an argument that is an appeal to cognitive authority as though it derives its weight as an argument not from reason, but from a sanctioned institutional kind of authority structure that leaves you no choice but to obey the command to follow the course of action indicated or to take the opinion given as mandatory and unchallengeable.

The source of the fallacy, according to this explanation, is the equivocation on the ambiguity of the two meanings of 'authority' outlined in Chapter 3, section 5. Such an explanation of the logical difficulties arising from this ambiguity was given by Cohen and Nagel.

> We may distinguish two forms of the appeal to authority. One form is inevitable and reasonable. It is employed whenever we are unable for lack of time or training to settle some problem, such as, What diet or exercise will relieve certain distressing symptoms? or, What was the system of weights which the

Egyptians used? We then leave the resolution of the problem to experts, whose authority is acknowledged. But their authority is only relatively final, and we reserve the right to others (also competent to judge), or to ourselves (finding the time to acquire competence), to modify the findings of our expert. The second form of the appeal to authority invests some sources with infallibility and finality and invokes some external force to give sanction to their decisions. On questions of politics, economics, and social conduct, as well as on religious opinions, the method of authority has been used to root out, as heretical or disloyal, divergent opinions. Men have been frightened and punished into conformity in order to prevent alternative views from unsettling our habitual beliefs. (1934, 194)

Cohen's and Nagel's aim here is not to evaluate the *ad verecundiam* fallacy but to study methods used for the fixation of belief, particularly in scientific reasoning. But what they say can be applied to the *ad verecundiam* fallacy. The error or deception is to take an expert opinion that should be treated as presumptive, subjective, and open to critical questioning and invest it with "infallibility and finality," even perhaps invoking "external force" to give it "sanction." The error is an unlicensed shift from one type of "authority" to another, portraying an argument as something it is not.

Citing Edward Gibbon, author of the *Decline and Fall of the Roman Empire* (1911), who wrote that intellectual disciplines should have "freedom of inquiry" and submit only "to the force of persuasion" (1992, 144), Charles Collier drew a distinction between two types of authority, intellectual authority and institutional authority.

What Gibbon termed the pure 'force of persuasion,' unaided and unhindered by institutional context, I refer to as 'intellectual authority.' This has been defined as 'the authority exerted by arguments that make their way simply by virtue of a superior rationality and do not depend for their impact on the lines of power and influence operating in an institution.' The contrasting notion of 'institutional authority' refers to the non-intellectual influence exerted by social, political, cultural, historical, legal, literary, education, religious, and other institutions. (145)

Collier makes the point that with arguments based on intellectual authority, you always have to be open to seriously and sympathetically considering the arguments on the other side, even if you are strongly inclined to be against them (146).

We may presume that what Collier calls intellectual authority is the same concept I defined as "cognitive authority" in Chapter 3, and that what Collier calls institutional authority is comparable to, or perhaps is even equivalent to, what I have called "administrative authority."

From this fundamental distinction between these two basic types of authority, an explanation of how the *ad verecundiam* fallacy works can be generated. Intellectual or cognitive authority need to be used (at least typically, or at least characteristically) as open to challenge, so that arguments resting on it are provisional and subjective in nature. They carry a weight of presumption, but it may need to be withdrawn if new evidence comes into consideration in a case. In contrast, administrative or institutional authority is often final and enforced coercively, so that it is not open to challenge in the same way. Thus treating the authority backing an argument as though it were of the latter sort, when it is really supposed to be of the former sort, is a serious and systematic misuse of argument from authority. It can be a bad error or, perhaps even worse, it can be used as a sophistical tactic to unfairly get the best of a partner in argumentation.

Thus we have three ways an appeal to authority fallacy can occur: (1) an appeal to institutional authority can be presented in such a way that it appears to be more absolute (less open to critical questioning) than it really is; (2) the same thing can happen with an appeal to expert opinion (an appeal to cognitive authority); or, (3) the two types of appeals can be confused. In particular, the most common type of fallacy occurring here is the kind of case where an appeal to expertise (cognitive authority) is confused with an appeal to institutional authority, particularly where the institutional authority is portrayed as having a finality or absolute authority that admits of no critical questions. This is the *ad verecundiam* fallacy I have primarily been concerned with.

What is common to all three ways, as a fundamental basis of the *ad verecundiam* fallacy, is the suppression of critical questioning by making the appeal to authority seem more absolute than it really is. But how is this factor of suppression of critical questioning evident in a case where appeal to expert opinion has been used as an argument? What sort of evidence can be collected and then used to back up a claim that an *ad verecundiam* fallacy has been committed (as opposed to the kind of case where the appeal to expert opinion is merely weak, or open to critical questioning, as opposed to being fallacious)? Obviously such evidence must come somehow from the way the argument has been used in a context of dialogue. But is there any more specific way of linking the given argument to the 'suppression factor'?

8. Profiles of Dialogue

In evaluating cases of an appeal to expert opinion used in an argument, one important tool is the sets of critical questions I have given in Chapter 7, section 9. But there is another tool available (currently being developed [see Walton 1989a; Krabbe 1992]) that can be used as well. A *profile of dialogue* is a relatively short sequence of question-reply exchanges in a dialogue that represents how a sequence of exchanges should proceed (Walton 1989c, 67) at a local level of some type of global dialogue the participants are supposed to be engaged in (Walton 1989a, 37–38). According to Krabbe, profiles of dialogue can be described as "tree-shaped descriptions of sequences of dialectic that display the various ways a reasonable dialogue could proceed," that can be used to analyze or discuss fallacies or critical moves "without having to go through all the technical preliminaries for the complete definition of a dialogue system" (1992, 277). Such profiles of dialogue can be used to model the dynamics, in a dialogue exchange, both of how a proponent has put an argument forward in a dialogue, and how a respondent has replied or reacted to the putting forward of the argument.

In evaluating particular cases of the use of appeal to expert opinion as an argument, the mark of the fallacious type of case is the dogmatic or "suppressing" way of putting the argument by the proponent that interferes with the respondent's asking of appropriate critical questions at the next move, or moves, appearing to leave the respondent no room to pose critical question. For example, consider the following schematized sequences of a dialogue.

Case 8.1:   Respondent: Why A?
            Proponent: Because E asserts that A, and E is an expert.
            Respondent: Is E's assertion based on evidence?
            Proponent: How could you evaluate such evidence? You are not an expert in this field of scientific knowledge.
            Respondent: No, I'm not an expert, but surely I have the right to ask what evidence E based her opinion on.

Proponent: The assessment of this kind of clinical
              evidence is the solemn responsibility of
              the scientists. You are not even a scientist!

To evaluate the sequence of argumentation in this case of a somewhat
abstracted text of a dialogue exchange, one needs to go back to the list
of critical questions given in Chapter 7, and cite the sixth critical question, 'Is E's assertion based on evidence?' Then one needs to recall the
general instructions given in Chapter 7, section 10, on how critical
questions should be used for evaluation of a case. When critical question 6 is asked by a respondent, the proponent who has put forward an
appeal to expert opinion at the prior move, in order to properly answer
the critical question, must (1) cite the evidence the expert's assertion
was based on, or (2) if that is not known, or (3) if the assertion was not
based on any specific evidence that can be cited, then the proponent
needs to admit such a lack of evidence. The necessity of these branch-
ing options, set into place in a dialogue by an asking of a critical question 6, sets up a profile of dialogue that represents how the sequence of
dialogue should ideally go in this kind of juncture in a dialogue.

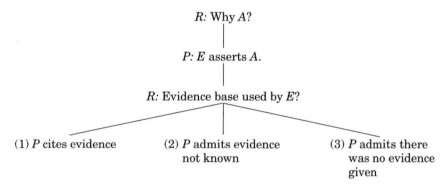

R: Why A?

P: E asserts A.

R: Evidence base used by E?

(1) P cites evidence   (2) P admits evidence   (3) P admits there
                                  not known   was no evidence
                                                                  given

Fig. 8.2. Example of a Profile of Dialogue

The rough sketch of a profile given in Figure 8.2 shows the proper
sequence the exchange should take into account as evidence the local
moves surrounding this kind of case of an appeal to authority.
    To evaluate whether a fallacy of the *ad verecundiam* type has been
committed in an argument having the general outline of the sequence
of dialogue indicated in Case 8.1, the profile of dialogue in Figure 8.2 is
applied to see how it fits the actual sequence of dialogue in the case.
The abstracted outline of a dialogue sequence represented in Case 8.1

represents the way the sequence of dialogue actually went in a real case (presumably), and the profile of dialogue represents a normative model of how the sequence of dialogue should have gone, according to the goals and rules of a particular type of dialogue. As Krabbe shows by other examples (1992, 80), the task of using the profile to relate to these rules and goals of a global dialogue is frequently complicated by one type of dialogue being embedded in another. In evaluating a case like 8.1, the sequence of argumentation presumes a somewhat complex framework of the kind outlined in Chapter 5. The given persuasion dialogue is based on the presumption of a prior information exchange between the proponent (*P*) and the expert (*E*), and also needs to allow for peirastic questioning by the respondent (*R*). Within such a global dialectical context of use, the argument can be evaluated, using the profile as a tool.

9. Subfallacies

According to our analysis, then, an appeal to authority argument can be (a) reasonable (presumptively acceptable), (b) weak (presumptively unacceptable because inadequately supported by appropriate evidence), or (c) fallacious. The (c) category arises when the argument is put forward in a dogmatic way, making it appear to be conclusive when it is really not. As we saw in Chapter 3, sometimes appeals to expert opinion are (legitimately) conclusive as arguments. But normally, and in the vast majority of cases where they are used in everyday argumentation of the kind studied in the logic textbooks' sections on fallacies, they are not (Rescher 1976).

So I propose a revision of the textbooks so that the generic *ad verecundiam* fallacy be analyzed as a fallacy of the dogmatic use of the argument from authority. This involves changing the standard treatment, because some textbooks currently treat dogmatic authority as only one subspecies of the generic *ad verecundiam* fallacy.

Schipper and Schuh distinguish five fallacies of authority: (1) *sweeping authority,* where the source is not specified well enough, or identified; (2) *dogmatic authority,* where the authority is held to be "ultimate" or "infallible"; (3) *misplaced authority,* where the field is wrong; (4) *misrepresented authority,* where what the authority said is changed in meaning; and (5) *venerable authority,* where veneration or glamour is substituted for real authority (1959, 38–45). Schipper and Schuh see these five fallacies as best examined separately, even though they all come under the general heading of "illicit appeal to authority" (38).

Michalos takes the entirely different approach of defining the *fallacy of irrelevant authority* as failure (2) above, and the *fallacy of misplaced authority* as the kind of case where either (4) or (5) occurs (1986, 43). Michalos classifies (something closer to) what we call the generic *ad verecundiam* fallacy under an entirely different fallacy name. "The fallacy of deceiving people with a confident manner is committed when, in the absence of a legitimate argument, one behaves as if one had a conclusive demonstration of one's view" (37). This seems to be an even more general category of fallacy, under which our generic *ad verecundiam* fallacy would fall as a special type of case.

Kilgore distinguishes three subtypes of the fallacy of misusing appeal to authoritative sources: (1) *misplaced authority,* where the field, or subject area, is wrong; (2) *appeal to celebrity,* where fame or popularity, rather than competence, is relied upon; (3) *appeal to common consensus,* where "alleged general belief of mankind" is the basis (1968, 59–60). The third fallacy would normally, and probably more properly, be dealt with under the heading of the *ad populum* fallacy. Kilgore's (1) corresponds to Schipper's and Schuh's (3), even in the name, 'misplaced authority' (Michalos uses the same name differently). And (1), also a common category found in the textbook treatments, seems to be pretty much the same as what Schipper and Schuh call 'venerable authority.'

Needless to say, this go-it-alone heterogeneity of treatments and classifications of *ad verecundiam* fallacies in the textbooks is a symptom of the failure to base these accounts on results of any research on appeal to authority as a type of argumentation. However, the basic idea of having several subfallacies under the generic *ad verecundiam* fallacy is useful. Based on my analysis of the fallacy, I propose the following set of five specific subfallacies.

If critical question 1 (How credible is E as an expert source?) is blocked, this is to be called the *fallacy of nonauthority.* Subfallacies under this fallacy are the *fallacy of appeal to celebrity* and the *fallacy of unidentified authority,* where the name of the expert is not given (and the appeal is presented in such a way that it is presumed there is no need to give the name, and that to ask for it would be inappropriate). Under critical question 2 (concerning the field), the *fallacy of misplaced authority* is a subfallacy that occurs where the field is definitely wrong. Under critical question 3 (on what the authority asserted), the *subfallacy of misrepresented authority* is said to occur where what E said has definitely been changed in meaning, in a deceptive way. Under this same heading we can have fallacies of *misquoting an authority* and *wrenching what an authority said out of context,* where there is definite evidence of a changing of the real meaning intended by the expert and using the shift in meaning as a deceptive argument Under critical question 4 (the personal reliability of the authority), we have the three subfallacies of *concealing the dishonesty of an authority, concealing the bias of an authority,* and *concealing the lack of conscientiousness of an authority,* as tactics to block the asking of this critical question. Under critical question 5 (consistency with what other experts said), there is *DeMorgan's subfallacy* of putting together two propositions—each one of which is the opinion of a separate expert—and drawing a conclusion (a third proposition) from the two propositions as a conclusion "vouched for by authorities." Under this same critical question there is also the *subfallacy of concealing deviance of an expert opinion,* where the opinion given is presented as if it were generally accepted in the field in question but is really an unusual or "maverick" opinion that lacks general acceptance in the field.

The above list is not meant to be complete or cast in stone. I have only recognized and classified what appear to be the most important of the subfallacies of the general or generic *ad verecundiam* fallacy. The work of classifying this network of fallacies and subfallacies has just begun. I have given a basis for carrying it on in a systematic and coherent fashion, flowing from an analysis of the fallacy, in the hope of giving some order to the textbook treatments.

10. Summary

Many textbooks either presume or even state explicitly that if an appeal to authority is weak or suspect (open to critical questioning), it is therefore an *ad verecundiam* fallacy. This, in my view, is a mistake, and a distinction should be drawn between cases where an *ad verecundiam* argument is open to critical questioning and cases where the *ad verecundiam* argument is fallacious.

On the other hand, it is quite justifiable to follow the practice that some textbooks do, of staying away from the word 'fallacy' altogether and only distinguishing between the appeals to authority that are weak or suspect (open to appropriate critical questions that have not yet been answered adequately) and those that are strong or justified arguments, and that have supplied the information necessary to answer the appropriate critical questions. This approach can be justified because the term 'fallacy,' although used traditionally, is not entirely clear or precise and admits of different interpretations. Even so, the term 'fallacy' appears to be best reserved for a kind of systematic failure of arguments worse than that of a mere blunder or weakness that is easily remedied by supplying more specific information needed to support the argument.

So there are really two problems: a prior and primary problem of evaluation and a secondary evaluation problem to determine whether a weak argument is sufficiently badly off (as committing a serious type of error or deception) that we are justified in calling it a fallacy.

My recommended solution to the first problem is the following. An appeal to expert opinion is reasonable or warranted if the argument is put forward by its proponent in the following form.

> (G7) E is an expert in domain D.
> E asserts that A is known to be true.
> A is within D.
> Therefore, A may (plausibly) be taken to be true.

The three premises are presumptive claims made by the proponent from which he draws the conclusion of (G7) as a proposition that the respondent in the dialogue should (provisionally) accept.

But the respondent has the right to ask any one or more of six (general) critical questions, listed again below, as found in Chapter 7, section 9.

Critical Questions for Appeal to Expert Opinion

Expertise Question	How credible is E as an expert source?
Field Question	Is E an expert in the field that A is in?
Opinion Question	What did E assert that implies A?
Trustworthiness Question	Is E personally reliable as a source?
Consistency Question	Is A consistent with what other experts assert?
Backup Evidence Question	Is A's assertion based on evidence?

If, when asked any one or more of these questions, the proponent gives no reply, or gives no answer that responds appropriately by citing the required evidence, the appeal to authority is evaluated as *weak* or *suspect*. However, if appropriate answers are given, the argument is evaluated as plausible (or is said to carry presumptive weight in the dialogue).

How much weight it should be judged to carry depends on the type of dialogue, on how strong the premises were to begin with, and on how well the critical questions have been answered in the given case.

Round one in the evaluation occurs when the argument is brought forward in form (G7). Round two occurs when the appropriate critical questions are posed, and replied to (or not). Round three can occur when subquestions to a critical question are posed by the respondent, once that critical question has been raised and responded to, in a previous round. Thus the evaluation of an *ad verecundiam* argument can have three dialectical layers, depending on the depth to which it has been investigated. These various subquestions have been set out in Chapter 7, section 9.

Up to this point in the evaluation process, no mention has been made of fallaciousness. We now go on to summarize the conditions under which such an argument can be judged to be fallacious.

In general, an argument of the form (G7) is an instance of the *ad verecundiam* fallacy in a case where the proponent has put it forward in a dogmatic manner, meaning that it is evident from his way of presenting the argument that it is meant to preempt or block the asking of one or more of the appropriate critical questions above. The evidence of this dogmatic attitude is to be found in "dialogical clues," of the kind studied by Snoeck Henkemans (1992, chap. 7), particularly in the use of qualifiers like "certainly," "necessarily," "beyond doubt," "obviously," and so forth. These ways of presenting the argument imply, in advance, that it is inappropriate to question the argument from authority.

The other kind of evidence is contextual. One needs to ask what type of dialogue the argument is supposed to be part of, in a given case. One also has to see how another type of dialogue may be embedded in this originating dialogue, and how the embedded dialogue proceeded. If the experts or their advocates who are using expert opinions to support their arguments refuse to countenance any critical questioning of a kind that would be appropriate in the case, then that is contextual evidence of the committing of an *ad verecundiam* fallacy. To gather this contextual evidence, one has to study the profile of dialogue as applied to the sequence of argumentation used by the arguers in their dialogue exchanges, showing how each reacted to the moves of the other in the given case. In particular, you need to look for repeated attempts to block off the asking of critical questions by saying that such questioning is not appropriate in the dialogue the participants are said to be engaged in.

The basis of this tactic is the *blocking move,* cited by Black (1946, 235; see also section 5), which, in effect, says that there is no need to go into the evidence on why A can be said to be known to be true, because it is enough to just say (flatly) that A is true, because E believes A is true (and that is the end of the matter). This type of closure-of-dialogue move is to be identified with the committing of the generic *ad verecundiam* fallacy. As Toulmin, Rieke, and Janik (1979, 171) put it, the authority is invoked as the *last word* on the subject.[3]

But what makes the *ad verecundiam* argument seem valid or reasonable? How does the psychology of it work, as a sophistical tactic that is, in fact, a powerful device of deceptive persuasion? Our analysis found the explanation of the *apparentia* (appearing to be reasonable) aspect of the *ad verecundiam* fallacy by combining two phenomena investigated in social psychology—the halo effect, and Milgram's experiments on obedience to authority (1974). With appeals to scientific expert opinion, in particular, there is a powerful institutional halo effect that seems to exclude critical questioning by a nonscientist, and make the claim seem to be unchallengeable by reasoned argumentation. The setting, or way the argument is presented in context, makes it seem impolite and socially inappropriate—here the halo effect explains Locke's notions of "respect" and "submission"—to question the say-so of an authority (see section 5). In such a context, it is made to seem impolite (or as Locke said, "insolent") to critically question the say-so of an authority. In the Lorenzo's Oil case, the chairpersons of the ALD meeting claimed that the Odones were showing insufficient respect for the "solemn responsibility" of the scientists, who have to follow clinical protocols.

In reality, however, appeals to expert opinion, when put forward in form (G7), are presumptive arguments, properly seen as plausible rules for action, or rules of thumb that are open to critical questions (Collier 1992). However, because of the halo effect, combined with normal contextual expectations of social obedience, it is easy to often take them for much stronger arguments having a binding deductive or inductive form. This confusion is precisely what is exploited by the *ad verecundiam* fallacy, and is the explanation of its real power as an effective, yet deceptive, tactic of persuasion.

Under various subquestions of the basic critical questions, I proposed the following subfallacies of the generic *ad verecundiam* fallacy: the fallacy of nonauthority, the fallacy of appeal to celebrity, the fallacy of unidentified authority, the fallacy of misplaced authority, the fallacy of misrepresented authority, the fallacy of misquoting an authority, the fallacy of wrenching what an authority said out of context, the fallacy

3. Particularly where the argument is of the form (G7), which is inherently presumptive in nature.

of concealing the dishonesty of an authority, the fallacy of concealing the bias of an authority, the fallacy of concealing the lack of conscientiousness of an authority, DeMorgan's fallacy, and the fallacy of concealing deviancy of an expert opinion.

The relationship of these fallacies to other related fallacies outside the category of appeal to authority remains as a subject for future research. One might note, however, the special affinity between the generic *ad verecundiam* fallacy and the *secundum quid* fallacy, as analyzed by Walton (1990a; 1992a). Both fallacies share the common defining characteristic of dogmatism. However, with the *ad verecundiam*, the other defining characteristic is the use of appeal to authority as a type of argumentation. The *secundum quid* fallacy of ignoring qualifications is the more general fallacy of making a presumptive argument based on a rule of thumb warrant seem like a deductively valid argument based on an (absolute) universal generalization, marked by the universal quantifier of first-order, deductive logic.

One might also note that the *ad verecundiam* is a source-based type of argument, like the *ad hominem,* but the *ad verecundiam* is positive while the *ad hominem* is a negative type of argument. In appeal to expert opinion, the credibility of the source upgrades the plausibility of the argument put forward by that source. In an *ad hominem* argument, the lack of credibility of the source downgrades the plausibility of the argument put forward by that source. The two types of argument share a similar structure, but one is positive while the other is negative. The credibility of the expert as a source relates to two critical questions (of the set given in Chapter 7, section 9)—the first question, 'How credible is E as an expert source?' and the fourth question, 'Is E personally reliable as a source?' In fact, the fourth question reveals the exact main point of linkage between the *ad hominem* and the *ad verecundiam*.

BIBLIOGRAPHY

Amabile, Teresa M., and Albert H. Hasdorf. 1976. "Person Perception." In Bernard Seidenberg and Alvin M. Snadowsky, eds., *Social Psychology,* 239–78. New York: Free Press.

American Psychiatric Association. 1980. *Diagnostic and Statistical Manual of Mental Disorders,* 3d ed. Washington, D.C.: American Psychiatric Association.

Angeles, Peter A. 1981. *Dictionary of Philosophy.* New York: Harper and Row.

Annis, David B. 1974. *Techniques of Critical Reasoning.* Columbus, Ohio: Charles E. Merrill.

Anonymous. 1992. "Rebel Without a Cause" [Review of Huber 1991a]. *Harvard Law Review* 105: 935–40.

Aristotle. 1937. *The Art of Rhetoric,* trans. John H. Freese. Loeb Library edition. Cambridge, Mass.: Harvard University Press.

———. 1928. *Topica,* trans. W. Pickard-Cambridge. In W. D. Ross, ed., *The Works of Aristotle Translated into English,* vol. 1. Oxford: Clarendon Press.

Arnauld, Antoine. 1964. *The Art of Thinking,* trans. James Dickoff, Patricia James, and Charles Hendel. Indianapolis: Bobbs-Merrill.

Audi, Robert. 1989. *Practical Reasoning.* London: Routledge.

Ayala, Francisco J., and Bert Black. 1993. "Science and the Courts," *American Scientist* 81:230–39.

Bailey, William S. 1993. "Expert Witnesses in the Sound-Bite Era," *Trial* 29:65–69.

Barker, Stephen F. 1965. *The Elements of Logic.* New York: McGraw-Hill.

Barnes, Jonathan. 1980. "Aristotle and the Methods of Ethics," *Revue Internationale de Philosophie* 34:490–511.

Beardsley, Monroe C. 1966. *Thinking Straight,* 3d ed. Englewood Cliffs, N.J.: Prentice-Hall

———. 1950. *Practical Logic.* New York: Prentice-Hall.

Begley, Sharon, with Kendall Hamilton. 1993. "The Meaning of Junk," *Newsweek,* March 22, pp. 62–64.

Bentham, Jeremy, 1971. *Handbook of Political Fallacies* (1816), ed. Harold Larrabee. New York: Thomas Crowell.

Black, Max. 1946. *Critical Thinking.* New York: Prentice-Hall.

Blair, J. Anthony. 1988. "What is Bias?" In Trudy Govier, ed., *Selected Issues in Logic and Communication,* 93–103. Belmont, Calif.: Wadsworth.

Block, Alan J. 1990. "Rape Trauma Syndrome as Expert Scientific Testimony," *Archives of Sexual Behavior* 19:309–23.

Blyth, John W. 1957. *A Modern Introduction to Logic.* Boston: Houghton Mifflin.

Bochenski, J. M. 1974. "An Analysis of Authority." In Frederick J. Adelman, ed., *Authority,* 56–85. The Hague: Martinus Nijhoff.

Bolton, Robert. 1990. "The Epistemological Basis of Aristotelian Dialectic." In Daniel Devereux and Pierre Pellegrin, eds., *Biologie, Logique et Métaphysique chez Aristote,* 185–236. Paris: Éditions du Centre National de la Recherche Scientifique.

Bratko, Ivan. 1986. *Prolog Programming for Artificial Intelligence.* Reading, Mass.: Addison-Wesley.

Brooks, Juanita R. 1993. "Fighting Back: Defense Use of Experts," *Trial* 29:42–45.

Bumiller, Elisabeth. 1995. "How Report Cards for Surgeons are Shaking Up the Medical Elite," *The Globe and Mail,* September 9, D8.

Burgess, A., and L. Holmstrom. 1974. "Rape Trauma Syndrome," *American Journal of Psychiatry* 131:980–86.

Byerly, Henry C. 1973. *A Primer of Logic.* New York: Harper and Row.

Capaldi, Nicholas. 1971. *The Art of Deception.* New York: Donald W. Brown.

Caplan, Paula J. 1994. *You're Smarter Than They Make You Feel: How the Experts Intimidate Us and What We Can Do About It.* New York: The Free Press.

Carney, James D., and Richard K. Scheer. 1964. *Fundamentals of Logic.* New York: Macmillan.

Cederblom, Jerry, and David W. Paulsen. 1982. *Critical Reasoning.* Belmont, Calif.: Wadsworth.

Cherwitz, Richard A., and Thomas J. Darwin. 1995. "On the Continuing Utility of Argument in a Postmodernist World," *Argumentation* 9:181–202.

Cialdini, Robert B. 1988. *Influence: Science and Practice.* Glenview, Ill.: Scott, Foresman.

Clancey, W. J. 1979. "Tutoring Rules for Guiding a Case Method Dialogue," *International Journal of Man-Machine Studies* 11:25–49.

Clarke, David S., Jr. 1985. *Practical Inferences.* London: Routledge and Kegan Paul.

Cohen, Morris R., and Ernest Nagel. 1934. *An Introduction to Logic and Scientific Method.* New York: Harcourt, Brace.

Coleman, Julian, and David Concar. 1993. "Pouring Cold Water on Lorenzo"s Oil," *New Scientist* 137:23–24.

Collier, Charles W. 1992. "Intellectual Authority and Institutional Authority," *Inquiry* 35:145–81.

Collins, Allan, Eleanor H. Warnock, Nelleke Aiello, and Mark L. Miller. 1975. "Reasoning from Incomplete Knowledge." In Daniel G. Bobrow and Allan Collins, eds., 383–415. *Representation and Understanding: Studies in Cognitive Science.* New York: Academic Press.

Copi, Irving M. 1953. *Introduction to Logic.* New York: Macmillan (7th ed., 1986; 8th ed., with Carl Cohen, 1990).

Creighton, James Edwin. 1904. *An Introductory Logic.* New York: Macmillan.

Crossen, Cynthia. 1994. *Tainted Truth: The Manipulation of Fact in America.* New York: Simon and Schuster.

Crossley, David J., and Peter A. Wilson. 1979. *How to Argue: An Introduction to Logical Thinking.* New York: McGraw-Hill.

Damer, T. Edward. 1980. *Attacking Faulty Reasoning.* Belmont, Calif.: Wadsworth.

De George, Richard T. 1985. *The Nature and Limits of Authority.* Lawrence: University Press of Kansas.

Degnan, Ronan E. 1973. "Evidence," *Encyclopaedia Britannia,* 15th ed., 8:905–16.

DeMorgan, Augustus. 1847. *Formal Logic.* London: Taylor and Walton.

Denning, Peter J. 1986. "Towards a Science of Expert Systems." *IEEE* Expert 1, no. 2: 80–83.

Devereux, Daniel. 1990. "Comments on Robert Bolton's The Epistemological Basis of Aristotelian Dialectic." In Daniel Devereux and Pierre Pellegrin, eds., *Biologie, Logique et Métaphysique chez Aristote,* 263–86. Paris: Éditions du Centre National de la Recherche Scientifique.

Diggs, Bernard J. 1960. "A Technical Ought," *Mind* 69: 301–17.

Drake, Stillman. 1967. "Galileo Galilei." *The Encyclopedia of Philosophy,* vol. 3., ed. Paul Edwards. New York: Macmillan.

Dreyfus, Hubert, and Stuart Dreyfus. 1986. "Why Expert Systems Do Not Exhibit Expertise," *IEEE Expert* 1, no. 2: 86–90.

Dyk, Timothy B., and Gregory A. Castanias. 1993. "Daubert Doesn't End Debate on Experts," *The National Law Journal* 15:17–20.

Eliot, Lance B. 1986. "Analogical Problem-Soling and Expert Systems," *IEEE Expert* 1, no. 2: 17–26.

Erickson, Bonnie, E. Allan Lind, Bruce C. Johnson, and William M. O'Barr. 1978. "Speech Style and Impression Formation in a Court Setting: The Effects of 'Powerful' and 'Powerless' Speech," *Journal of Experimental and Social Psychology* 14:266–79.

Evans, John D. G. 1977. *Aristotle's Concept of Dialectic.* Cambridge: Cambridge University Press.

Facione, Peter A., and Donald Scherer. 1978. *Logic and Logical Thinking.* New York: McGraw-Hill.

Fairweather, James S. 1988. "Reputational Quality of Academic Programs: The Institutional Halo," *Research in Higher Education* 28:345–56.

Fearnside, W. Ward. 1980. *About Thinking.* Englewood Cliffs, N.J.: Prentice-Hall.

———, and William B. Holther. 1959. *Fallacy: The Counterfeit of Argument.* Englewood Cliffs: Prentice-Hall.

Feteris, Eveline T. 1989. *Discussieregels in het recht. Een Pragma-dialectische Analyse van het Burgerlijk Proces en het Strafproces* (Rules for discussion in law: A pragma-dialectical analysis of the civil and criminal processes). Dordrecht: Foris Publications.

———. 1987. "The Dialectical Role of the Judge in a Legal Process." In J. W.

Wenzel, ed., *Argument and Critical Practice, Proceedings of the Fifth SCA/AFA Conference on Argumentation,* 335–39. Annandale, Va.: Speech Communication Association.

Finocchiaro, Maurice A. 1989. *The Galileo Affair.* Berkeley and Los Angeles: University of California Press.

———. 1980. *Galileo and the Art of Reasoning.* Dordrecht: Reidel.

Flew, Anthony. 1979. *A Dictionary of Philosophy.* New York: St. Martin's Press.

Flint, Anthony. 1995. "The Scientists and the Radicals Square Off," *The Globe and Mail,* June 3, D8.

Fowler, Thomas. 1870. *The Elements of Inductive Logic.* Oxford: Clarendon Press.

Frye, Albert Myrton, and Albert William Levi. 1969. *Rational Belief: An Introduction to Logic.* New York: Greenwood Press.

Galilei, Galileo. 1967. *Dialogue Concerning the Two Chief World Systems,* trans. Stillman Drake. 2d ed. Berkeley and Los Angeles: University of California Press.

Gardner, Martin. 1993. "Notes of a Fringe-Watcher," *Skeptical Inquirer* 17:370–75.

Gensler, Harry J. 1989. *Logic: Analyzing and Appraising Arguments.* Englewood Cliffs, N.J.: Prentice-Hall.

Giannelli, Paul C. 1993. "Junk Science: The Criminal Cases," *Journal of Criminal Law and Criminology* 84:105–28.

———, and Edward J. Imwinkelried. 1986. *Scientific Evidence.* Charlottesville, Va.: Michie.

———. 1981. "General Acceptance of Scientific Tests: Frye and Beyond. " In Edward J. Imwinkelried, ed., *Scientific and Expert Evidence,* 2d ed., 11–35. New York: Practicing Law Institute.

Gibbon, Edward. 1811. *Decline and Fall of the Roman Empire,* vol. 7 of 12 vols. Edinburgh: Printed for Bell & Bradfute, Peter Hill, Sylvester Doig, A. Stirling and John Ogle.

Glare, P. G. W., ed. 1982. *Oxford Latin Dictionary.* Oxford: Clarendon Press.

Gleason, Robert W. 1966. *The Essential Pascal.* New York: New American Library.

Goldstein, Abraham S. 1967. *The Insanity Defense.* New Haven: Yale University Press.

Govier, Trudy. 1992. *A Practical Study of Argument,* 3d ed. Belmont, Calif.: Wadsworth.

Grady, Denise. 1996. "The Whiplash Syndrome Loses its Validity," New York Times Service, *The Globe and Mail,* May 11, D8.

Graham, Michael H. 1977. "Impeaching the Professional Expert Witness by a Showing of Financial Interest," *Indiana Law Journal* 53:35–53.

Guthrie, William K. C. 1981. *A History of Greek Philosophy.* 6 vols. Cambridge: Cambridge University Press.

Hamblin, Charles L. 1970. *Fallacies.* London: Methuen. Reprinted, Newport News, Va.: Vale Press, 1993.

Hansen, Mark. 1993. "Believe it or Not," *American Bar Association Journal* 79:64–67.

Hart, Anna. 1986. *Knowledge Acquisition for Expert Systems.* New York: McGraw-Hill.

Haskell, Thomas L. 1984. "Introduction." In Thomas L. Haskell, ed., *The Authority of Experts,* 9–39. Bloomington: Indiana University Press.

Hastings, Arthur C. 1962. "A Reformulation of the Modes of Reasoning in Argumentation." Ph.D. diss., Northwestern University, Evanston, Illinois.

Hendel, Charles. 1964. "Forward" to Arnauld's *The Art of Thinking.* Indianapolis: Bobbs-Merrill.

Hensler, Deborah R. 1991. "Science in the Court: Is There a Role for Alternative Dispute Resolution?," *Law and Contemporary Problems* 54:171–93.

Herrera, René J., and Martin L. Tracey, Jr. 1992. "DNA Fingerprinting: Basic Techniques, Problems, and Solutions," *Journal of Criminal Justice* 20:237–48.

Hibben, John Grier. 1906. *Logic: Deductive and Inductive.* New York: Charles Scribner's Sons.

Hoffman, Herbert C. 1979. "The Cross-Examination of Expert Witnesses." New York: Planning, Zoning and Eminent Domain Institute, 3:313–49.

Holmström-Hintikka, Ghita. 1995. "Expert Witnesses in Legal Argumentation," *Argumentation* 9:489–502.

Howard, Michael N. 1991. "The Neutral Expert: A Plausible Threat to Justice," *The Criminal Law Review,* February 1, pp. 98–105.

Huber, Peter. 1991a. *Galileo's Revenge: Junk Science in the Courtroom.* New York: Basic Books, 1991.

———. 1991b. "Junk Science in the Courtroom," *Forbes,* July 8, pp. 68–72.

Hurley, Patrick J. 1991. *A Concise Introduction to Logic,* 4th ed. Belmont, Calif.: Wadsworth.

Hyslop, James H. 1899. *Logic and Argument.* New York: Charles Scribner's Sons.

Imwinkelried, Edward J. 1993. "The *Daubert* Decision: *Frye* is Dead, Long Live the Federal Rules of Evidence," *Trial* 29:60–65.

———. 1991. "A Comparativist Critique of the Interface Between Hearsay and Expert Opinion in American Evidence Law," *Boston College Law Review* 33:1–35.

———. 1986. "Science Takes the Stand: The Growing Misuse of Expert Testimony," *The Sciences* 26:20–25.

Inlander, Charles B., Lowell S. Levin, and Ed Weiner. 1988. *Medicine on Trial: The Appalling Story of Ineptitude, Malfeasance, Neglect and Arrogance.* New York: Prentice Hall.

Intelliware. 1986. *Experteach* (Software and Manual). Los Angeles: Intelligence Ware.

Johnson, Paul E. 1983. "What Kind of Expert Should a System Be?," *Journal of Medicine and Philosophy* 8:77–97.

Johnson, Ralph H. 1990. "Hamblin on the Standard Treatment," *Philosophy and Rhetoric* 23:153–67.

———, and J. Anthony Blair. 1983. *Logical Self-Defense,* 2d ed. Toronto: McGraw-Hill Ryerson.

Kelley, David. 1988. *The Art of Reasoning.* New York: Norton.

Kenny, Anthony. 1983. "The Expert in Court," *Law Quarterly Review* 99:197–216.

Kilgore, William J. 1968. *An Introductory Logic.* New York: Holt, Rinehart and Winston.

Klawans, Harold L. 1991. *Trials of an Expert Witness: Tales of Clinical Neurology and the Law.* Boston: Little, Brown.

Kneale, William, and Martha Kneale. 1962. *The Development of Logic.* Oxford: Clarendon Press.

Knight-Ridder Newspapers. 1986. "Pauling Braces for Foes of Views on Use of Vitamins," *Winnipeg Free Press,* March 19, p. 39.

Krabbe, Erik. 1992. "So What? Profiles for Relevance Criticism in Persuasion Dialogues," *Argumentation* 6:271–83.

Kretzmann, Norman, and Eleonore Stump. 1988. *The Cambridge Translations of Medieval Philosophical Texts.* Cambridge: Cambridge University Press.

Kreyche, Robert J. 1961. *Logic for Undergraduates.* New York: Holt Rinehart and Winston.

Krueger, Alice. 1990. "Nutritionist's Ph.D. Debunked," *Winnipeg Free Press,* October 27, p. 1.

Laghi, Brian. 1996. "Joudrie Cleared in Attack," *The Globe and Mail,* May 10, A1 and A4.

Laplace, Pierre Simon. 1951. *A Philosophical Essay on Probabilities* (1795), trans. Frederick W. Truscott and Frederick L. Emory. New York: Dover Publications.

Latta, Robert, and Alexander MacBeath. 1956. *The Elements of Logic.* London: Macmillan.

Lincoln, Bruce. 1994. *Authority: Construction and Corrosion.* Chicago: University of Chicago Press.

Little, J. Frederick, Leo A. Groarke, and Christopher W. Tindale. 1989. *Good Reasoning Matters.* Toronto: McClelland and Stewart.

Little, Winston W., W. Harold Wilson, and W. Edgar Moore. 1955. *Applied Logic.* Boston: Houghton Mifflin.

Locke, John. 1961. *An Essay Concerning Human Understanding* (1690), 2 vols., ed. John W. Yolton. London: Dent.

MacDonald, Helen. 1985. *Eating for the Health of It.* Priddis, Alberta: Austin Books.

Mackenzie, Jim. 1988. "Authority," *Journal of Philosophy of Education* 22: 57–65.

Makin, Kirk. 1994. "Morin Lawyers Say Study on Clothing Fibres Misread," *The Globe and Mail,* September 23, A6.

Mander, Alfred E. 1936. *Clearer Thinking.* London: Watts & Co.

Martin, R. Niall D. 1991. "The Trouble with Authority: The Galileo Affair and One of Its Historians," *Modern Theology* 7:269–80.

Mazur, Allan. 1973. "Disputes Between Experts," *Minerva* 11:243–62.

Mervis, Jeffrey. 1993. "Supreme Court to Judges: Start Thinking Like Scientists," *Science* 261:22.

Michalos, Alex C. 1986. *Improving Your Reasoning,* 2d ed. Englewood Cliffs, N.J.: Prentice-Hall.

Milgram, Stanley. 1977. *The Individual in a Social World.* Reading, Mass.: Addison-Wesley.

———. 1974. *Obedience to Authority.* New York: Harper & Row.

Mitchell, Alanna. 1996. "Doctors' Testimony Key for Joudrie Jury," *The Globe and Mail,* May 7, A7.

Moore, W. Edgar. 1967. *Creative and Critical Thinking.* New York: Houghton Mifflin.

Murphy. Susan. 1992. "Assisting the Jury in Understanding Victimization: Expert Psychological Testimony on Battered Woman Syndrome and Rape Trauma Syndrome," *Columbia Journal of Law and Social Problems* 25:277–312.

Mussi, Silvano. 1993. "A Method for Putting Strategic Common Sense into Expert Systems," *IEEE Transactions on Knowledge and Data Engineering* 5:369–85.

Naftulin, Donald, John E. Ware, Jr., and Frank A. Donnelly. 1973. "The Doctor Fox Lecture: A Paradigm of Education Seduction," *Journal of Medical Education* 48:630–36.

Pascal, Blaise. 1966. "Reflections on Geometry and the Art of Persuading." In Robert W. Gleason, ed., The *Essential Pascal,* 297–327. New York: New American Library.

Patel, Kam. 1995. "Science Losing Its Cutting Edge," *The Times Higher Education Supplement,* July 7, p. 7.

Peirce, Charles S. 1958a. "The Fixation of Belief," *Popular Science Monthly* 12 (1877): 1–15. Reprinted in Philip P. Wiener, ed., *Charles S. Peirce: Selected Writings*, 91–112. New York: Dover.

———. 1958b. "How to Make Our Ideas Clear." Popular Science Monthly, January 1878: 286–302. Reprinted in Philip P. Weiner, ed., *Charles S. Peirce: Selected Writings,* 113–36. New York: Dover.

Perelman, Chaim, and Lucie Olbrechts-Tyteca. 1969. *The New Rhetoric.* Notre Dame: University of Notre Dame Press.

Peter of Spain (Pope John XXI). 1990. *Language in Dispute: An English Translation of Peter of Spain's Summulae Logicales,* trans. Francis P. Dineen. Amsterdam: John Benjamins.

Plato. 1961. *Collected Dialogues,* ed. Edith Hamilton and Huntingdon Cairns. New York: Random House.

———. 1936. *The Works of Plato,* 4 vols., trans. Benjamin Jowett. New York: Dial Press.

Poser, Charles M. 1991. "Review of *Trials of an Expert Witness," Journal of the American Medical Association* 266:1142.

Purtill, Richard L. 1972. *Logical Thinking.* New York: Harper & Row.

Reese, William L. 1980. *Dictionary of Philosophy and Religion.* Atlantic Highlands, N.J.: Humanities Press.

Reiter, Raymond. 1987. "Nonmonotonic Reasoning," *Annual Review of Computer Science* 2:147–86.

Rescher, Nicholas. 1976. *Plausible Reasoning.* Assen-Amsterdam: Van Gorcum.
———. 1964. *Introduction to Logic.* New York: St. Martin's Press.
Review [anonymous]. 1992. "Rebel Without a Cause: Review of *Galileo's Revenge,*" *Harvard Law Review* 105:935–40.
Robinson, Daniel Sommer. 1947. *The Principles of Reasoning,* 3d ed.,New York: D. Appleton-Century.
Robinson, Richard. 1953. *Plato's Earlier Dialectic,* 2d ed. Oxford: Clarendon Press.
Ruby, Lionel. 1950. Logic: *An Introduction.* Chicago: J. B. Lippincot.
Runes, Dagobert D. 1984. *Dictionary of Philosophy.* Totowa, N.J.: Rowman and Allanheld.
Runkle, Gerald. 1991. *Good Thinking: An Introduction to Logic.* Fort Worth: Holt, Rinehart and Winston.
Russow, Lilly-Marlene, and Martin Curd. 1989. *Principles of Reasoning.* New York: St. Martin's Press.
Salmon, Merrilee H. 1989. *Introduction to Logic and Critical Thinking,* 2d ed. San Diego: Harcourt Brace Jovanovich.
Salmon, Wesley C. 1963. *Logic.* Englewood Cliffs, N.J.: Prentice-Hall.
Saltzburg, Stephen A., and Michael M. Martin. 1990. *Federal Rules of Evidence Manual,* 5th ed. Charlottesville, Va.: Michie.
Samuelson, Robert J. 1995. "A Nation of Experts," *Newsweek,* June 5, p. 49.
Sawyers, Mike. 1985. "Sunday Hunting Update," *Outdoor Life* 176:4.
Schank, Roger G. 1982. *Dynamic Memory.* Cambridge: Cambridge University Press.
Schipper, Edith W., and Edward H. Schuh. 1959. *A First Course in Modern Logic.* New York: Henry Holt and Co.
Schrof, Joannie. 1992. "Courtroom Conundrum," *U.S. News & World Report,* October 26, pp. 67–69.
Simon, Ron. 1992. "How to Win the Battle of the Experts," *Trial* 28:36–41.
60 Minutes. 1994. "Right on Fred Zain!," CBS News, New York, April 24. Transcript, Burrelle's Information Services, Livingston, N.J., vol. 26, no. 32.
———. 1992. "Zapped." CBS News, New York, June 21. Transcript, Burrelle's Information Services, Livingston, N.J., vol. 24, no. 40.
Smith, Robin. 1993. "Aristotle on the Uses of Dialectic," *Synthese* 96:335–58.
Snoeck-Henkemans, A. Francisca. 1992. *Analysing Complex Argumentation.* Amsterdam: SICSAT.
Soccio, Douglas J., and Vincent E. Barry. 1992. *Practical Logic,* 4th ed. Fort Worth: Harcourt Brace Jovanovich.
Spellman, Howard Hilton. 1968. *Direct Examination of Witnesses.* Englewood Cliffs, N.J.: Prentice-Hall.
Thorndike, Edward. 1920. "A Constant Error in Psychological Ratings," *Journal of Applied Psychology* 4:25–29.
Thouless, Robert H. 1936. *Straight and Crooked Thinking.* London: English Universities Press.
Toulmin, Stephen, Richard Rieke, and Allan Janik. 1979. *An Introduction to*

Reasoning. New York: Macmillan.

Trevor-Roper, Hugh R. 1967. *Religion, The Reformation and Social Change.* London: Macmillan.

van Eemeren, Frans H., and Rob Grootendorst. 1992. *Argumentation, Communication and Fallacies.* Hillsdale, N.J.: Lawrence Erlbaum.

———. 1987. "Fallacies in Pragma-Dialectical Perspective." *Argumentation* 1:283–301.

———. 1984. *Speech Acts in Argumentative Discussions.* Dordrecht: Foris.

Vatz, Richard E., and Lee S. Weinberg. 1992. "Psychiatric Excuses for Criminal Behavior: The Public is Losing Patience," *USA Today,* March 1, 63–64.

Veitch, John. 1885. *Institutes of Logic.* Edinburgh: William Blackwood and Sons.

Vernon, Thomas S., and Lowell A Nissen. 1968. *Reflective Thinking: The Fundamentals of Logic.* Belmont, Calif.: Wadsworth.

von Wright, Georg H. 1983. "On So-Called Practical Inference." In his *Practical Reason,* vol. 1 of *Philosophical Papers,* 18–34. Ithaca: Cornell University Press.

Waller, Bruce N. 1988. *Critical Thinking: Consider the Verdict.* Englewood Cliffs, N.J.: Prentice-Hall.

Walton, Douglas N. 1996a. *Arguments from Ignorance.* University Park: The Pennsylvania State University Press.

———. 1996b. *Argumentation Schemes.* Mahwah, N.J.: Erlbaum.

———. 1995. *A Pragmatic Theory of Fallacy.* Tuscaloosa: University of Alabama Press.

———, and Erik C. W. Krabbe. 1995. *Commitment in Dialogue.* Albany: State University of New York Press.

———. 1992a. "Nonfallacious Arguments from Ignorance," *American Philosophical Quarterly* 29:381–87.

———. 1992b. *The Place of Emotion in Argument.* University Park: The Pennsylvania State University Press.

———. 1992c. *Plausible Argument in Everyday Conversation.* Albany: State University of New York Press.

———. 1991. "Bias, Critical Doubt, and Fallacies," *Argumentation and Advocacy* 28:1–22.

———. 1990a. "Ignoring Qualifications (*Secundum Quid*) as a Subfallacy of Hasty Generalization," *Logique et Analyse* 129–30:113–54.

———. 1990b. *Practical Reasoning.* Savage, Md.: Rowman and Littlefield.

———. 1989a. *Informal Logic.* Cambridge: Cambridge University Press.

———. 1989b. "Problems in the Use of Expert Opinion in Argumentation," *Communication & Cognition* 22:383–89.

———. 1989c. *Question-Reply Argumentation.* New York: Greenwood Press.

———. 1989d. "Reasoned Use of Expertise in Argumentation," *Argumentation* 3:59–73.

———. 1987. "What is a Fallacy?" In Frans H. van Eemeren, Rob Grootendorst, J. Anthony Blair, and Charles A. Willard, eds., *Argumentation: Across the Lines of Discipline: Proceedings of the Conference on Argumentation 1986,* 323–30. Dordrecht, Foris.

———. 1985a. *Arguer's Position,* Westport, Conn.: Greenwood Press, 1985.

———. 1985b. *Physician-Patient Decision-Making* Westport, Conn.: Greenwood Press.

———, and Lynn M. Batten. 1984. "Games, Graphs and Circular Arguments," *Logique et Analyse* 106:133–64.

———, and John Woods. 1982. *Argument: The Logic of the Fallacies.* Toronto: McGraw-Hill Ryerson.

———. 1975. "Philosophical Perspectives on the Insanity Defense," *The Human Context* 7:546–60.

———, and John Woods. 1974. *"Argumentum ad Verecundiam," Philosophy and Rhetoric* 7:135–53.

Waterman, Donald A. 1986. *A Guide to Expert Systems,* Reading, Mass.: Addison-Wesley.

Watts, Isaac. 1725. *Logick, or the Right Use of Reason in the Enquiry after Truth, with a Variety of Rules to Guard Against Error, in the Affairs of Religion and Human Life, as well as in the Sciences.* London. Printed for John Clark and Richard Hett.

Weber, O. J. 1981. "Attacking the Expert Witness," *Federation of Insurance Counsel Quarterly* 31:299–319.

Werkmeister, William H. 1948. *An Introduction to Critical Thinking.* Lincoln, Neb.: Johnsen Publishing.

Wilensky, Robert. 1983. *Planning and Understanding: A Computational Approach to Human Reasoning.* Reading, Mass.: Addison-Wesley.

William of Sherwood. 1966. *Introduction to Logic,* trans. Norman Kretzmann. Minneapolis: University of Minnesota Press.

Wilson, Patrick. 1983. *Second-Hand Knowledge: An Inquiry into Cognitive Authority.* Westport, Conn.: Greenwood Press.

Windelband, Wilhelm. 1901. *A History of Philosophy.* New York, Macmillan.

Windes, Russel R., and Arthur Hastings. 1965. *Argumentation and Advocacy.* New York: Random House.

Woods, John, and Douglas Walton. 1982. *Argument: The Logic of the Fallacies.* Toronto: McGraw-Hill Ryerson.

———. 1974. *"Argumentatum ad Verecundiam,"* Philosophy and Rhetoric 7:135–53.

Yanal, Robert J. 1988. *Basic Logic.* St. Paul: West Publishing.

Yang, Catherine. 1993. "Under Attack: Testimony for Hire," *Business Week,* January 18, pp. 60–61.

Yankelovich, Daniel. 1991. *Coming to Public Judgment.* Syracuse: Syracuse University Press.

Younger, Irving. 1982. "A Practical Approach to the Use of Expert Testimony," *Cleveland State Law Review* 31:1–42.

INDEX

a priori method, 3, 15

ad judicium argument, 115, 239

ad verecundiam
  argument, 239, 261; *de facto* form of, 102; deductive, 103; deductively valid, 92–93; evaluating, 126, 157; inductive, 103; power of, 175; presumptive, 103; strategy of deception, 143
  fallacy, 45, 230, 232, 260

Adair, Eleanor, 127–32, 188

advice-giver, 83

advocacy groups, 11

Aiello, Nelleke, 96

Amabile, Teresa, 244

Angeles, Peter A., 59

Annis, David B., 99

appeal, 80
  abuse of, 75
  ad populum, 90, 116
  to authority, 34, 47, 71, 87, 115; adequacy of, 207; conditions for, 207; credibility of, 208; dogmatic, 239–40, 255; as a fallacy, 28, 45, 87, 228–29, 232, 236; form as an argument, 200; illicit, 256; misused, 204, 236; three ways the fallacy can occur, 252; weak, 232, 258
  to celebrity status, 82–83
  to deontic authority, 78–79
  to emotions, 64, 66, 73, 90, 249
  to epistemic authority, 78
  to evidence, 249
  to experience, 82–83
  to expert opinion, 28, 32, 90, 245;

abuses of, 25; complex type of argument, 19–22; fallacious appeal, 75; in politics, 140–44; presumptive type of, 103; problem with, 29–30; types of reasoning used, 18; weak, 139, 142–43
  to expertise, 92; six adequacy conditions, 101
  to faith, 116
  to the feeling of reverence, 80
  to knowledge, 75
  legitimate critical questioning of, 148
  personal, 79
  to pity, 66
  to popular opinion. See *argumentum ad populum*
  to popularity, 81
  to prestige, 70
  to reason, 65
  to reverence, 64, 66, 73
  to scientific expert opinion, 260
  to testimony, 70
  testimonial, 80
  to tradition, 83, 116

Appleton, Nancy, 8

argument
  from authority, 33–34, 43, 46–48, 55, 87, 89, 202; good, 210; presumptive, 235, 241
  appeal to authority: stronger than justified, 248; types of, 40
  cumulative, 13
  deductive, 61
  deductively valid, 45, 261
  demonstrative, 40, 42

argument *(continued)*
  dialectical, 29, 40, 42–44
  from extrinsic grounds, 43; treated as
    a fallacy, 33
  from illegitimate authority, 243
  inductive type of, 99
  from negative evidence, 44
  peirastic, 42–43
  from position to know, 83
  presumptive, 260
  from reverence, 87, 89
  weak, 44, 231, 233, 258
Argument: The Logic of the Fallacies,
    101
argumentation
  based on testimony, 157
  from consequences, 161
  inductive, 87, 98
  question-reply, 113
  scheme, 223
  universal, 161
argumentum ad hominem, 69, 261
argumentum ad ignorantiam, 44, 52,
    69, 94–95, 97
argumentum ad judicium, 52–54, 56, 68
argumentum ad personam, 68–69
argumentum ad populum, 40, 69, 81
argumentum ad rem, 68
argumentum ad verecundiam, 32,
    52–54, 58–59, 90
  complex negative form, 95
  deductive form of, 95
  defined, 64, 67–69
  dismissed, 74
  fallacious use of, 60, 64–66, 71
  first usage of, 33–34, 52
  inferiority of, 67
  simple positive form, 95
Aristotle, 14–15, 19, 33, 38–43, 47, 119
  valued argument from appeal to
    expert opinion, 38
Arnauld, Antoine, 48–51, 56
The Art of Rhetoric, 39
The Art of Thinking, 48–50
artificial intelligence (AI), 107, 119 164,
    166
assumption
  closed world, 94, 96, 100; implicit
    premise of, 94
attacks, personal, 21
attitude of reverence. See *verecundia*

attorney, aggressively hostile, 168
audience, 148, 151
authority, 20, 33, 80, 209, 235
  administrative, 40, 76–78, 121, 252
  of Aristotle, 34, 44–45, 48
  attack on, 35
  cognitive, 76–78, 84, 86, 121, 250, 252
  concept of, 89
  de facto, 77
  de jure, 77
  defined, 45, 85
  deontic, 77
  displacement of authorities, 34
  dogmatic, 255
  epistemic, 77, 84
  evaluating, 205–6
  expert, 240
  expertise of, 213
  four types of force of, 56
  government, 28
  intellectual, 251
  institutional, 40, 46, 190, 245, 250–52
  legal, 28
  medical, 77
  method of, 3, 15
  misplace, 255
  misrepresented, 255
  misuse of, 80
  political, 78, 85
  power of, 46, 76, 78
  qualifications of, 203–4
  reliability of, 116, 203, 213–14, 216
  religious, 28, 34, 46, 49, 76, 78, 85
  respect for, 69
  reverence to, 89
  of science, 17, 35
  sweeping, 255
  venerable, 255, 256
  veneration of, 65
  versus persuasion, 20
  weight of, 206
axioms, 51–52
  fundamental, 14

Bailey, William S., 150, 167
Barker, Stephen F., 235
Barry, Vincent E., 233
  three questions, 209
Batten, Lynn, 105–6
Beardsley, Monroe C., 85–86, 202,
    207–8, 243

three conditions of, 202, 217
Bentham, Jeremy, 55–57, 68
bias, 12, 17, 29, 115, 195, 202–4, 206–8,
    213–15, 227, 236, 261
  biasing halo, 249
  critically bad, 216
  cultural, 10–11, 15, 31
  expert, 115
  institutional, 216
  nonbiased, 133, 210
  subjective, 18
  unanticipated, 193
Big Brother, 2, 28
Black, Max, 70–71, 73, 82, 239, 259
Blair, J. Anthony, 85, 222, 238
  five rules, 207–8, 215–16, 221
  violation of conditions, 237
Block, Alan J., 190
blocking move, 259
Blyth, John W., 235
Bochenski, J. M., 77
Brooks, Juanita R., 150
burden of proof, 88, 108, 122, 160
  legally appropriate, 21
  prosecution's, 168
  shifted, 134, 143, 158, 228
Burgess, A., 190
Byerly, Henry C., 208, 222
  three conditions of, 205, 221

Calvin, choice of authorities, 34–35
Capaldi, Nicholas, 215
  eight qualifications of, 205–6, 218–19
Caplan, Paula J., 22
Carney, James, 74, 236
Cederblom, Jerry, 243, 247
celebrity, 154, 235, 256
chaining, forward or backward, 105
Charmides, 36–37
Cherwitz, Richard A, 11
Cialdini, Robert B., 244
circumstances, internal versus external,
    51
Clancey,W. J., 107
clinical ecology, 176–78
closure-of-dialogue move, 260
Cohen, Morris R., 250–51
Collier, Charles W., 248–49, 251–52
Collins, Allan, 96
commitment(s), 21, 31, 122, 162
  arguer's set of, 107

communication, 20
computer science, 91, 94, 101
conclusions, relativistic, 29
condition, completeness (closure), 95
conditionals, 117
conflict resolution, 106
conscientiousness, 214
Copernicus, Nicolaus, 46, 70
Copi, Irving, 79, 87–88, 226, 234
Creighton, James Edwin, 64, 154,
    239
Crossen, Cynthia, 6, 9
Crossley, David J., three questions of,
    205
culture of technical control, 12–13
Curd, Martin, 215
  three factors of, 209

Damer, T. Edward, 75, 85
  three factors of, 236
Darwin, Thomas J., 11
data base, closed, 117
Daubert v. Merrill Dow
    Pharmaceuticals Inc., 184–85
De George, Richard, 76–77
De L'Esprit Geometrique, 14
Decline and Fall of the Roman Empire,
    251
DeMorgan, 155–57, 207, 212–13
Degnan, Ronan E., 169
debate, political, 140, 160
deliberation. See dialogue, deliberation
Descartes, René 2, 13–14
dialectic, 37, 42
  exetastic, 42
  peirastic, 42
  shifts, 195
dialogue, 20
  advice-giving, 161, 166
  advice-seeking, 122, 161
  critical discussion, 220, 226
  deliberation, 5, 124, 144–45, 160
  dual nature of context of, 228
  eristic, goal of, 21
  expert consultation, 21, 121, 124, 145,
    220; advice-giving, 25
  expert-user, 225
  face-to-face, 149
  goals of, 125, 250
  information-seeking, 21, 121–22, 145,
    161, 166, 196, 226; goal of, 123

dialogue *(continued)*
  information-seeking question-reply
    dialogue, 145
  multiple types of, 22
  negotiation, goal of, 122–23
  persuasion, 122, 255; goal of, 21;
    two basic types of, 122
  profile of, 253
  question-reply, 106, 161, 229
  reasonable, 107, 109
  sequence of, 127
  shift, 124
  six basic types, 21
*Dialogue on the Two Chief Systems of
  the World,* 47
Dickoff, 52
Diggs, B. J., 163
DNA profiling, 15
Doctor Fox Lecture experiment, 152–53
dogmatic attitude, 242
Drake, Stillman, 46
Dreyfus, Hubert, 110–11
Dreyfus, Stuart, 110–11

eikos, 13, 40
Elements of Inductive Logic, The, 67
elenchus, 38
endoxa, 15, 40 n. 2, 41
Enlightenment, 2, 14
Erickson, Bonnie, 151–52
*Essay Concerning Human
  Understanding, An,* 33, 52
ethos, 150
Euclidean
  geometry, 4, 14
  model of demonstration, 61
European witch craze, 27, 238
evidence, 155
  anecdotal, 165
  direct, 57
  hearsay, 185–86
  inconclusive, 57
  lack of, 44
experience, personal, 207
expert, 202
  battle of the experts, 167, 171–72,
    195, 220, 222
  cross-examination of, 151, 196
  defined, 21
  features of, 112
  functions of, 112

genuine, 120, 212
go-it-alone, 179–81, 198
handwriting, 188
human, 115, 118–19
knowledge, 49
medical, cross-examining, 25
opinion, 12, 115; increase in demand
  for, 178; outside of special field,
  234; problems when used in
  argumentation, 145
paradox of expertise, 113–14
scientific, 6, 216; not a, 12
skill acquisition, 111, 212
skills that typify, 110–11
stylometry, 188
systems, 91, 104, 107, 117; bias of,
  115; machine-based, 118;
  reasoning structure, 105;
  rule-based, 104; shell, 107
testimony, 17–19, 178–80; abuse of,
  177
trial by, 167
war of, 167
exetasis, 38

Facione, Peter, 72
  three factors of, 236
Fairweather, James S., 244
fallacious, 231
  defined, 28
  versus weak, 238
fallacy, 233. *See also* subfallacy
  defined, 231
  dialectical view, 250
fallacy of appeal to authority, 32
  of appeal to celebrity, 256
  of appeal to illegitimate authority, 86
  of irrelevant authority, 256
  of misplaced authority, 256
  of misquoting an authority, 256
  of nonauthority, 256
  of prestige of great names, 80
  of *secundum quid,* 161
  of testimonials, 80
  of unidentified authority, 256
  of wrenching what an authority said
    out of context, 256
Fearnside, W. Ward, 75, 115–16, 203–6,
  213, 215–16, 231
  criteria for judging reliability of a
    soure, 116, 218

three reliability factors of, 214
Federal Rules of Evidence, 16, 167, 181–84, 185
"Fixation of Belief," 2–5
fixation of belief, 251
Flew, Anthony, 58–59
Flint, Anthony, 10
48 Hours, 179
Fowler, Thomas, 67–68, 248
Frye, Albert M., 66
Frye Rule, 177–78, 183–84, 194, 204, 218–19
  described, 182
Frye test, 16, 190, 193

Galilei, Galileo, 2, 34, 46–48
  -like conflict, 4
Galileo's Revenge: Junk Science in the Courtroom, 15
Gardner, Martin, 26, 238
gatekeeper, 184
generalization, 100, 248
  inductive, 117
  statistical, 100
  universal, 117, 261
Gensler, Harry J., 101, 232
Giannelli, Paul C., 15, 182, 216
Gibbon, Edward, 251
goals, 162
goal-oriented structure, 166
Greeks, 13, 35
  dialectical concept of argument, 61
  science, 46
Govier, Trudy, 200
Groarke, Leo A., 233
  five factors of, 210, 233
Grootendorst, Rob, 195
Guthrie, W. K. C., 42–43

halo effect, 243–44, 246–47, 260
  of authority, 50, 70, 85
  of general merit, 244
  institutional, 244, 260
  of personal appearance, 152
Hamblin, Charles L., 32–34, 43, 46, 52–53, 57, 62, 92–93, 125, 164, 233
  criticized, 63
Handbook of Political Fallacies, 55
Hansen, Mark, 179
Hart, Anna, 112
Hasdorf, Albert H., 244

Haskell, Thomas L., 24
Hastings, Arthur, 121, 157, 160, 202–3
  five critical questions of, 157, 203
Hendel, Charles, 52
Henkemans, Snoeck, 259
Hibben, John Grier, 64
Hinckley, John, Jr., 173–74
Hoffman, Herbert, 169
Holmstrom, L., 190
Holmström-Hintikka, Ghita, 171
Holther, William, 75, 115–16, 203, 205–6, 213, 215–16, 231
  three reliability factors of, 214
Huber, Peter, 15, 176–78, 193
human expertise, 110
Hurley, Partick, 87–88, 99, 234
Hyslop, James, 68–69

ignoratio elenchi, 69
impeachment, 169–70
Imwinkelried, Edward J., 159–60, 167
inaccessibility thesis, 110
inference, 86
  defeasible, 101
  lack of knowledge, 97
  negative, 94
  presumptive, 248
  warrant, 39
Inlander, Charles B., 246
inquiry, 13–14, 17, 19–21, 122
  cumulative, 122
  goal of, 165
  scientific, 72
Inquisition, 47
insanity plea, 172–73
institutions, 245
  institutional aura, 247
intersubjective testing procedure, 195
Introduction to Logic, 79
Introductiones in Logicam, 43
ipse dixit, 115

James, 52
Janik, Allan, 84, 241, 260
Johnson, Paul E., 110–11, 113
Johnson, Ralph, H. 63, 85, 222, 238
  five rules, 207–8, 215–16, 221
  violations of conditions, 237
Johnson, Bruce C., 151–52

Kelley, David, 232
  three conditions, 208
Kenny, Anthony, 189–90
Kepler, Johannes, 46
Kilgore, William J., 71, 73, 256
Klawans, Harold L., 170, 174
Kneale, Martha, 45
Kneale, William, 45
knowledge, 36
  advancement of, 178
  base, 107, 162, 197
  -based opinion, 37
  cumulative body of, 197
  indirect claim to, 114
  inquiry into, 67
  lack-of-, 96
  scientific, 68, 165
Krabbe, Erik, 21, 122, 255
Kretzmann, Norman, 45
Kreyche, Robert, 73, 75

Laches, 35
language, technical jargon, 22, 226
Laplace, Pierre Simon, 61–62
Latta, Robert, 74
layperson, 111, 113
  ability to refute an expert, 38–39
  argument between two, 144
legal
  evidence, 5
  trials, 150, 159
Lettres Provinciales, 13
Levi, Albert W., 66
Levin, Lowell S., 246
Lincoln, Bruce, 20
Lind, E. Allan, 151–52
Little, J. Frederick, 233
  five factors of, 210, 233
Little, Winston, 80–81, 234
Locke, John, 33–34, 51, 52–61, 68–69,
    85, 89, 115, 226, 228, 242
  notion of reverence, 64
Lockean
  analysis, 88, 148
  concept of fallacy, 147
  concept of respect, 243, 260
  distinction, 239
logic, Stoic, 14
Logick, 33, 54
Lorenzo's Oil Case, 134, 146, 149, 158,
    163–65, 241–42, 260

MacBeath, Alexander, 74
MacDonald, Helen, 6–7
Mackenzie, Jim, 102–3
Mander, A. E., 115, 202
  four conditions of, 202
Mansfield, Lord, 188
Marshal, Barry, 4
Mazur, Allan, 97
medical treatment, 149
media, 12, 137–39
medicine, aura about, 246–47
Menendez brothers, 18
Michalos, Alex, 256
Middle Ages, 34, 43, 45
  conflict between religion and science,
    49
Milgram, Stanley, 244–45, 260
Miller, Mark, 96
Moore, W. Edgar, 80–81, 204, 234
  three questions of, 204
MYCIN, 106, 108

Nagel, Ernest, 250–51
*1995 Yearbook of Experts, Authorities
    and Spokespersons,* 137–38
Nissen, Vernon, 101

oat bran mania, 6
O'Barr, William M., 151–52
Olbrechts-Tyteca, Lucie, 34, 46
On Sophistical Refutations, 33, 42
opinion, 40 n. 2, 41
  conflicts of, 173
Oxford Latin Dictionary, 58

Pascal, Blaise, 2, 13–15, 19, 28
Patel, Kam, 8
Pauling, Linus, 8, 219–20
Paulsen, David W., 243, 247
peirastic interval, 147, 227, 241–42
Peirce, Charles Saunders, 2, 3–5, 14–15,
    19, 21
  Fixation of Belief, 3
Perelman, Chaim, 34, 46
persuasion, 20
Peter of Spain, 45
physician, 24, 169, 186, 217, 246
Plato, 35–38
phronesis, 119
Port-Royal Logic, 48, 51–52
positivism, 28

Posner, Charles M., 170
power, 28, 56, 151–52, 156, 228, 246, 260
powerless, 22–23, 151–52
Practical Study of Argument, A, 200
premises, 14, 122, 162, 258
  error of missing, 242
  negative, 93
prestige, 69–71, 154, 204
presumptions, 18, 163
  burden of, 197
  weight of, shifted, 133, 158, 201, 222
proof, 122
  satisfactory, 14
  scientific, 14
propaganda, 65
propositions, 16, 117
psychiatry, 186–87, 189, 217
  defense for criminal behavior,
    174–75
psychology, 23
Ptolemy, Claudius, 46
Purtill, Richard L., 207, 233
  five questions of, 206, 217

question-reply sequence, 25
question
  backup evidence, 228
  consistency, 227
  critical, 30–31, 101, 126, 136, 143,
    155, 163, 165–66, 196, 214, 222,
    241–42, 245, 249; blocked
    legitimate, 229; closing off, 228,
    242; for evaluating *ad
    verecundiam* arguments, 201, 211;
    general, 218, 221, 223, 227, 254,
    258; matching the argument from
    authority, 157; peirastic, 146; for
    practical reasoning, 162; sets of,
    199; subquestions, 209–12, 218,
    224, 225; suppression of, 252
  cross-examination, 213
  deterred from asking, 245
  knowledge, 214
  loaded, 141
  opinion, 225
  reliability, 214
  yes and no, 145
  why, 145
question-reply exchanges, 253
quotations, common errors in use of,
  156

Radar Guns case, 127–34, 146, 148, 158,
  165, 188
reasoning
  axiomatic method of, 2
  bad, 3
  casuistic based on probability, 13
  circular, 106
  collaborative practical, 163
  defeasible presumptive, 228
  as a demonstration, 41 n. 2
  dialectic, 14, 40 n. 2
  discursive, 162
  as a discussion, 41 n. 2
  expert, logic of, 165
  geometric, 13
  goal-directed practical, 119, 124, 160
  good, 3, 232
  internal, 165
  methodical, 14
  modus tollens, 96
  negative, 97; by exclusion, 94
  objective logical, 14
  persuasive, 14
  plausible, 101, 143
  practical, 5, 108, 119–20, 160–63,
    165–66
  projective practical, 162
  presumptive, 100
  quarrel, 124
  scientific, 5, 28; inquiry model of, 14;
    knowledge-based, 19
  sign, 157
  technical, 19
  used by expert, 144
receiver, 89
Reese, William L., 58–59
Reiter, Raymond, 94, 101
relativism, 30–31
  extreme, 18
relevance, 184, 243
reliable, 184
Rescher, Nicholas, 101, 235
reverence, 69, 89
Rieke, Richard, 84, 241, 250, 260
Robbins, Louise, 179–80
Robinson, Daniel Sommer, 38, 65
Ruby, Lionel, 66, 243
rules
  artificial intelligence, 117
  conclusion of the, 107
  domain, 106

rules *(continued)*
  of evidence in trials, 168, 196
  legal, 194; of argumentation, 195; of
    courtroom dialogue, 169
  of politeness, 195
  of procedure for dialogue, 107
  of thumb, 248
  tutorial, 106
Runes, Dagobert D., 59
Runkle, Gerald, 80
Russow, Lilly-Marlene, three factors of,
  209

Salmon, Merrillee, 99–100
Salmon, Wesley, 98, 101, 126, 204, 218,
  249
Samuelson, Robert, 137–38
Schank, Roger, 118
Scheer, Richard K., 236
Scherer, Donald, 72–74
  three factors of, 236
Schipper, Edith W., 240, 255–56
SCHOLAR, 96, 103
Schrader, Dr. Harald, 9–10
Schuh, Edward H., 240, 255–56
scientific argument, 12, 19
  investigation, 17
  research, 17, 19
science
  defining criteria, 189
  empirical, 46
  fads, 178
  junk, 167, 176–77, 192–95, 218, 247
  method of, 2, 3
  postacademic, 8–9
  scientific investigation, 3, 4
scrutiny, 38
Soccio, Douglas J., 233
  three questions, 209
Socrates, 35–38, 40, 228
  method of questioning, 37–38
sophism, 88
sophoi, 40
speech style, 151–53
stage, discovery, 14
Stump, Eleonore, 45
subfallacy
  of appeal to celebrity, 260
  of concealing the bias of an authority,
    257, 261
  of concealing deviancy of an expert

    opinion, 257, 260
  of concealing the dishonesty of an
    authority, 257, 260
  of concealing the lack of
    conscientiousness of an authority,
    257, 260
  DeMorgan's subfallacy, 257
  of misplaced authority, 260
  of misquoting an authority, 260
  of misrepresented authority, 256, 260
  of nonauthority, 260
  of unidentified authority, 260
  of wrenching what an authority said
    out of context, 260
Summulae Logicales, 45
syllogism, 14
  statistical, 99–100
syndrome, 18, 191–92, 218
  battered woman, 15, 191
  child abuse, 15
  chronic whiplash, 9–10
  evidence, 15
  False Memory Syndrome Foundation,
    27
  rape trauma, 15, 190
  scientific, 16
subdialogue, peirastic, 153, 165, 171

tactics, 21, 147, 228, 259
  dialectical, 148
  of persuasion, 69
  sophistical, 53, 60, 143, 148, 252
television, 59, 79–80, 178
tenacity, method of, 3, 15
testimonials
  advertising, 80–82
  celebrity, 90
testimony
  extremist, 192
  human, 121
  scientific, 167
  witness, 116
thesis, 122
Thorndike, Edward, 244
Thouless, Robert, 69–70
Tindale, Christopher W., 233
  five factors of, 210, 233
Topics, 14, 38, 40–42
Toulmin, Stephen, 84, 241, 260
traumatists, 25–26, 238
trial, 150–51, 20

adversary system, 168–71, 195
  structure of argumentation in, 196
trust, 150–51
trustworthiness, 215
Twinkie Defense, 174
Tycho, 46

user interface, 106–7, 144, 164

Van Eemeren, Frans H., 195
Vatz, Richard E., 174
Veitch, John, 68
verecundia, 88–89
  defined, 32, 54–55, 58–59
Vernon, Thomas, 101
viewpoints
  foundationalism, 13
  modern, 2, 28
  postmodernist, 2, 10–11, 18, 22,
    28–30

Waller, Bruce N., 173, 213
Walton, Douglas N., 21, 77–78, 94–95,
    101–2, 105–6, 109, 113, 122–23,
    164, 210, 223, 225, 250, 261
  critical subquestions of, 211–12, 223
  five conditions of, 207
  six critical questions of, 211, 213, 217
Warnock, Eleanor, 96
Waterman, Donald, 114
Watts, Isaac, 33, 54

Weinberg, Lee S., 174
Weiner, Ed, 246
Werkmeister, William, 75–76
whiplash in Lithuania case, 9–10, 192
William of Sherwood, 43–45, 61
Wilson, Harold, 80–81, 234
Wilson, Patrick, 76
Wilson, Peter A., three questions of, 205
Windelband, Wilhelm, 43
Windes, Russel R., 160
wisdom, 36, 118, 246
  conventional, 28, 48, 142
  distinct from knowledge, 40
  first-order, 37
  practical, 40
  second-order, 36
  Socratic, 37–38
Woods, John, 77–78, 101–2, 109, 113,
    155, 164
  five conditions of, 207

Yanal, Robert, 99, 232
Yankelovich, Daniel, 12
Yang, Catherine, 180
*You're Smarter Than They Make You
  Feel,* 22
Younger, Irving, 171, 186–87

Zain, Fred, 181
Ziman, John, 8